Subject Access to Information

SUBJECT ACCESS TO INFORMATION

An Interdisciplinary Approach

Koraljka Golub

LIBRARIES UNLIMITED

AN IMPRINT OF ABC-CLIO, LLC
Santa Barbara, California • Denver, Colorado • Oxford, England

Library of Congress Cataloging-in-Publication Data

Golub, Koraljka.
Subject access to information : an interdisciplinary approach / Koraljka Golub.
pages cm
Includes bibliographical references and index.
ISBN 978-1-61069-577-0 (pbk.) — ISBN 978-1-61069-578-7 (ebook)
1. Classification. 2. Subject headings. 3. Information organization. 4. Information storage and retrieval systems. I. Title.
Z696.A4G65 2015
025.4'7—dc23 2014027052

ISBN: 978-1-61069-577-0
EISBN: 978-1-61069-578-7

19 18 17 16 15 1 2 3 4 5

This book is also available on the World Wide Web as an eBook.
Visit www.abc-clio.com for details.

Libraries Unlimited
An Imprint of ABC-CLIO, LLC

ABC-CLIO, LLC
130 Cremona Drive, P.O. Box 1911
Santa Barbara, California 93116-1911

This book is printed on acid-free paper ♾
Manufactured in the United States of America

Contents

Preface

The interdisciplinary nature of library and information science has made it evident that there is considerable potential for joint efforts to create effective and user-friendly information retrieval systems—in particular between the fields of library and information science and computer science. Generally speaking, library and information science professionals build the theory and practice of organizing information, drawing on more than two millennia of practical experience in library organization. Computer science professionals build algorithms that enable users to search the vast spaces of digital information resources via tools such as search engines. Both scientific disciplines share common aims, a major one being that of supporting information retrieval of resources by subjects or topics.

The two disciplines have rather different epistemological backgrounds, which is both an advantage and a disadvantage in relation to joining efforts to create user-friendly information-retrieval systems. One advantage would be that merging the two disciplines' theories, methodologies, and approaches appropriately could bear excellent solutions to certain problems. For example, library and information science has invested much effort into studying end users' needs and information-retrieval behaviors. Computer scientists could use the results of such studies to build the systems.

One major disadvantage might be that the differing theories, methodologies, and approaches could create obstacles to communication and understanding between the two disciplines. Computer science and library and information science fields often use different terminology to mean the same thing and can have innate conceptual differences. For example, "indexing" in computer science often refers to automated extraction of terms from an electronic document, which then enables the document's retrieval when the same terms are used in a search. "Indexing" in library and information science encompasses an act of intellectual examination of a document, assigning index terms from a controlled vocabulary (e.g., subject headings), and doing so in accordance to indexing policies predefined for a given collection.

Epistemological differences can lead to problems including not examining what has been done previously or excluding what is written in related disciplines. At an invited presentation given by David De Roure at the second European Semantic Web Conference in 2005, De Roure suggested that Semantic Web researchers should examine library science literature—a clear indication that they had not been doing so. Even in narrower fields—such as automated text classification—there are different communities (e.g., machine learning, information retrieval, library science) which generally do not cite each other's work and which use different terminology for the same concepts (e.g., text categorization, automatic indexing, automated classification).

The purpose of this book is to provide an interdisciplinary overview that encompasses current and potential approaches to organizing information by subject. It is hoped that, as such, this work will enhance communication and understanding between the library and information science and the computer science communities, and will increase collaboration between the different industry professionals—thus yielding common solutions to practical problems and reducing the duplication of efforts. The book includes contributions from computer science professionals and from library and information science professionals and practitioners (including those who consider themselves to be interdisciplinary and cross-sector specialists), each of whom has added to the glossary at the end of each chapter. This effort could help to further bridge the gap between the two disciplines as well as between the theory and practice of each.

The content of this book is organized into five chapters. Chapter 1 introduces the importance of information organization in general, and organization by subject in particular. The latter topic provides the perspectives of library and information science and computer science disciplines. The chapter discusses major terms, and provides the rationale for subsequent chapters. The importance of understanding and supporting users of information systems is shown through a state-of-the-art review of user behavior.

Chapter 2 deals with systems for knowledge organization by subject, such as classification schemes, thesauri, and subject headings that have been used in libraries and bibliographic databases for more than a century. It also examines more recent developments pertaining to the World Wide Web (the Web) such as "folksonomies" (a group of terms which occur naturally in the language of system users and are designed by the users) and ontologies of the Semantic Web. Also discussed are design, applicability, advantages, disadvantages, and suggested improvements.

Chapter 3 covers technological standards for representation, storage, and retrieval of various knowledge organization systems, and their constituent elements. It examines XML (Extensible Markup Language), RDF (Resource Description Framework), SKOS (Simple Knowledge Organization System), and OWL (Web Ontology Language), among others. The chapter reviews various discovery standards, such as SRU (Search/Retrieval via URL) and CQL (Contextual Query Language) protocols. Also considered are registries of knowledge organization systems and their concepts and terms.

An unavoidable topic is that of automated tools for subject information organization, thus Chapter 4 examines selected related topics: Bibliometrics-based subject representation, document clustering, and text categorization.

The book closes with Chapter 5, which discusses the differences between the disciplines of library and information science and computer science and their approaches to organizing information, as well as the necessity for these two disciplines to combine their efforts further to prevent duplication. Directions for future research are also presented.

Each chapter follows the same structure:

- Presents major questions that the chapter aims to answer;
- Provides answers to these questions structured around headings and subheadings;
- Provokes further thought based on the information discussed in the chapter in the "chapter review" section; and
- Includes a glossary of terms used in the chapter.

The book is geared toward graduate and undergraduate students studying information and knowledge organization, information retrieval, information architecture, information management, and related areas within the disciplines of library and information science, computer science, business informatics, and information technology. These students are the next generation of researchers and practitioners, and would benefit greatly from acquiring the basic knowledge of learning the other discipline's approaches. The text is written as simply as is possible for ease of understanding. As such, it primarily aims to be an introductory text. (Entire books have been written on topics such as subject indexing or algorithms for information retrieval in library and information science and computer science, respectively.)

This work also can be useful to researchers in the two major disciplines in general, and to developers dealing with information retrieval systems and digital libraries in particular. Computer engineers, information system designers, and information professionals working in the field of information organization also can benefit from the information presented.

Acknowledgments

First and foremost I would like to thank Marta Deyrup for suggesting that I write this book, and for believing in my competence to complete the task. Marta is an experienced editor, and her suggestions and comments on the first draft of this book were very thorough and they impacted the writing significantly. Claudio Gnoli, one of the contributors, also has been ever so supportive and made an important difference by providing edits to early versions of the manuscript.

Very special thanks to Gordon Dunsire, Antoine Isaac, and Anders Ardö whose knowledge and recommendations—in particular on Semantic Web topics and Chapter 3 (Technological Standards)—yielded a vast improvement to the work. Riccardo Ridi provided useful comments on Chapter 2 (Knowledge Organization Systems). My brother-in-law, Goran Vukušić, offered friendly advice on this work from the perspective of an end user of the book. My friend and colleague, Drahomira Gavranović, helped immensely with editorial work on references and index creation.

I am most grateful to all the contributors for their hard work, prompt communication from a distance, and for putting up with all my suggestions—it has been a true pleasure to work with you all. The contributors, in the order of their contributions, are David Elsweiler, Claudio Gnoli, Fredrik Åström, Ingo Frommholz, Muhammad Kamran Abbasi, Dunja Mladenić, Marko Grobelnik, and Isto Huvila. I also wish to express thanks to Greg Janée, James Reid, Aida Slavić, and Mike Taylor for their generosity in providing expert feedback related to technological standards and issues.

Finally, many thanks are offered to Barbara Ittner and Emma Bailey of Libraries Unlimited, ABC-Clio, for their constant support throughout the process. I am also indebted to the Technology Innovation Centre of Međimurje, Croatia, for providing me with a space and excellent conditions to work on the book.

1

Organizing Information by Subject

MAJOR QUESTIONS

- Why should information be organized?
- Why is organizing information by subject the most challenging type of information organization?
- How should information be organized?
- How do library and information science professionals organize information by subject?
- How do algorithms organize information by subject?

ORGANIZATION OF INFORMATION

Sorting the world around us is a fundamental activity of the human mind. At home, at work, in stores, and even on computers, humans tend to group things together. Tools are stored in one place, food in another; we organize photographs, files, and folders in certain orders.

Recognizing similar items and distinguishing them from others is part of how we make sense of the world and is part of our cognition. The activity of grouping objects that are alike starts at a very early age. For example, small children refer to people who somehow roughly are similar to other people they know by using the same name. A child whose grandfather rides a bike, for example, might refer to another cyclist as "grandfather." This also is true for objects; a child who learns what a kitchen towel is might also call similar items—such as a blanket or a shawl—a kitchen towel. This classification process continues, and as people grow older they tend to make finer distinctions between objects of the world—both abstract and concrete—based on the totality of their experiences of the world. Because we are exposed to different educational, societal, and other experiences, an individual's classification of objects often differs from the classification of others. A computer scientist, for example, would group animals in more general categories than a zoologist would.

In stores, museums, libraries, on the Web, and in various specialized databases and catalogs, objects which share major characteristics are placed together. In stores, objects are grouped based on type, size, discount, and brand. In museums, objects might be exhibited according to the period during which they were made or according to their practical use. In libraries, books on shelves primarily are organized by topic, but online catalogs can be browsed and searched using a variety of aspects including topic, author, publisher, medium, and year of publication. Similar options are available in commercial databases of research articles. In contrast, search engines support searching primarily by automatically extracting significant words or phrases from information resources they automatically have collected (crawled) into a database.

Here, a distinction is made between formal and informal information systems. "Formal" implies that systematic guidelines and standards are closely followed in selecting, organizing, and providing access to resources. To make information resources findable in information retrieval systems that are designed with a more formal purpose in mind, it is necessary to apply efficient approaches and methods of organizing them. The longest record of experience in organizing information lies within the library and information science and profession; the first known library catalog was created in the third century BCE. The catalog of the Library of Alexandria organized scrolls by authors and subject categories—a system devised by Callimachus (Eliot and Rose 2009). Library catalogs have been used since that time, and contemporary versions implement guidelines and standards based on centuries of research and practice. Adaptations still are underway to integrate them with the Semantic Web and Web 2.0, including more varied types of information resources and services for more heterogeneous user populations.

Apart from library catalogs, other formal information retrieval systems commonly used today include:

- Databases of journal articles and eBooks, which often are integrated with university and academic library catalogs;
- Professional subject gateways such as Infomine (1994) and the Internet Public Library (IPL2) (IPL2 2012) which include quality Web-based information resources;
- Digital collections of cultural heritage institutions, including large ones such as Europeana (Europeana 2014), which integrates records and digitized holdings of more than 2,000 European libraries, galleries, museums, and archives; and

- Digital collections of specific purpose, such as institutional or subject repositories of research papers and of theses and dissertations, which tend to be enlarged by collections of research-related data sets.

Informal information-retrieval systems, that is, those that do not tend to follow systematic guidelines and standards in selecting, organizing, and providing access to resources, are Web search engines and similar information organization systems based on automated approaches. Search engines (e.g., Google, Bing, Yahoo!) apply algorithms to automatically select and index Web resources. These sites have become the main points for information searching, which leads to some problems. Many end users, for example, tend to believe that any information a search engine finds is correct and trustworthy, that what is listed in the top 10 results is the most relevant information, and that few other relevant resources exist beyond the top 10. This is in contrast to what can be found in formal systems such as library catalogs or databases of research articles, which follow standards and guidelines in selecting and organizing resources.

As part of Web 2.0 (also known as the Social Web), many information retrieval systems—both formal and informal—now include support for the social interaction of their end users. Some sites offer users to, for example, leave comments, provide reviews, write summaries, and tag (index) various resources.

What information should be organized in an information retrieval system? Opinions differ. Some researchers argue that the organizational categories should be somewhat abstract and include, among other things, data, information, knowledge, or wisdom. These often are presented as a hierarchy, whereby data is the least processed and wisdom is the most processed, analyzed, synthesized, and integrated. Others claim that these categories should be more concrete, and include things such as information resources, documents, or information objects. Further, there are various definitions of each of those terms.

Bates's (2009) review of definitions of "information," for example, is drawn from various disciplines—including information science, cognitive science, computer science, and philosophy—and demonstrates how the definition of information remains hotly contested. Related is Foskett's (1996) distinction between "reference retrieval" which refers to retrieval of library catalog records, database records, or snippets in search engines; "document retrieval" whereby full documents are retrieved (e.g., a complete eBook, a full-text research paper); and "information retrieval," referring to finding the needed information in the retrieved document.

The discussions herein use the term "information resource" to refer to a book, a journal article, an image, a museum object, or any other object from which information can be extracted and be of potential use to the end user of an information retrieval system. In Chapters 3 and 4, "document" is the term used more often in the context of technological standards and various computational techniques and approaches.

A quality information-retrieval system should provide enough information about a resource in the form of a metadata record for the user to be able to decide whether to pursue it. In creating metadata records and describing information resources, two major aspects can be distinguished: Formal characteristics of the information resource, such as its title, author, publisher, and year of publication; and those focusing on the topic or theme of the information resource. In librarianship, the former often is known as "descriptive cataloging" and the latter as "subject cataloging" or "subject indexing."

Subject cataloging includes verbal subject indexing, subject classification, and abstracting. Verbal subject indexing refers to the representation of topics from the information resource using keywords. In library catalogs and databases of journal articles, these keywords primarily are taken from language-controlled subject heading systems or thesauri, although common keywords also can be assigned in social tagging. In subject classification, topics are represented using classification systems. This traditionally was done to group together information resources having similar topics, and to enable systematic and hierarchical browsing on library shelves. Abstracting involves writing a high-quality synopsis of the information resource, and commonly is included in article databases.

The following example is a catalog record from the Library of Congress for a book on growing an indoor garden (available at a unique URL, http://lccn.loc.gov/80021657). The book is described using a number of elements, listed below.

- Identification number of the catalog record in the Library of Congress catalog ("LC control no.")
- Type of information resource ("type of material")
- Author ("personal name")
- Title and main authors and contributors as listed on the main title page of the book ("main title")
- Publication details ("published/created")
- Physical description details (e.g., the number of pages and illustrations) ("description")
- ISBN (International Standard Book Number)
- Subject terms, which in this example are drawn from the Library of Congress Subject Headings ("subjects")
- Classmarks or classification numbers, Library of Congress Classification ("LC classification"), and Dewey Decimal Classification ("Dewey class no.") are the classification systems commonly used in U.S. libraries

LC control no.	80021657
Type of material	Book
Personal name	Hardigree, Peggy Ann, 1945–
Main title	The edible indoor garden: a complete guide to growing over 60 vegetables, fruits, and herbs indoors / Peggy Hardigree, drawings by Peggy Ellen Reed.
Published/Created	New York: St. Martin's Press, c1980.
Description	298 p. : ill.; 26 cm.
ISBN	0312236891: $16.95 0312236905 (pbk.): $7.95
Subjects	Vegetable gardening. Fruit-culture. Indoor gardening.
LC classification	SB324.5 .H37
Dewey class no.	635

The last three elements of the record are common examples of subject access points used in library catalogs. An obvious improvement for end users would be to use captions that translate the classmark in place of or alongside the classmark, e.g., "garden crops (Horticulture)" alongside "635." Library catalogs typically do not include abstracts because of the substantial production costs of creating them.

Metadata records in other formal information retrieval systems are similar, in that a number of formal and subject elements are provided, and abstracts sometimes are included. Search engines provide only an automatically extracted title and snippet of information. There is no quality control. Summaries and tags produced by end users as part of Social Web services are similar in that there is no quality control of the assigned tags or summaries. Existing standards and guidelines for organizing resources used in formal information retrieval systems are based upon centuries of practice and research, including research about how people search for information and how they use information-retrieval systems.

A search for an information resource starts with an information need or a specific question, although it also is common for users to simply look for something that catches their interest. An individual sees the world through his or her own knowledge structures, and a verbal information request is formulated based on a number of processes, including:

- Perception of the information need,
- Conceptualization of the information need (recognizing major concepts of that information need),
- Verbalization (putting those various concepts into words),

- Choice (establishing a search strategy for an information retrieval system), and
- Translation (translating the information need into the language of the information retrieval system).

Information retrieval systems of today deal with the last item only: the translation. If a user makes an error in any of the first four stages, then the search will fail (Olson and Ball 2001, 265–269). Translating an information need into a search strategy consists of a number of steps. These steps can include:

- Deciding whether to search by entering search terms and/or to browse a given structure;
- Choosing terms to use in the search;
- Determining which synonyms to use to retrieve more results or which narrower terms to use to get more precise results; and
- Deciding whether to use Boolean operators, proximity operators, wild characters, truncation, or phrase searching.

The system effectively must support these steps and modifications to the search strategy.

Retrieved results should be relevant to the original information need. Often users find partial and inadequate information without realizing that better answers are available (Foskett 1996, 426). For example, teachers sometimes describe students who want to change their seminar topics because they believe "there is no information about it," even though they searched for information on the topic using Google only. Further, when using Web search engines, users have the additional burden deciding on the quality of retrieved resources, as there is no selection control.

Users' characteristics strongly influence the search strategy and the evaluation of retrieved results. These include demographic characteristics as well as the situation of the information need; for example, whether the purpose of the search is to find practical information or to find a complete reference list for writing a term paper.

Rapid developments in information and communication technology necessitate more research to determine how—in this distributed network of information resources—end users from around the globe and with very differing backgrounds search for information resources. It is important to determine how people in general, and specific user groups in particular, search for information resources; how users organize information resources for their own home and work use; and which knowledge organization systems are best suited for which purposes in organizing information resources—and how to redesign them to be more compatible with end user needs.

The section on user information behavior (below) addresses the first two questions based on current research findings. The third question briefly is introduced in the section that follows, and is discussed in more detail in Chapter 2, although the topic remains open to interpretation.

ORGANIZATION OF INFORMATION BY SUBJECT

It is very common for end users to look for what is available about their topic of interest instead of having a particular information resource and a known title or author in mind. Ensuring appropriate subject-based access points long has been a recognized major objective of information retrieval systems. As mentioned, the catalog of the Library of Alexandria in the third century BCE organized scrolls by subject categories. In 1876, Charles Ammi Cutter's guidelines for library catalogs stated that one of the major objectives is to enable end users to find what the library has on a particular subject (Cutter 1876). In the same year, the Dewey Decimal Classification (DDC), a classification scheme covering all subject areas, was published in its first edition. At the time of this writing, the latest printed version of the DDC is in its twenty-third edition—including numerous translations to other languages and adaptations for specialized collections.

Subject-based searches often are the most challenging type. This search method, for example, tends to be more difficult than searching for an information resource with a known title and looking for its location or preferred edition. Further, different people, end users, and authors often use different terms to refer to the same concept. A user can search for one concept using a term that the author might not even have mentioned in the text. This is one of the primary reasons that algorithms cannot retrieve that text in response to the search. False hits, too few hits, too many hits, or hits that are not specific enough are what end users commonly find when using Web search engines.

Any natural language includes many words that have multiple meanings; this is known as "polysemy." The word "bank," for example, can have 18 different meanings according to the WordNet 3.1 dictionary (WordNet 2014). Only a small fraction of the words in a language have only one or two meanings; for example, the scientific names of species. Many words have completely unrelated meanings, for example "jaguar," which can refer to the animal and to the car. This is referred as "homonymy." Further, a concept can be represented using different terms—for example, "automobile," "motor car," or "car"—or might use spelling variants. This phenomenon is known as "synonymy."

To address the issues of using natural language in retrieval some language control must be imposed. For this purpose, subject headings systems, thesauri, and similar systems have been designed to ensure that each concept is represented and assigned to the information resource using one term only, and at the same time references other terms by which the concept can be found. The terms "cars," "automobiles," and "motor cars" all should be linked to one another, and one of these terms should be prescribed as the authorized term which always is assigned in a metadata record to denote that concept.

A user also might want information resources that deal with related or narrower topics than that specified in the search. Someone searching for books on cats in the local public library, for instance, also might want books on pets in general; or the user might want a book on a more specific type of cats, such as the Siamese breed. In this example, the information system could provide terms that a user might find appropriate—such as domestic cats, cats, Siamese cats, and pets—based on an underlying system of cross-referenced terms.

Additionally, end users might not know exactly what they need or want. In such cases, users would appreciate browsing the shelves in a library where books are arranged by hierarchical topics according to an established classification scheme, such as the Library of Congress Classification (LCC), Dewey Decimal Classification, or Universal Decimal Classification (UDC). In an online information organization system the classification scheme could be represented as a hierarchical browsing tree with assigned information resources.

Systems used in subject indexing to link the content of information resources are known as "controlled vocabularies" and "indexing languages." "Controlled vocabularies" is a broader concept in that it includes any controlled set of terms used in creating metadata records, such as author names. Indexing languages refers to a specific type of controlled vocabulary representing formalized languages designed and used to describe the subject content of information resources for information retrieval purposes.

There are two main types of indexing languages: alphabetical, using natural language terms and thus requiring terminology control (e.g., thesauri and subject headings), and classification schemes, using symbols. They all provide control for synonyms and distinguish among homographs and group-related terms, but they use different methods to do so. Classification schemes have a systematic and hierarchical arrangement as the primary control and an alphabetical arrangement in the index as a secondary control. Subject headings and thesauri both have alphabetical order as the primary control, and hierarchical order is present in a cross-reference structure.

The main characteristics of indexing languages are that they primarily are used to organize the subject content of documents. The term "knowledge organization system" (KOS) now is used more and more often to include controlled vocabularies as well as folksonomies, ontologies, and other systems which could be used for various aspects of organizing information. Chapter 2 discusses different types of KOS and implications for their application; they also are briefly addressed below.

Apart from indexing languages which are applied for indexing the content of information resources, KOS types include the following as well (which also can have other purposes).

- Lists (a simple group of terms used, for example, in website pick lists).
- Synonym rings (a list of synonyms or near-synonyms used interchangeably for retrieval).
- Authority files (names for countries, individuals, and organizations).
- Glossaries (usually a subject-specific list of terms with definitions).
- Dictionaries (a more general subject list of terms and their definitions).
- Encyclopedias.
- Gazetteers (dictionaries of place names).
- Taxonomies (similar to classification schemes, but the term more often is used in knowledge management systems to indicate any grouping of objects based on a particular characteristic).
- Lexical databases or semantic networks (with more defined relationships between terms used in natural language applications, a major example being WordNet).
- Ontologies (with even more defined relationships between terms as well as the rules and axioms, often applied in data mining and knowledge management).
- Search-engine directories of Web pages (e.g., http://dir.yahoo.com/).
- Folksonomies (a contraction of "folk" (person) and "taxonomy' (the science or technique of classification into ordered categories); a decentralized, social approach to creating subject index terms.

The different KOS types overlap and vary in their purpose, structure, functionality, and field of application, as well as in other characteristics. The wide range of characteristics enables a KOS to be used in a variety of applications. The most prominent use is for improved information retrieval through searching, disambiguation, query expansion and reformulation, or browsing. Different knowledge organization systems serve different functions, which is why ideally more than one KOS should be used in information retrieval applications. Classification schemes generally group together topically related information resources into classes and list them in conceptually meaningful sequences—and, as such, they are better suited to subject browsing than are other KOSs. Thesauri are used to denote a number of detailed topics and thus are better suited for searching (although examples of knowledge organization systems which aim to integrate both functions do exist).

Other uses include aiding in the general understanding of a subject area, serving as semantic maps by showing interrelationships between concepts, and helping to provide definitions of terms. A KOS also can help improve automated classification and indexing, semantic reasoning, text mining, and information extraction. Topical crawlers or harvesters can utilize a KOS to define topics using high-quality terms for those topics. A KOS also can provide support for social tagging—and consequently improve information retrieval and knowledge organization in social Web applications.

Subject indexing and classification languages are expensive to produce and maintain. Subject indexing also is resource intensive. These are some of the reasons that the discussion often is sharply divided between those in favor of pure automated solutions such as used in Web search engines, and those in favor of the expert subject indexing and classification from standardized indexing languages.

Simple keyword searching used by Web search engines is successful to the degree that:

- End users know which terms to use in the search query;
- Terms used are the same as those used by the authors of relevant information resources;
- Relevant information resources are appropriately indexed by the algorithm; and
- Relevant information resources are ranked high enough by the algorithm.

These conditions can be fulfilled more completely when a user is looking for specific websites. When searching for information on a certain topic, such as a health issue or a college paper theme, however, Web search engines probably will retrieve results that are not completely relevant, comprehensive, or even accurate. The resources retrieved are those that the searching and indexing algorithm considers relevant, based on factors such as the number of Web pages linking to the resources and the number of times the keyword is used in the full text of the resource. Additionally, the resources retrieved only include those which are available in digital form, are accessible to the search engine's crawler, and are selected by the crawler.

When criticizing the Google Print project aimed at digitizing millions of books, with some even claiming the project would replace libraries, T. Mann said, "Searching for all relevant book texts via a simple Internet-type search box would be like trying to get an overview of a whole country while looking at it only though a bombsight" (Mann 2008, 183). Substituting systematic cataloging and indexing as done in libraries with basic search mechanisms such as those offered by Google produces results that are "superficial, incomplete, haphazard, indiscriminate, biased toward recent works, and largely confined to English-language sources" (Mann 2008, 188). The loss of information and knowledge which are not possible to retrieve probably would be immense.

As compared to Web search engines, the following example illustrates the richness of options for clarifying a search query and providing relevant results as enabled by the Library of Congress Subject Headings (LCSH) in the Library of Congress catalog. If, for example, a researcher is looking into history of the Republic of Macedonia, then entering the term "Macedonia" results in a note appearing which says that the retrieved results refer to Macedonia covering both the Greek province and the Former Yugoslav Republic of Macedonia, which were one entity up until 1912–1913, and for

Macedonian regions from periods thereafter different headings are used. Entering the terms "former" and "Macedonia," with the aim of locating resources about the former Yugoslav Republic of Macedonia, results in a cross reference pointing to "Macedonia (Republic)." By choosing the suggested term, an alphabetical list of subjects narrowed by specific subtopics is provided. Below is an extract of the "Macedonia (Republic)" subtopics, with each subtopic linked to resources discussing it.

Macedonia (Republic)—Ethnic identity.
Macedonia (Republic)—Ethnic relations.
Macedonia (Republic)—Ethnic relations—21st century.
Macedonia (Republic)—Ethnic relations—Congresses.
Macedonia (Republic)—Ethnic relations—History—20th century.
Macedonia (Republic)—Ethnic relations—Political aspects.
Macedonia (Republic)—Ethnic relations—Press coverage.
Macedonia (Republic)—Ethnography.

This illustrates how the LCSH allows end users to distinguish between information resources which deal with the current Republic of Macedonia and not with Macedonia that is a Greek province. It teaches the end user that the region of the Republic of Macedonia was joined with what is today's Greek province and was divided in 1912–1913; and it provides a detailed list of specific topics and their subdivisions related to the Republic of Macedonia. If libraries—with their extensive practices of subject description—did not exist, then the end user would be left with search capabilities of Web search engines that do not allow any of these distinctions or granularity.

Disadvantages of natural-language searching include the following (Olson and Boll 2001, 48–51).

- It retrieves many irrelevant results due to highly exhaustive indexing.
- It leads to information overload.
- It does not retrieve information resources with concepts which are not denoted using search terms.
- Concepts not explicitly mentioned in the text are not searchable.
- Vocabulary control is shifted to the user, who must think of the possible relations with other terms and concepts, including how up to date the information is; for example, users unaware of the change of a country name will not include the new name in a search.

In comparison to a KOS, automated searching based on natural language has a number of advantages. The human effort and cost needed to create and maintain a KOS and to index applying it are minimal. The automatically derived index terms will be up to date in new information resources, often in contrast to KOSs, which are usually slow to include new terms and concepts. Additionally, full-text indexing is exhaustive—almost all terms used in the information resource could serve as index terms, in contrast to intellectual indexing in which a selection is made. This is useful when searching across information retrieval systems which each use a different KOS and there is no mapping between them.

Algorithm-based indexing works better for natural sciences, such as chemistry and physics, and is less effective for social sciences such as philosophy, for which the terminology used is much more polysemic (*see* Buxton and Meadows 1977). Because of the advantages and disadvantages of each approach, many users would agree that the best approach is the one that combines natural language with controlled language indexing and searching, whereby the end user can choose which options to use.

Another more recent development comes from Web 2.0, in which end users can enrich the record with reviews and comments, write summaries, and add tags. Tags can be added to various information resources such as images, videos, books, bookmarks, and others in services such as Flickr, YouTube, and LibraryThing—hence the name "social tagging." Groups of tags are called "tag clouds" or "folksonomies." An increasing number of library catalogs (the first one being the University of Pennsylvania Library's PennTags project which began in 2006) and library software vendors also offer this option.

Research focusing on tags has particularly picked up in recent years. Because they are manually assigned by end users, tags potentially provide a cheap add-on to metadata created by professional indexers, allowing for multiple end-user perspectives. The focus also could be different. Lin et al. (2006), for example, show that tags in Connotea were more focused on specific subject matter, rather than on the overall subject assigned by Medical Subject Headings (MeSH). Additionally, compared to subject indexing whereby terms are assigned from a standard KOS, tags can be more up to date and more likely to use end-user terminology. Choi (2013) also emphasizes the potential for assigning emotional tags, which are especially popular on Flickr for photographs.

There are, however, two major disadvantages of social tags: They are not assigned by trained, professional indexers, following an index policy, and there is no language control as is provided by a KOS. Additionally, many tags only are personally significant (such as the tag "to_read"). Spiteri (2007) still found that tags are in line with some of the National Information Standards Organization (NISO) guidelines on indexing, such as the predominance of nouns and single tags.

Taking into account all the advantages and disadvantages of tags, combining tags with index terms from KOSs has been suggested. One way forward is to provide a KOS from which to select tags and modify them as needed. One study (Golub, Lykke, and Tudhope 2014) explored using the Dewey Decimal Classification with mappings from the Library of Congress Subject Headings as the source of tags. The study compared tagging with the KOS index terms against other forms of tagging. The results of the study demonstrated the importance of KOS suggestions for indexing and retrieval. These suggestions helped to determine which tags to use and made it easier to find a focus for the tagging, to ensure consistency and to increase the number of access points in retrieval. The value and usefulness of the tags proved to be dependent on the quality of the suggestions, both as to conceptual relevance to the user and as to appropriateness of the terminology.

Another possibility is to allow end users to contribute alongside KOS index terms as is the case in many library catalogs. There has been an increase in end-user contributions which help show the end user's views of the topicality, use, and usefulness of information resources (Miksa 2013). It has also been shown, however, that few users are contributing (Ho and Horne-Popp 2013). Options such as providing guidance on tagging or having expert indexers monitor tagging are only two of the topics that could be researched further, as well as studying the motivation of end users to contribute their own terms.

Another often-discussed alternative to manual subject indexing using a KOS is automated subject indexing. Research on automated subject indexing began with the availability of electronic text in the 1950s (Luhn 1957; Baxendale 1958; Maron 1961) and still is a challenging and relevant topic today. Automatically derived subject terms cannot entirely replace manual indexing due to problems similar to those of search engines (described above). Like social tags, however, they have the potential to enrich existing metadata records and improve indexing quality and consistency.

Some commercial software vendors and researchers claim to have achieved results in which it would be possible to entirely replace manual subject indexing in certain subject areas (e.g., Purpura and Hillard 2006; Roitblat, Kershaw, and Oot 2010). Others recognize the need for both human and automated indexing and note the advantages and disadvantages of each method (Anderson and Perez-Carballo 2001; Hagedorn 2001; Lykke and Eslau 2010). Reported examples of operational information systems include machine-aided indexing. NASA's machine-aided indexing system was shown to increase production and improve indexing quality (Silvester 1997); the Medical Text Indexer system at the U.S. National Library of Medicine was shown to be consulted by indexers in about 40% of indexing throughput (Ruiz, Aronson, and Hlava 2008).

Hard scientific evidence on the success of automated subject indexing tools in operative information environments is scarce, however. A major reason for this is that related research usually is conducted in laboratory conditions, excluding the complexities of real-life systems and situations. Having reviewed a large number of automatic indexing studies, Lancaster concluded that the research comparing automatic versus human indexing is seriously flawed (Lancaster 2003, 334). There are a number of concerns with current methods of evaluation which are due to the subjective nature of "aboutness" relative to context, described below.

Subject Indexing and Evaluation

The challenges of subject indexing and its evaluation seem to be inherent to any subject-indexing process. The ISO 5963:1985 standard, "Documentation—Methods for examining documents, determining their subjects, and selecting indexing terms" (International Organization for Standardization 1985) defines subject indexing as a process involving three steps: (1) determining the subject content of an information resource; (2) a conceptual analysis to decide which aspects of the content should be represented; and (3) translation of those concepts or aspects into a KOS.

This standard gives a resource-oriented definition of subject indexing whereby the topics are determined in relation to the resource only, in contrast to user-oriented indexing (Soergel 1985) where the indexer's task is to anticipate what topics or resources at hand would be relevant to end users. In user-oriented indexing, many cognitive factors such as interest, task, purpose, knowledge, norms, opinions, and attitudes can determine the meaning that the information resource might have for a user (Moens 2000, 12).

In a similar vein, Hjørland (2009) argues that concepts are viewed differently based on different epistemological theories (empiricism, rationalism, historicism, or pragmatism), each of which gives context to the concept. In biological systematics, for example, the concept of "species" for an empiricist is a group of organisms that look similar to each other and distinct from other groups. For a historicist, "species" is the smallest group of organisms that share a pattern of descent. Terminology in any given field also is not consensual; for example, the concept of "information" in library and information science. Social tagging offers the potential of indexing an information resource from a larger number of perspectives.

The second and third steps in the ISO definition are based on an indexing policy concerning information resource collection and target user groups. The indexing policy prescribes exhaustivity—the number of concepts to index, and specificity—the depth of detail to index. Both are dependent on the number of information resources and the major theme of the collection. A collection of several thousand information resources on general topics, such as that found in a small school library, for example, would not need to be very deep or specific; a university library with hundreds of thousands of information resources would have a more exhaustive and specific indexing policy.

Subject indexers might make errors such as (Lancaster 2003, 86–87) assigning too many or too few subjects, selecting subjects that are not the most specific ones available, omitting important subjects, and assigning obviously incorrect subjects. Also—because of different indexing policies—a subject correctly assigned in a high-exhaustivity system could be erroneous in a low-exhaustivity system (Soergel 1994). This is why it is important to bear in mind the indexing policy when evaluating indexing, including the differences between automated indexing and human indexing. Related to this is the question of indexing consistency between different indexers ("inter-indexer consistency") or between different sessions conducted by the same indexer ("intra-indexer consistency"). It has been reported that different people, whether end users or professional subject indexers, assign different subjects to the same information resource. For an overview see Lancaster (2003, 68–82).

The purpose of quality subject indexing is improved information retrieval; therefore evaluating subject indexing in this context can prove illuminating. A key concept in information retrieval, however, is relevance. Like "aboutness," relevance also is context-dependent and involves a degree of subjectivity. This is discussed, for example, by Borlund (2003), who argues that relevance is multidimensional and dynamic. Dynamic because the user's perception of relevance can change over time; and multidimensional because users employ many different criteria in assessing relevance, plus there are different classes, types, degrees, and levels of relevance.

Soergel (1994) lists three types of relevance as being central to good subject indexing and to assessing retrieval performance: topical relevance, pertinence, and utility. Topical relevance is defined as a relationship between an information resource and a topic, question, function, or task, whereby the information resource is topically relevant for a question if it can shed light on the question. "Shedding light" implies different degrees of relevance which depend on a number of factors, such as the amount of relevant information given, the strength of the relationship between the information given and the question, and the strength of the contribution to the quality or surety of the answer. The information resource is pertinent if it is topically relevant and if it is appropriate for the person, that is, if the person can understand the information resource and apply the information gained. Finally, the information resource has utility if it is pertinent and makes a useful contribution beyond what the user already knew. Soergel says that a pertinent information resource could lack utility; for example, the user already might know the information provided.

In spite of the dynamic and multidimensional nature of relevance, in practice evaluation of information retrieval systems has been reduced to comparison against the gold standard—a set of pre-existing relevance judgments which are taken out of context. An early study on retrieval conducted by Gull in 1956 powerfully influenced the selection of a method for obtaining relevance judgments. Gull reported that two groups of judges could not agree on relevance judgments. Since then it has become common practice to not use more than a single judge or a single object for establishing a gold standard (Saracevic 2008, 774). The effect of inconsistency on retrieval evaluation has not yet been studied in depth (Saracevic 2008).

Furthermore, end users might need a few information resources that are highly relevant, all information resources that are relevant, or information resources that are immediately available even if they are not the most relevant. There could be errors in the user's perception, conceptualization, verbalization, choice, and translation of the specific need into the query. The interface can play a role because of a number of factors, such as usability, aesthetics, and speed of response. The degree to which the system allows users to ask very precise questions, the system's coverage of many specific topics rather than just a single broad one, the indexing policy, the indexing quality, and the KOS applied all influence the performance of an information retrieval system and make evaluation of any of its aspects increasingly complex.

Knowledge Organization Systems in the Online Environment

The Internet and the Web environment have significantly changed the nature of information systems use. End users themselves now can search information systems to the same extent as information professionals can. Additionally, end users come from all age groups and educational backgrounds, and have differing abilities. It therefore is necessary to accommodate all users when designing and creating an interface and search options (e.g., basic or advanced search). User expectations also have increased—end users want quick access to information. New tools, techniques, and standards have been developed to organize and process digital information available on the Internet and on intranets, including metadata standards and new versions and types of KOSs. There also is the move toward the Semantic Web, which would enable advanced machine-processing of information as compared to what is available today on the Web (discussed below).

The early days of library automation (the 1980s) showed an increase in patrons performing subject searches of online library catalogs compared to subject searching in card catalogs (Olson and Boll 2001, 2). Since the 1980s, many more options have become available, including combined term searching, usage of Boolean and proximity operators, combined field searching, and the limitation by field values such as language and date. The online environment has made it possible to enhance KOS-based subject searching in many ways. For example, although classification schemes in traditional libraries primarily have been used for shelving books, they now also can be used in searching and as synthetic languages: Any combination of classifications or of individual facets could be made searchable.

Classification schemes—being systematic and hierarchical—support directory-style browsing of classes and subclasses as well as enabling the collocation of similar items. Although this is similar to shelf browsing in libraries in that a book has only one location there, if the book deals with several major topics, then in the online environment it easily can be listed as belonging to all the relevant classes. The importance of browsing is evidenced in the number of developed taxonomies which serve the same function. Further, classification schemes use a system of notation to represent the concepts and their hierarchical structure, which provides the potential for interoperable searching and browsing access to multilingual databases when the databases use the same classification schemes. Figure 1.1 shows an example of the Universal Decimal Classification class structure. The left side of the screen shows a hierarchical list of classes, and the right side of the screen contains notes on usage, definitions, and similar items.

Subject access in online information systems could be provided to include the following (Golub 2003).

- Browsing by subject access points: Titles, subjects from KOSs (e.g., subject headings, captions from classifications systems, classmarks with captions), free keywords, and tags.
- Searching by individual words from various metadata elements and by words from subject access points and full-text (if available).
- Searching and browsing by facets and individual concepts and facets from KOSs, such as individual terms from subject headings and individual notations from combined classmarks.
- Combining the search strategies above, including allowing unique searches by major and minor themes represented by KOSs if supported by the indexing policy.
- Presenting and browsing multiple classification hierarchies for each component concept of a classmark.
- Linking to other bibliographic records containing the same subject access points.
- Suggesting corrected versions of mistypes.
- Suggesting auto-completion of search terms once the user begins typing.
- Suggesting authorized KOS versions of entered search terms, presenting all the relationships and allowing further choice on browsing or searching the KOS.
- Combining subject searching with searching by other bibliographic fields (e.g., author, publication year, medium).
- Searching by citing or cited resources (if citations are available).
- Highlighting search terms in retrieved metadata and resources.
- Advanced searching by Boolean and proximity operators, truncation, and stemming.
- Choosing the type of sorting desired.
- Suggesting changes or describing automatic steps such as stemming if no results are returned.
- Combining previous search formulations.
- Providing help in simple end-user language.

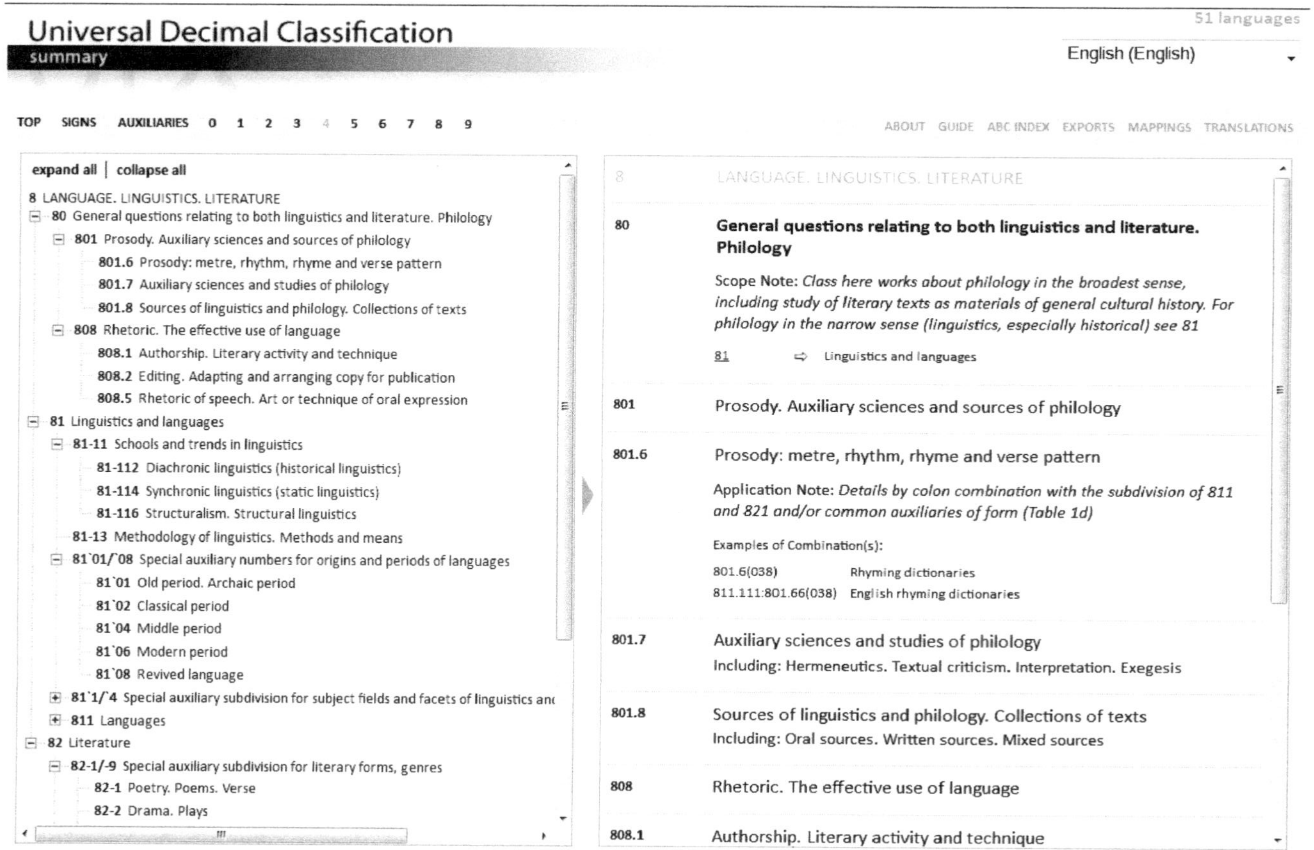

Figure 1.1. A segment of the UDC browsing tree.

Users also should be made aware of what influences the information retrieved—which very rarely is the case for automated systems such as Web search engines.

Search interfaces also must support novice end users. This includes adapting the existing KOS in a number of ways. One thought is that there should be more end-user and layman language included in the KOS, cross-referenced with terms used to index information resources in a given collection. These adaptations would allow support for search (re)formulation by disambiguating homographs and suggesting related, broader, or narrower terms. Information-science terminology used in interfaces must be simple and be defined in an easy-to-use manner for end users. For example, using terms such as "captions" or "uniform title" without explaining them in a search interface could perplex the end user. Classification classmarks (e.g., 821.111, a UDC classmark for English literature) must be replaced or accompanied by captions (this example would use "English literature").

Because KOSs now could be used by the general public, it would be important to simplify complex KOSs through the use of search terms, the possibility of browsing, and the application of social tags. Replacing complex built-in concepts (which are present in some KOSs) with a structure based on combinations of concepts such as that found in the Universal Decimal Classification (see Chapter 2 for more details), would allow greater flexibility in building new specific concepts both at the time of searching and at the time of subject indexing. Concurrently, it would reduce the size of the KOS.

The traditionally slow maintenance and updating of some KOSs is an issue for end users who cannot find new concepts and terms or who cannot find out how to use them because of outdated structures or hierarchies. A primary reason that classification systems are updated slowly is that it requires re-indexing or reclassification and reshelving in libraries, which are expensive tasks. Changing the structure also would cause problems for end-users, as they would have to learn the new structures to browse either an online or a physical collection. It is easier to make minor changes to a KOS, however, now that they are maintained in a digital format and are available online.

There are other reasons that it is so difficult to change the structure of KOSs. A librarian analyzing search logs of library patrons, for example, discovered that many end users searched using the term *Maritime Indians*—which is not cross-referenced in LCSH. When the librarian asked the Library of Congress to add the term as a "*see*" reference, the request was rejected on the grounds that it would involve too much time to create all the references of that type (Cann Casciato 2008). The librarian decided to add it in the local library system along with some other terms, including references resulting from common misunderstandings and misspellings discovered in the search logs (e.g., for "Klu Klux Klan" there is now a "see" reference to its correct name, "Ku Klux Klan").

Knowledge organization systems do not simply represent information, they also construct that information. In many KOSs there persists a historical bias on the basis of gender, sexuality, race, age, ability, ethnicity, language, and religion, which limits the representation of diversity and library service for diverse populations. Native American topics, for example, are segregated into the category of a historic people and into a single area of the Library of Congress classification schedule, regardless of discipline. Medicine, history, art, and tribal philosophy, for example, all are found in one area. This is especially problematic in a collection that focuses on this subject matter (Webster and Doyle 2008). The Dewey Decimal Classification—the most widespread classification system in the world—also has been criticized (Olson 2002) for its bias toward Western and Anglo-American views and topics. Such KOSs, which are used globally and in interoperable systems, should be restructured to address these issues.

Generally speaking, too little research has been conducted related to KOSs and their use. To inform their design and incorporation into information flows, much more research is needed. One stream of research in knowledge organization that focuses on informing the development of KOSs is domain analysis (Hjørland 2002). It emphasizes unique domain-specific needs and related meanings of concepts. For example, the topic "infection" can be approached from a medical, pharmaceutical, or public health viewpoint, which might not transfer to another domain's point of view. End users' tags also could provide feedback about which terms and concepts the KOS should include and thus allow the user perspective to be represented.

The online environment created the possibility of easier integration of information systems. Thus, the boundaries of online library catalogs no longer are clear. Academic and university library catalogs now can include eJournal and eBook databases, repositories of preprints, and various other collections of information resources. Integrating information systems involves considerable cost if quality subject access is to be maintained. Indeed, databases often follow different metadata formats and standards. To enable cross searching and browsing these differing metadata must be mapped to one another, merged, or transformed to match the structure, domain, language, or granularity.

Mapping different KOSs is complex when they are in different languages, because mapping involves the translation of concepts, not terms, and there often is significant variation between languages. Different cultural perspectives also should be integrated. On one hand, communities develop KOSs specific to their needs. Conversely, end users want to use a single search interface to find resources in multiple databases serving different domains and different KOSs, across which there might be no consensus regarding concepts, terminology, and knowledge organization.

Figure 1.2 shows an example of an existing multilingual searching interface. When searching for "booksellers" in all fields, the search retrieved 101

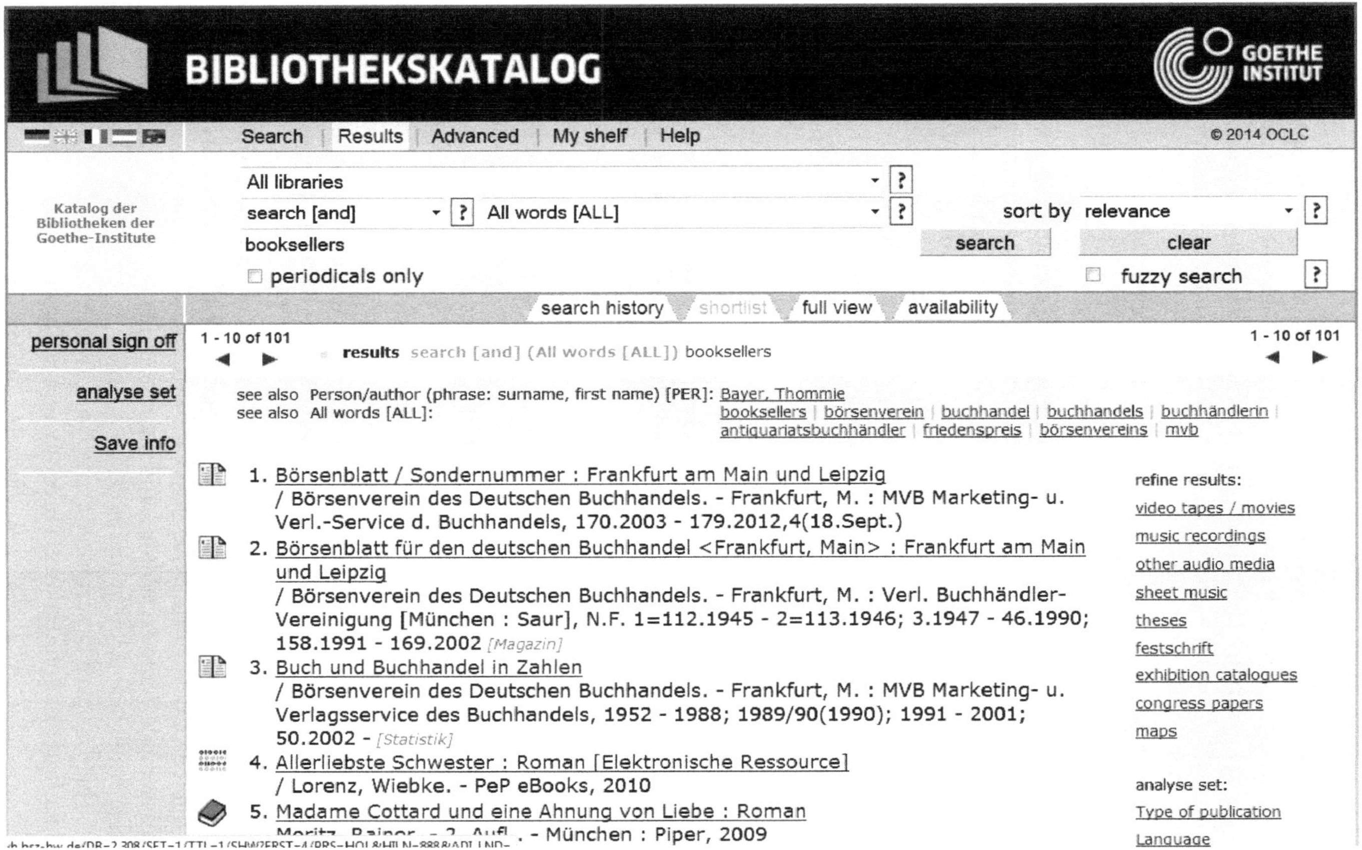

Figure 1.2. The multilingual subject search example from the Library of the Goethe Institute.

information resources with catalog records in the German language, and also suggests additional subject terms—in German—related to the search term.

The interoperability problem also exists at a technical level as there must be interoperability with other platforms as well as other applications. KOSs also ideally should work with search engines, content management systems, and Web publishing software. To allow for this, the KOS must be available in existing formats and protocols for data exchange and have URIs for unique identification of the KOS, its concepts, and terms. This is discussed in more detail in Chapter 3.

The Web has grown faster than any other technology and now has entered into and influenced virtually all areas of modern life—from the school child to the professional; from big companies to academic institutions, governments, and nonprofit organizations. Transforming the Web into the Semantic Web would enable computers to integrate and process data semantically across the Internet. In the words of Tim Berners-Lee—the inventor of the Web and the creator of the Semantic Web vision—it would be the Web of "machine-readable information whose meaning is well defined by standards" (Berners-Lee 2003, xi).

As compared to the Web of today, the Semantic Web would allow for establishing and recognizing more connections between the data contained within the distributed information resources, which in turn would support more advanced computer-based reasoning based on that data. Today's Web consists of information resources which link to other information resources via hyperlinks which often are not based on the content of these linked resources. As discussed above, retrieval in Web search engines is based on word matching rather than on meaning, which is why there are many false hits and incomplete results returned. More importantly, neither in Web search engines nor in library catalogs do results integrate data from different Web pages or websites. The Semantic Web requires that data which are part of those information resources (for example, structured data in tables) are presented in a standardized fashion that is understood by computers and are linked with other data. A table listing dates of major historical events at one website, for example, ideally would link to data in other websites that mention the same dates in a historical context. Then a synthesis or analysis of these data could be performed by computers and the results could be presented to the end users. Data connected in this manner are known as "Linked Data" (World Wide Web Consortium 2013). Today, existing examples include commercial hotel and flight booking websites, as they integrate data from various flight and hotel companies.

The Resource Description Framework (RDF) is a standard for encoding data (information resources) in a way that computers can process them. The data are represented and identifiable as Hypertext Transfer Protocol (HTTP) Universal Resource Identifiers (URIs). HTTP is the major Web protocol, and

URIs are used as unique identifiers for any information resource, such as a Web page or any datum on the page. The HTTP URIs link data about information resources on the Web to an interconnected graph of data and information resources.

Furthermore, OWL (Web Ontology Language) and SKOS (Simple Knowledge Organization Systems) are used to represent ontologies, thesauri, and other KOS types in a manner that can be used on the Semantic Web—primarily to allow for grouping together different names for the same concepts and thus ensuring semantic interpretation by computers. For more details on all standards, see Chapter 3.

Ontologies are defined as a special type of KOS which allows for advanced semantic information processing, including logical inferencing. To do this, ontologies define relationships and mappings between concepts using specialized properties, more formally and in more detail in comparison to, for example, thesauri and classification schemes. For many uses of the Semantic Web, however, traditional KOSs suffice, provided that they are available in RDF and that their data are identified as URIs. As such, in the future a KOS could be accessed by advanced search engines via Web services, which then could map the terms from all the information resources to the same concept and retrieve all the resources. A KOS also could allow for inclusion or exclusion of broader, narrower, and related terms.

Mapping different KOSs available in RDF and enriched with URIs would spread their usage further and enable searching across disciplines, thus promoting interdisciplinary access to resources. Including mappings to social tags potentially could broaden the set of retrieved information resources to include those that were not initially covered by the KOS. Another advantage of mapping is ensuring multilingual access—if each concept has a URI, then for many concept terms the URI could be the same in all languages, or URIs could be mapped. Although KOSs long have been restricted to the library and information science and profession, they now could realize their full potential and be used by other communities and thus enhance their visibility and importance.

New standards, conceptual models, and services are being developed in cultural heritage institutions and in the library and information science and profession to transfer the existing metadata into the Semantic Web. This would enable the exploitation of their full potential and increase their visibility. For example, CIDOC CRM is an ISO standard (21127) (International Organization for Standardization 2006) which defines an ontology for the exchange of rich cultural-heritage data.

The Functional Requirements for Bibliographic Records (FRBR) (IFLA Study Group on the Functional Requirements for Bibliographic Records 1998) is a recommendation of the International Federation of Library Associations and Institutions (IFLA) to restructure existing catalog databases into databases based on an entity-relationship model of catalog records which would better serve Semantic Web purposes, among others. The FRBR model covers three groups of entities. Group 1 is composed of "the products of intellectual or artistic endeavour that are named or described in bibliographic records: work, expression, manifestation, and item." Group 2 covers "those entities responsible for the intellectual or artistic content, the physical production and dissemination, or the custodianship of such products: person and corporate body." Group 3 is composed of the "entities that serve as the subjects of intellectual or artistic endeavour: concept, object, event, and place" (IFLA Study Group on the Functional Requirements for Bibliographic Records 1998, 13).

Similarly, the FRAD (Functional Requirements for Authority Data) (Patton 2009) describes the entity-relationship model for authority data, and the FRSAD (Functional Requirements for Subject Authority Data) (Zeng, Žumer, and Salaba 2011), the entity-relationship model for subjects data. In the FRSAD model, all entities of all three groups defined by FRBR can be the subject of a work. All the entities from all three groups (work, expression, manifestation, item; person, corporate body; concept, object, event, place) in FRSAD are called "*thema*" (Latin for topic) which is designated by a "*nomen*" (Latin for name). Work has as subject *thema*, which has a name *nomen*. *Thema*-to-*thema* relationships can be hierarchical (e.g., partitive, generic, instance with further details such as whether it has an acronym or is an acronym) and associative; other context-specific relationships are also defined. The *thema-nomen* model allows for separating concepts from their names or other types of strings such as classification number or code used to represent them, thus ensuring better interoperability across the library catalogs and beyond.

Zeng and Žumer (2010) discuss mapping FRSAD to other models such as SKOS and OWL. They show how subject authority data that follow the FRSAD model are easily encoded in SKOS or OWL, and thus can become part of the Linked Data and the Semantic Web. For a detailed overview and discussion of these matters in the library sphere, including guidelines and applications, refer to "Bibliographic Information Organization in the Semantic Web" (Willer and Dunsire 2013).

Today, a major effort of the Semantic Web is dedicated to developing standards and technologies needed to facilitate the creation, sharing, and querying of Linked Data. A major issue is the scalability of the human efforts needed to make the relevant part of the Web available in these standards. Although some claim that the Semantic Web still is a concept far from reality, others—including the World Wide Web Consortium (W3C), which develops the (Semantic) Web standards—claim that there already are a number of tools and appropriate technologies that can be used to realize at least some Semantic Web goals. Most work has been carried out in funded research projects (e.g., Europeana, DBpedia, DBLP, Geonames).

USER INFORMATION BEHAVIOR
(by David Elsweiler)

The field of Human Information Behavior (HIB)—an active area of research since the 1960s—studies "how people need, seek, manage, give and use information in different contexts" (Fisher, Erdelez, and McKechnie 2005). The HIB literature clearly shows that people are heterogeneous in the information behavior that they exhibit and that the exact way that people behave can differ depending on user aspects (e.g., the user's cognitive abilities or experience), task aspects (e.g., the kind or complexity of task), and a wide range of contextual factors (including situational and sociocultural aspects).

This section provides a brief overview of the HIB literature, taking examples from the related domains of information seeking (IS) and personal information management (PIM), where research has investigated how people acquire and manage information and the factors that influence these and related behaviors.

Barreau (1995) divided PIM behavior into four separate activities: (1) The acquisition of information items to form or add to a collection (this stage is the focus of the IS literature); (2) the organization of items into a personal collection; (3) the maintenance of the collection; and (4) the retrieval of items for reuse.

This section is structured around three of these four activities (1, 2, and 4). Each stage is examined in turn and evidence is collated from the findings of relevant publications, presenting an overview of current knowledge of the behavior associated with each activity. Each activity represents a well-studied research area, therefore it is not possible to cover the complete literature in depth herein. Rather, an array of important findings is presented for each activity, and provides insight into how people think about, organize, and manage information they possess or wish to possess. This is of relevance to the overarching theme of this book: how information collections should be organized for optimal access.

Acquiring Information

One common starting point for IS behavior is the user recognizing that he or she has insufficient knowledge on a given topic or for the completion of a specific task. Belkin et al. (1983) refer to this concept as an "Anomalous State of Knowledge" (ASK). Typically, the response is to address the anomaly by locating appropriate information. The individual then repeatedly reassesses the situation to determine whether the ASK has been resolved, possibly generating additional ASKs in the process. Other scholars characterize the motivation for seeking information in other ways, such as the desire to reduce uncertainty, which is associated with negative emotions

(Kuhlthau 1991), or by the intrinsic wish to understand and derive meaning from the world (Cornelius 1996; Dervin 1992).

Information seeking—the behavior performed in response to these situations—is well understood to be a dynamic activity that consists of several often cognitively demanding processes, such as the construction of search queries, the navigation of an information space, and the assessment of relevance.

It is clear that no one-size-fits-all approach to information seeking exists. Instead, researchers have identified various strategies that people apply. The strategies go beyond a user simply submitting queries and evaluating returned documents independently for relevance—the behavior classically modeled in information retrieval experiments. Strategies have been described at different levels of abstraction, ranging from the level of operations performed with a specific system (sometimes referred to as "tactics" (Bates 1979), for example, "remove Boolean operators" (Ford et al. 2009) to more general, system-agnostic strategies describing how actively the user communicates with the system (Ramirez et al. 2002).

Many scholars emphasize browsing as an IS strategy (Ellis 1989; Marchionini 1995; Pejtersen 1984). Bates (2007) characterizes browsing as "the activity of engaging in a series of glimpses, each of which might or might not lead to closer examination of a (physical or represented) object, which might or might not lead to (physical and/or conceptual) acquisition of the object." Bates argues that browsing reflects the intrinsic inquisitive and exploratory nature of humans. Browsing can be goal based or non–goal based, but the key properties of the strategy are that it is opportunistic and data driven (Marchionini 1995). The user starts in an area of interest—this could be anything from a magazine shelf to a subject of relevance in a classification scheme—and via such glimpsing behavior, attempts to drift toward relevant or interesting information objects.

Pejtersen (1984) identified four strategies in addition to browsing.

1. An "analytical strategy" requires the user to draw comparisons between the information problem and the technical functionalities of the system, actively translating a need into a "language" the system can use. Keyword search would be a prototypical example of such a strategy.
2. An "empirical strategy" is based on the user's past experience of what works. The user learns from previous attempts and derives rules and tactics that have allowed past tasks to be completed successfully. One instance of such a strategy—collected from a child—is the approach of modifying URLs to locate the information required: "When I want to buy something I just put it [in] as a URL. For example, if I need to buy a flag, I'll enter 'www.flags.com'" (Fidel 2012, 105).
3. A "known-site" strategy is applied when the user knows where the sought-after information is located or is likely to be located (e.g., a particular bookshelf or website) and a local search of that location must be performed.

4. A "similarity" strategy is performed when the user has difficulty describing what is needed, but has an example of a similar item. Pejtersen discovered this strategy to be a common way of finding fiction books. The user articulates what he or she wants by presenting the librarian with a book that the user has enjoyed previously and asking the librarian for suggestions for books that have similar content or properties.

A further strategy that goes beyond those suggested by Pejterson, and indeed could go outside the bounds of an information system, is the decision to use people as a source of information (Shah 2010). People often are associated with topics or areas of expertise and can be a means of quickly accessing reliable information.

The dynamic nature of IS behavior, how the strategies a user applies can change and merge into one another is characterized in Bates's "berry picking" metaphor, which models behavior as humans searching for berries, moving from bush to bush depending on how satisfied they are with the berries they pick. Several observational studies support the model (Ellis 1989; O'Day and Jeffries 1993).

The literature demonstrates that the exact strategy chosen by a user when presented with the task of finding information can vary depending on a number of different factors. Some of these are reviewed below.

When examining the information-seeking behavior of engineers, Hertzum and Pejtersen (2000) discovered that they search for documents to find people, search for people to get documents, and interact socially to get information without engaging in explicit searches. Thus, the way that people search is influenced by the task in which they are engaged.

Byström and Järvelin (1995) demonstrated that the complexity of the task is an important factor in determining information seeking behavior. Their study found that the more complex an information task appeared, the more likely it was that the person performing the task would ask another person rather than make use of an information system.

In the context of Web searching, White and Drucker (2007) identified two classes of extreme searchers, who they refer to as "navigators" and "explorers." Navigators tackle problems serially and are more likely to revisit Web pages from the same site. Explorers tend to submit many more queries while visiting pages from several different websites. The majority of Web searchers exhibit both traits, and both could be necessary for the user to complete the task at hand. With respect to the task classification proposed by Marchionini (2006), navigation might be better suited to well-defined lookup tasks for which the user requires explicit facts or must answer a well-defined question. Conversely, exploration could benefit tasks involving complex learning activities or the investigation of topics about which the user has minimal knowledge.

Other studies emphasize factors influencing behavior that are more associated with the users themselves. There are clear differences, for example, in the behavior of expert and novice search-engine users: Experts spend less time generating queries, take less time clicking on results, but explore results more thoroughly and ultimately are more successful (Aula, Jhaveri, and Käki 2005; White and Morris 2007).

The level of cognitive and motor skills the user possesses also can have an impact. The information behavior of children who are less developed in both of these respects, for example, has been shown to differ significantly from that of healthy adults (Bilal 2000; Hutchinson et al. 2005). The difficulties children have with cognitively challenging behaviors—such as the construction of search queries—seems to make browsing strategies more typical and also more successful for young users as compared to using analytical strategies (Schacter, Chung, and Dorr 1998).

Beyond experience and user skills, the personality of the user can be decisive. Heinström (2003) shows that users' personalities could be connected to the way they search for information. Heinström investigated five personality dimensions: neuroticism, extraversion, openness to experience, competitiveness, and conscientiousness. He found correlations between these and behavioral traits. Neuroticism—the vulnerability to negative emotions—for example, was related to having a preference for confirming information, feeling that lack of time was a barrier to information retrieval, having difficulties with relevance judgment, and exhibiting insecurity regarding database searching. Competitiveness was related to experiencing lack of time as a barrier to information retrieval, and to competence in critical analysis of information. Extraversion was found to be related to informal information retrieval as well as a preference for finding thought-provoking documents rather than documents which confirmed the ideas being researched.

The literature emphasizes that information-seeking behavior is highly contextual (Järvelin and Ingwersen 2004). Behavior simultaneously can be shaped by immediate influences—such as friends, family, and other trusted sources—as well as by wider socio-cultural influences, including media, technology, and politics (Burnett and Jaeger 2011). Contextual factors, in turn, can influence the task being performed. Elsweiler, Wilson, and Lunn (2011) showed how what people require or want and the information that satisfies these needs and desires differs in leisure scenarios as compared to more traditional work contexts. User behavior adapted accordingly.

Finally, it is important to mention that not all information acquisition results from the explicit seeking of information. Studies such as those by Erdelez (1997) and Toms (2000) revealed examples of what is referred to as "information encountering." This is the accidental or serendipitous discovery of information when the user is attempting to resolve another ASK, has some background interest or task (i.e., a general interest not related to the task at hand), and is aware of a need or interest of another person (Rioux 2005). Information encountering often is associated with a browsing strategy (Bawden 2011).

This section has demonstrated the existence of diverse information acquisition behavior that can be influenced by a multitude of various factors. The following section examines what people do after they have acquired information, in terms of how it can be organized and managed, revealing another layer of complexity.

Organizing Information

Several studies have investigated the classificatory choices made by different groups of people including office workers (Cole 1982), researchers (Kwasnik 1989), and historians (Case 1991). These investigations endorse the claim that the topical content of an item is important when organizing personal information.

A participant in Case's study, for example, described part of his organization stating that "over there you have some things on American literature and most of these middle files concern legal history" (Case 1991). Case noted that participants had a regular desire to keep topically related documents together. Articles and books, for instance, which are physically difficult to intersperse were grouped using "paper-bound containers."

Kwasnik's investigation provided the strongest evidence for the importance of topic as a classification dimension, with "topic" featuring frequently in the participants' explanations for their classification choices. Nevertheless, all three studies show that other dimensions such as document attributes and, in particular, situational attributes can be and often are more important. Document attributes include the author or the person most associated with the item and the form or type of item, for example, whether it was a book or a magazine. Situational attributes include the document's source (that is, where the item came from: Was it downloaded from the Web or suggested by Fred?), the reasons for its creation (e.g., a project report, an invitation to a party), or its predicted future use (e.g., it will be needed to claim expenses later).

The literature makes it clear that no single dimension prevails even for individual users. Instead, a complicated weighting system of priorities determines the dimension used to classify an item. Even if an individual tends toward a topic-based organization, for example, other factors (such as the form of item and space constraints) can overrule that tendency. Further, it is common for individuals to attempt to "keep (important) things close at hand" (Case 1991).

Similar to the findings of information seeking studies, scholars have observed that organization behavior can be very different at a user level. Users often are grouped by the strategies they utilize, reflecting the level of organization they exhibit and their dedication to maintaining that organization. Malone (1983), for example, distinguished between neat and messy people. Neat people designate a category for every document and place it in a location corresponding to that category; the location could be a folder inside a filing cabinet, a paper tray, or a named pile. Messy people, conversely, pile up documents over time and in a less-structured way. Whittaker and Sidner (1996) classified email users into filers, non-filers, and spring-cleaners (users who periodically tidy their inbox by moving messages into folders). Abrams, Baecker, and Chignell (1998) grouped users of bookmark organizations into no-filers, creation-time filers (organize bookmarks immediately), end-of-session filers (organize after the Web browsing session is completed), and sporadic filers (organize when they feel like it). Although these categories relate to effort exerted in organizing, the effort individuals apply can be different across tools (Boardman and Sasse 2004). Therefore an individual's strategy also might have to do with task-level factors, that is, what the user wants to achieve with the tool.

One of the principal reasons for collecting and organizing personal information is the prediction of a utility for information in the future (Bruce, Jones, and Dumain 2004). The act of re-accessing previously seen information in response to an ASK is referred to in the HIB literature as information re-finding. The following section provides an overview of the research characterizing this behavior.

Re-Finding Information

Re-accessing information has been shown to be an activity people undertake regularly. For example, 60% to 80% of Web page visits are re-accesses (McKenzie and Cockburn 2001) and approximately 40% of Web searches are performed with the aim of finding something that the user previously had found (Teevan et al. 2007). Similar patterns of reuse have been shown for other objects, ranging from library books (Burrell 1980), to files on computer systems (Dumais et al. 2003), to email messages (Elsweiler, Harvey, and Hacker 2011).

Most of the items that are re-found were created or accessed recently. The distribution of time between accessing and re-accessing has a long and fat tail, however, as information items can have very long life spans (Dumais et al. 2003; Elsweiler, Harvey, and Hacker 2011). Re-finding also tends to be performed in bursts; an item might not have been accessed for a while and then is accessed several times within a short period (Tyler and Teevan 2010; Elsweiler, Harvey, and Hacker 2011).

The task of re-finding is different from looking for new information and uses different cognitive processes. Whereas finding new information involves recognizing that retrieved resources are useful, re-finding utilizes recollection to guide the search for specific resources that are known to be useful (Capra and Perez-Quinones 2005).

In the same vein as the information-seeking literature, several re-finding strategies have been revealed. People can have a strong preference for location-based finding, orienteering, or simply browsing as a primary means to return to specific information (Barreau and Nardi 1995; Marchionini 1995; O'Day and Jeffries 1993). Capra and Perez-Quinones (2003) observed that, when re-finding, users often take a two-stage iterative approach. In the first stage the user identifies an appropriate information source, and in the second the user focuses on narrowing toward specific information from within that source (similar to Pejtersen's "known-site" strategy).

Similarly, Teevan et al. (2004) described orienteering behavior, which "involves using contextual information to narrow in on the actual information target, often in a series of steps." Teevan et al. also observed a second approach to re-finding, which they refer to as "teleporting." In this approach, users attempt "to take themselves directly to the information they are looking for" (Teevan et al. 2004). An example of a teleporting strategy would be using a remembered URL to directly access a Web page or using extensive, detailed search queries to locate a Web page with one attempt. When people employ a search strategy, the queries they submit tend to be very short and frequently contain person names or parts of person names (Dumais et al. 2003; Elsweiler, Harvey, and Hacker 2011). Aula, Jhaveri, and Käki (2005) argued that searching to re-find data is necessarily an iterative task, largely because it is nearly impossible to accurately recreate original queries.

Strategies for re-finding, therefore, seem to involve searching, browsing, or a combination of the two. The literature suggests, however, that the type of information item someone is trying to re-find will influence the strategy used. For documents and other computer files, users prefer browsing (Barreau and Nardi 1995; Bergman et al. 2008); for email, users prefer searching (Elsweiler, Harvey, and Hacker 2011; Whittaker et al. 2011); and for Web references a mixture of auto-complete, searching, and browsing seems to be the preferred approach. The evidence suggests that strategies are honed over time for regularly re-found objects; the more often an object or type of object is found, the better defined the strategy for that object becomes (Tyler and Teevan 2010).

As with the other behaviors discussed, the strategy that the user employs depends on a number of factors beyond the tool. There is evidence to suggest that the behavior exhibited will be influenced by the time elapsed between accessing and re-accessing the information (Tyler and Teevan 2010), the experience of the user (Elsweiler et al. 2011), and exactly what the user remembers, which will in turn be influenced by other contextual factors (Elsweiler, Baille, and Ruthven 2008). Thus, a complex web of variables influences re-finding behavior.

SUMMARY

As part of making sense of the world, people attempt to organize everything around them. The library and information science and profession hold the longest record of organizing information. The first known library catalog comes from the third century BCE and organizes scrolls by authors and subjects.

Searching for information on a certain topic is very common and yet often is the most difficult to achieve in an information retrieval system, mainly because concepts can take various names and these names can take various forms (e.g., plural or singular, noun or verb). Additionally, there is more room for error when conceptualizing an information need and then translating it into a search query, as compared to a known-item search.

To establish control over the natural language, subject indexing languages such as subject headings systems, thesauri, and classification systems are used in libraries and other quality information systems. They control synonyms, distinguish among homonyms and group-related concepts, thus ensuring indexing consistency as well as high precision and high recall in retrieval. With transition to an online environment, "knowledge organization systems" became a term that includes ontologies, folksonomies, taxonomies, and other systems. These systems are used to ensure a level of language control on the (Semantic) Web, although other functionalities are also fulfilled by KOSs.

Automated subject indexing and social tagging are two options often discussed as alternatives to manual subject indexing. Automated subject indexing might extract terms from information resources, which often results in false hits and incomplete results, or it can automatically assign controlled subject index terms or classes from KOSs. The latter method also can produce false matches, again due to the problems of the natural language. Social tags lack even basic spelling and word-form control; there is no structure for concepts and no relationships among terms—many of which only are of personal significance. Regardless, both automated index terms and social tags could be used to provide additional perspectives on the "aboutness" of a work. For some machine-aided indexing systems satisfying results have been reported, and research also indicates the potential added value of social tags. More research is needed to examine these, however, including the development of a more reliable and contextualized evaluation methodology, as there are numerous factors that influence the subjective nature of aboutness.

The online environment has brought the potential for much-improved subject access, both within formal information systems such as library catalogs and across a variety of other information systems. The former includes a greater number of subject access points, which can be combined in library catalogs and in other information systems by applying KOSs. The latter includes the possibility for access across multilingual information systems (provided that they use the same classification scheme, which includes the same notation in all languages, or a multilingual thesaurus), or any other KOSs whose concepts have been mapped to one another.

Traditional KOSs need to be improved in a number of aspects. They need to be updated more quickly as new concepts are introduced and as end-user suggestions are provided (e.g., from search logs and social tags). The historical bias on the basis of gender, sexuality, race, age, ability, ethnicity, language, and religion should be excluded. Also, more research is needed to inform the development of KOSs, such as domain analysis or interdisciplinary research.

The Semantic Web has been envisioned as the Web of data, where Web-accessible resources of various types are encoded in such a way that computers can process them. These include RDF and HTTP URIs, which draw on ontologies, and KOSs where relationships and concepts also are encoded in established standards. Eventually, this will turn the Web into a large, structured, distributed database that can be queried in a precise way to retrieve relevant meaningful results. Libraries and cultural heritage institutions are developing and implementing new models and standards which would enable them to merge their high-quality catalogs into the Semantic Web.

CHAPTER REVIEW

1. Which formal and which informal information systems do you use? What are your tasks at hand when you use formal information systems? What tasks do you handle using informal systems?
2. What search strategies and techniques do you use when researching a certain topic?
3. What do you think about algorithms for automated searching and indexing? What value do they hold in comparison to KOSs?
4. What do you think about social tags? What value do they hold in comparison to KOSs?
5. What do you envision that the Semantic Web will do for you?

GLOSSARY (*Including Contributions by David Elsweiler*)

Anomalous state of knowledge: The state an individual experiences when recognizing that he or she has inadequate knowledge for completing a task.

Browsing: An exploratory information-seeking strategy often used when a user is unfamiliar with the information space. Browsing can be goal-based or non–goal-based, but the key properties of the strategy are that it is opportunistic and data driven.

Controlled vocabularies: Any authorized set of terms used in creating metadata records, such as author names; broader than indexing languages.

Document attributes: Metadata associated with a given document that influences classification decisions. These include the author or the person most associated with the item, and the form or type of item (for example, whether it is a book or a magazine, or whether it is blue or green).

Folksonomy: A list of all social tags in a service.

Formal information systems: Systems in which systematic guidelines and standards that are followed closely in selecting, organizing, and providing access to resources.

Indexing languages: A specific type of controlled vocabulary representing formalized languages designed and used to describe the subject content of information resources for information-retrieval purposes.

Informal information systems: Systems in which no particular standards or guidelines are followed in selecting, organizing, and providing access to resources.

Information encountering: The acquisition of information without explicitly seeking it. This can be desired or undesired.

Information organizing: The behavior exhibited to maintain order on an information space or collection.

Information organization: Grouping of descriptions of information resources according to specific principles.

Information re-finding: The information-seeking task of locating information previously seen or possessed in the past. This behavior tends to be driven by the user's recollection.

Information resource: A physical object or digital file containing information conveyed through language, image, sound, and other means accessible to the end user of an information-retrieval system.

Information seeking: The process or activity of using human or technological means in an attempt to obtain information.

Information-seeking strategy: A sequence of tactics which, viewed together, help achieve some aspect or subgoal of an individual's primary objective or task.

Information-seeking tactics: The immediate choices or actions taken in light of the current focus of attention and state of the information-seeking task.

Knowledge organization system (KOS): System which can be used for various aspects of organizing information. Now often includes controlled and indexing languages as well as folksonomies and other systems.

Personal information management: The behaviors an individual exhibits to acquire, keep, manage, organize, re-find, and reuse information.

Semantic Web: A vision of the current and future Web which includes encoding data describing information resources in a standard way and identifying them using HTTP URIs so as to create a network of linked data that can be processed by software agents.

Situational attributes: Contextual factors influencing classification decisions, which include the document's source or where the item came from (e.g., Was it downloaded from the Web? Was it suggested by Fred?), the reasons for its creation (e.g., a project report, an invitation to a party), or its predicted future use (e.g., needed later for claiming expenses).

Social tags: Index terms assigned by end users.

Subject gateways: Professional digital collections of Web resources which are selected and cataloged following guidelines and standards.

Subject indexing: Determining relevant topics of an information resource, selecting appropriate index terms or classes, and assigning them to the description of the resource as part of cataloging or metadata creation.

Subject-based information organization: Grouping of descriptions of information resources according to their topic, theme, or content.

Web 2.0: Web services with facilities enabling end users to contribute comments, reviews, social tags, and similar items.

REFERENCES

Abrams, David, Ron Baecker, and Mark Chignell. 1998. "Information Archiving with Bookmarks: Personal Web Space Construction and Organization." In *Proceedings of the ACM CHI 98 Human Factors in Computing Systems Conference*, edited by Clare-Marie Karat et al., 41–48. New York: ACM Press.

Anderson, James D., and Jose Pérez-Carballo. 2001. "The Nature of Indexing: How Humans and Machines Analyze Messages and Texts for Retrieval. Part II: Machine Indexing, and the Allocation of Human versus Machine Effort." *Information Processing and Management* 37: 255–77.

Aula, Anne, Natalie Jhaveri, and Mika Käki. 2005. "Information Search and Reaccess Strategies of Experienced Web Users." In *WWW '05 Proceedings of the 14th International Conference on World Wide Web*, 583–92. New York: ACM Press.

Barreau, Deborah. 1995. "Context as a Factor in Personal Information Management Systems." *Journal of the American Society for Information Science* 46 (5): 327–39.

Barreau, Deborah, and Bonnie Nardi. 1995. "Finding and Reminding: File Organization from the Desktop." *ACM SIGCHI Bulletin* 27 (3): 39–43.

Bates, Marcia J. 2009. "Information." In *Encyclopedia of Library and Information Sciences*, 3rd ed., edited by Marcia Bates, 2347–60. New York: Taylor and Francis.

Bates, Marcia J. 2007. "What is Browsing—Really? A Model Drawing from Behavioural Science Research." *Information Research* 12 (4). Accessed September 3, 2014. http://InformationR.net/ir/12-4/paper330.html.

Bates, Marcia J. 1979. "Information Search Tactics." *Journal of the American Society for Information Science* 30 (4): 205–14.

Bawden, David. 2011. "Encountering on the Road to Serendip? Browsing in New Information Environments." In *Innovations in IR: Perspectives for Theory and Practice*, edited by Allen Foster and Pauline Rafferty, 1–22. London: Facet Publishing.

Baxendale, P. B. 1958. "Machine-Made Index for Technical Literature—An Experiment." *IBM Journal of Research and Development* 2: 354–61.

Belkin, Nicholas, Thomas Seeger, and Gemot Wersig. 1983. "Distributed Expert Problem Treatment as a Model for Information Systems Analysis and Design." *Journal of Information Science* 5: 153–67.

Bergman, Ofer, Ruth Beyth-Marom, Rafi Nachmias, Noa Gradovitch, and Steve Whittaker. 2008. "Improved Search Engines and Navigation Preference in Personal Information Management." *ACM Transactions on Information Systems (TOIS)* 26 (4), paper 20.

Berners-Lee, Tim. 2003. "Foreword." In *Spinning the Semantic Web: Bringing the World Wide Web to Its Full Potential,* edited by Dieter Fensel, James A. Hendler, Henry Lieberman, and Wolfgang Wahlster, xi–vi. Cambridge, MA: The MIT Press.

Bilal, Dania. 2000. "Children's Use of the Yahooligans! Web Search Engine: Cognitive, Physical, and Affective Behaviors on Fact-Based Search Tasks." *Journal of the American Society for Information Science* 51 (7): 646–65.

Boardman, Richard, and M. Angela Sasse. 2004. "Stuff Goes into the Computer and Doesn't Come Out: A Cross-Tool Study of Personal Information Management." In *CHI '04: Proceedings of the SIGCHI Conference on Human Factors in Computing Systems,* edited by E. Dykstra-Erickson and M. Tscheligi, 583–90. New York: ACM Press.

Borlund, Pia. 2003. "The Concept of Relevance in IR." *Journal of the American Society for Information Science and Technology* 54 (10): 913–25.

Bruce, Harry, William Jones, and Susan Dumais. 2004. "Keeping and Re-Finding Information on the Web: What Do People Do and What Do They Need?" In *ASIST 2004: Proceedings of the 67th ASIST Annual Meeting* 41 (1). doi: 10.1002/meet.1450410115.

Burnett, Gary, and Paul T. Jaeger. 2011. "The Theory of Information Worlds and Information Behaviour." *Library and Information Science* 1: 161–80.

Burrell, Quentin. 1980. "A Simple Stochastic Model for Library Loans." *Journal of Documentation* 36 (2): 115–32.

Buxton, A. B., and A. J. Meadows. 1977. "The Variation in the Information Content of Titles of Research Papers with Time and Discipline." *Journal of Documentation* 33 (1): 46–52.

Byström, Katriina, and Järvelin, Kalervo. 1995. "Task Complexity Affects Information Seeking and Use." *Information Processing & Management* 31 (2): 191–213.

Cann Casciato, Daniel. 2008. "Respect My Authoritah!" In *Radical Cataloging,* edited by K.R. Roberto, 265–68. Jefferson, NC: McFarland and Co.

Capra, Robert G., and Manuel A. Perez-Quinones. 2005. "Using Web Search Engines to Find and Refind Information." *Computer* 38 (10): 36–42.

Capra, Robert G., and Manuel A. Perez-Quinones. 2003. "Re-Finding Found Things: An Exploratory Study of How Users Re-Find Information." Technical Report. Blacksburg, VA: Virginia Tech. Computer Science Dept.

Case, Donald Owen. 1991. "Conceptual Organization and Retrieval of Text by Historians: The Role of Memory and Metaphor." *Journal of the American Society for Information Science* 42 (9): 657–68.

Choi, Yunseon. 2013. "Social Indexing: A Solution to the Challenges of Current Information Organization." In *New Directions in Information Organization*, edited by Jung-Ran Park and Lynne C. Howarth, 107–35. Bingley: Emerald Group Publishing Limited.

Cole, Irene. 1982. "Human Aspects of Office Filing: Implications for the Electronic Office." In *Proceedings of the Human Factors and Ergonomics Society Annual Meeting*, 26 (1): 59–63. doi: 10.1177/154193128202600115.

Cornelius, Ian V. 1996. *Meaning and Method in Information Studies*. Norwood, NJ: Ablex Publishing Corporation.

Cutter, Charles A. 1876. *Rules for a Printed Dictionary Catalog*. Washington, DC: U.S. GPO.

Dervin, Brenda. 1992, "From the Mind's Eye of the User: The Sense-Making Qualitative-Quantitative Methodology." *Qualitative Research in Information Management* 6: 1–84.

Dumais, Susan, Edward Cutrell, J. J. Cadiz, Gavin Jancke, Raman Sarin, and Daniel C. Robbins. 2003. "Stuff I've Seen: A System for Personal Information Retrieval and Re-Use." In *SIGIR '03: Proceedings of 26th Annual International ACM SIGIR Conference on Research and Development in Information Retrieval*, edited by Mark Sanderson, 72–79. New York: ACM Press.

Eliot, Simon, and Jonathan Rose. 2009. *A Companion to the History of the Book*. Chicester: John Wiley and Sons.

Ellis, David. 1989. "A Behavioural Approach to Information Retrieval System Design." *Journal of Documentation* 45 (3): 171–212.

Elsweiler, David, David Losada, Jose Carlos Toucedo, and Ronald T. Fernandez. 2011. "Seeding Simulated Queries with User-Study Data for Personal Search Evaluation." In *Proceedings of the 34th International ACM SIGIR Conference on Research and Development in Information Retrieval*, 25–34. New York: ACM Press.

Elsweiler, David, Mark Baille, and Ian Ruthven. 2008. "Exploring Memory in Email Refinding." *ACM Transactions on Information Systems (TOIS)* 26 (4). doi: 10.1145/1402256.1402260.

Elsweiler, David, Max L.Wilson, and Brian Kirkegaard Lunn. 2011. "Understanding Casual-Leisure Information Behaviour." In *Library and Information Science* Vol. 1, edited by Amanda Spink and Jannica Heinström, 211–41. Bingley: Emerald Group Publishing Limited.

Elsweiler, David, Morgan Harvey, and Martin Hacker. 2011. "Understanding Re-Finding Behavior in Naturalistic Email Interaction Logs." In *Proceedings of the 34th International ACM SIGIR Conference on Research and Development in Information Retrieval*, 35-44. New York: ACM Press.

Erdelez, Sanda. 1997. "Information Encountering: a Conceptual Framework for Accidental Information Discovery." In Information Seeking in Context: Proceedings of an International Conference on Research in Information Needs, Seeking and Use in Different Contexts, edited by Pertti Vakkari, Reijo Savolainen, and Brenda Dervin, 412–21. London: Taylor Graham.

Europeana. 2014. "Europeana: Think Culture." *FAQs; About Europeana.* http://pro.europeana.eu/web/guest/europeana-faq.

Fidel, Raya. 2012. *Human Information Interaction: An Ecological Approach to Information Behavior.* Cambridge, MA: The MIT Press.

Fisher, Karen. E., Sanda Erdelez, and Lynne E.F. McKechnie (ed.). 2005. *Theories of Information Behavior.* Medford, NJ: Information Today.

Ford, Nigel, Barry Eaglestone, Andrew Madden, and Martin Whittle. 2009. "Web Searching By the 'General Public': An Individual Differences Perspective." *Journal of Documentation* 65 (4): 632–67.

Foskett, A. C. 1996. *The Subject Approach to Information.* 5th ed. London: Library Association Publishing.

Golub, Koraljka. 2003. "Predmetno pretraživanje u knjižničnim katalozima s web-sučeljem." MA thesis, University of Zagreb. Accessed July 21, 2014. http://koraljka.info/publ/Magisterij-hrv.pdf.

Golub, Koraljka, Marianne Lykke and Douglas Tudhope. 2014. "Enhancing Social Tagging with Automated Keywords from the Dewey Decimal Classification." *Journal of Documentation* 70 (5): 801–828.

Hagedorn, Kat. 2001. "Extracting Value from Automated Classification Tools: The Role of Manual Involvement and Controlled Vocabularies." White Paper. Accessed September 3, 2014. http://argus-acia.com/white_papers/classification.html.

Heinström, Jannica. 2003. "Five Personality Dimensions and Their Influence on Information Behaviour." *Information Research* 9 (1). Accessed September 3, 2014. http://www.informationr.net/ir/9-1/paper165.html.

Hertzum, Morten, and Annelise Mark Pejtersen. 2000. "The Information-Seeking Practices of Engineers: Searching for Documents As Well As for People." *Information Processing and Management* 36 (5): 761–78.

Hjørland, Birger. 2009. "Concept Theory." *Journal of the American Society for Information Science and Technology* 60 (8): 1519–36.

Hjørland, Birger. 2002. "Domain Analysis in Information Science: Eleven Approaches—Traditional As Well As Innovative." *Journal of Documentation* 58 (4): 422–62.

Ho, Birong, and Laura Horne-Popp. 2013. "VuFind: An OPAC 2.0?" In *New Directions in Information Organization,* edited by Jung-Ran Park, Lynne C. Howarth, 159–71. Bingley: Emerald Group Publishing Limited.

Hutchinson, Hilary, Allison Druin, Benjamin B. Bederson, Kara Reuter, Anne Rose, and Ann Carlson Weeks. 2005. "How Do I Find Blue Books About Dogs? The Errors and Frustrations of Young Digital Library Users." In *Proceedings of Human-Computer Interaction Lab (HCIL) 2005.*

IFLA Study Group on the Functional Requirements for Bibliographic Records. 1998. *Functional Requirements for Bibliographic Records.* München: K.G. Saur.

Infomine. 1994. *Infomine: Scholarly Internet Resource Collections.* University of California. Accessed September 3, 2014. http://infomine.ucr.edu.

International Organization for Standardization. 2006. *Information and Documentation—A Reference Ontology for the Interchange of Cultural Heritage Information: ISO 21127*. Geneve: International Organization for Standardization.

International Organization for Standardization. 1985. *Documentation—Methods for Examining Documents, Determining their Subjects, and Selecting Indexing Terms: ISO 5963*. Geneve: International Organization for Standardization.

Ipl2. 2012. *Ipl2: Information You Can Trust*. Drexel University. http://www.ipl.org/.

Järvelin, Kalervo, and Peter Ingwersen. 2004. "Information Seeking Research Needs Extension Towards Tasks and Technology." *Information Research* 10, 1: paper 212.

Kuhlthau, Carol C. 1991. "Inside the Search Process: Information Seeking from the User's Perspective." *Journal of the American Society for Information Science* 42 (5): 361–71.

Kwasnik, Barbara H. 1989. "How a Personal Document's Intended Use or Purpose Affects Its Classification in an Office." *SIGIR Forum* 23(SI): 207–10.

Lancaster, F. W. 2003. *Indexing and Abstracting in Theory and Practice*. 3rd ed. London: Facet.

Lin, Xia, Joan E. Beaudoin, Yen Bui, and Kaushal Desai. 2006. "Exploring Characteristics of Social Classification." In *Proceedings of the 17th Annual ASIS&T SIG/CR Classification Research Workshop*. Accessed September 3, 2014. http://faculty.cis.drexel.edu/~xlin/papers /ASIS2006.lin.pdf.

Luhn, Hans Peter. 1957. "A Statistical Approach to Mechanized Encoding and Searching of Literary Information." *IBM Journal of Research and Development* 1: 309–17.

Lykke, Marianne, and A. G. Eslau. 2010. "Using Thesauri in Enterprise Settings: Indexing or Query Expansion?" In *The Janus Faced Scholar: A Festschrift in Honour of Peter Ingwersen*, edited by B. Larsen, J. W. Schneider, F. Åström, and B. Schlemmer, 87–97. Copenhagen: Det Informationsvidenskabelige Akademi.

Malone, Thomas W. 1983. "How Do People Organize Their Desks? Implications for the Design of Office Information Systems." *ACM Transactions on Information Systems* 1 (1): 99–112. Accessed September 3, 2014. www.ischool.utexas.edu/~i385q/readings/Malone-1983-HowDoPeople.pdf.

Mann, Thomas. 2008. "What Is Going on at the Library of Congress?" In *Radical Cataloging: Essays at the Front*, edited by K. R. Roberto, 170–88. London: McFarland & Company.

Marchionini, Gary. 2006. "Exploratory Search: From Finding to Understanding." *Communications of the ACM* 49 (4): 41–46.

Marchionini, Gary. 1995. *Information Seeking in Electronic Environments*. Cambridge University Press.

Maron, M. E. 1961. "Automatic Indexing: An Experimental Inquiry." *Journal of the Association for Computing Machinery* 8 (3): 404–17.

Moens, Marie-Francine. 2000. *Automatic Indexing and Abstracting of Document Texts*. Boston, MA: Kluwer Academic Publishers.

O'Day, Vicki. L., and Robin Jeffries. 1993. "Orienteering in an Information Landscape: How Information Seekers Get from Here to There." In *CHI '93 Proceedings of the INTERACT '93 and CHI '93 Conference on Human Factors in Computing Systems*, 438–45. New York: ACM.

Olson, Hope A. 2002. *The Power to Name: Locating the Limits of Subject Representation in Libraries*. Dordrecht, Netherlands: Kluwer Academic.

Olson, Hope A., and John J. Boll. 2001. *Subject Analysis in Online Catalogs*. 2nd ed. Orlando, FL: Academic Press.

Patton, Glenn E. (ed.). 2009. *Functional Requirements for Authority Data—A Conceptual Model*. München: K. G. Saur.

Pejtersen, Annelise Mark.1984. "Design of a Computer-Aided User-System Dialogue Based on an Analysis of Users' Search Behavior." *Social Science Information Studies* 4 (2): 167–83.

Purpura, Stephen, and Dustin Hillard. 2006. "Automated Classification of Congressional Legislation." In *Proceedings of the 7th International Conference on Digital Government Research*, edited by José A. B. Fortes and Ann MacIntosh, 219–25. Digital Government Research Center.

Ramirez, Artemio, Joseph B. Walther, Judee K. Burgoon, and Michael Sunnafrank. 2002. "Information-Seeking Strategies, Uncertainty, and Computer-Mediated Communication." *Human Communication Research* 28 (2): 213–28.

Rioux, Kevin. 2005. "Information Acquiring and Sharing." In *Theories of Information Behavior*, edited by Karen E. Fisher, Sanda Erdelez, and Lynne E.F. McKechnie, 169–73. Medford, NJ: Information Today, Inc. (ASIST Monograph Series).

Roitblat, Herbert L., Anne Kershaw, and Patrick Oot. 2010. "Document Categorization in Legal Electronic Discovery: Computer Classification vs. Manual Review." *Journal of the American Society for Information Science and Technology* 61 (1): 70–80.

Ruiz, Miguel E., Alan R. Aronson, and Marjorie Hlava. 2008. "Adoption and Evaluation Issues of Automatic and Computer Aided Indexing Systems." In *Proceedings of the American Society for Information Science and Technology*, 46 (1): 1–4.

Saracevic, Tefko. 2008. "Effects of Inconsistent Relevance Judgments on Information Retrieval Test Results: A Historical Perspective." *Library Trends* 56 (4): 763–83.

Schacter, John, Gregory K.W. K. Chung, and Aimée Dorr. 1998. "Children's Internet Searching on Complex Problems: Performance and Process Analyses." *Journal of the American Society for Information Science* 49 (9): 840–49.

Shah, Chirag. 2010. "Collaborative Information Seeking: A Literature Review." *Advances in Librarianship* 32: 3–33.

Silvester, June P. 1997. "Computer Supported Indexing: A History and Evaluation of NASA's MAI System." In *Encyclopedia of Library and Information Services* 61, supplement 24: 76–90.

Soergel, Dagobert. 1994. "Indexing and Retrieval Performance: The Logical Evidence." *Journal of the American Society for Information Science* 45 (8): 589–99.

Soergel, Dagobert. 1985. *Organizing Information: Principles of Database and Retrieval Systems.* Orlando, FL: Academic Press.

Spiteri, Louise. 2007. "Structure and Form of Folksonomy Tags: The Road to the Public Library Catalogue." *Webology* 4 (2). Accessed July 21, 2014. http://www.webology.org/2007/v4n2/a41.html.

Teevan, Jaime, Christine Alvarado, Mark S. Ackerman, and David R. Karger. 2004. "The Perfect Search Engine Is Not Enough: A Study of Orienteering Behavior in Directed Search." In *Proceedings of the SIGCHI Conference on Human Factors in Computing Systems*, 415–22. New York: ACM.

Teevan, Jaime, Eytan Adar, Rosie Jones, and Michael A. S. Potts. 2007. "Information Re-Retrieval: Repeat Queries in Yahoo's Logs." In *Proceedings of the 30th Annual International ACM SIGIR Conference on Research and Development in Information Retrieval*, 151–58. New York: ACM.

Toms, Elaine G. 2000. "Understanding and Facilitating the Browsing of Electronic Text." *International Journal of Human-Computer Studies* 52 (3): 423–52.

Tyler, Sarah K., and Jaime Teevan. 2010. "Large Scale Query Log Analysis of Re-Finding." In *Proceedings of the Third ACM International Conference on Web Search and Data Mining*, 191–200. New York: ACM.

Webster, Kelly, and Ann Doyle. 2008. "Don't Class Me in Antiquities! Giving Voice to Native American Materials." In *Radical Cataloging: Essays at the Front*, edited by K. R. Roberto, 189–97. London: McFarland & Company.

White, Ryen W., and Dan Morris. 2007. "Investigating the Querying and Browsing Behavior of Advanced Search Engine Users." In *Proceedings of the 30th Annual International ACM SIGIR Conference on Research and Development in Information Retrieval*, 255–62. New York: ACM.

White, Ryen W., and Steven Drucker. 2007. "Investigating Behavioral Variability In Web Search." In *WWW '07 Proceedings of the 16th International Conference on World Wide Web*, 21–30. New York: ACM.

Whittaker, Steve, and Candace Sidner. 1996. "Email Overload: Exploring Personal Information Management of Email." In *Proceedings of the SIGCHI Conference on Human Factors in Computing Systems*, 276–83. New York: ACM.

Whittaker, Steve, Tara Matthews, Julian Cerruti, Hernan Badenes, and John Tang. 2011. "Am I Wasting My Time Organizing Email? A Study of Email Refinding." In *PART 5 Proceedings of the 2011 Annual Conference on Human Factors in Computing Systems*, 3449–58. New York: ACM.

Willer, Mirna, and Gordon Dunsire. 2013. *Bibliographic Information Organization in the Semantic Web*. Burlington, MA: Elsevier Publishing.

WordNet. 2014. "Bank." Accessed September3, 2014. http://wordnetweb.princeton.edu/perl/webwn?s=bank.

World Wide Web Consortium. 2013. "Linked Data." Accessed September 3, 2014. http://www.w3.org/standards/semanticweb/data.html.

Zeng, Marcia Lei, and Maja Žumer. 2010. "Introducing FRSAD and Mapping It with SKOS and Other Models." *International Cataloguing and Bibliographic Control* 39 (3): 53–55.

Zeng, Marcia Lei, Maja Žumer, and Athena Salaba, eds. 2011. *Functional Requirements for Subject Authority Data (FRSAD)—A Conceptual Model.* Berlin, München: De Gruyter Saur.

2

Knowledge Organization Systems (KOSs)

Claudio Gnoli

MAJOR QUESTIONS

- How does a thesaurus differ from a classification scheme and other knowledge organization systems (KOSs)?
- What is ontology in computer science as compared to ontology in metaphysics?
- What are facets?
- What are different applications of various KOSs?

AN ENCOMPASSING NOTION: KNOWLEDGE ORGANIZATION

Many different principles, techniques, and tools for organizing information by subject have been devised over time. These often have different names according to their distinctive features or, less consistently, according to the different research communities that have developed and used them. The fundamental problems they address are basically the same, however, and their principles can be described within a single general framework, as attempted by some authors (Foskett 1996; Fugmann 1993). Knowledge organization thus requires some unifying terminology that enables researchers to understand each other, avoid duplicating efforts as an effect of scientific isolation, and be working toward complementary techniques.

A useful phrase encompassing all the various approaches is "knowledge organization" (KO). This term first was used in the titles of two important books on these topics published by Henry Evelyn Bliss (Bliss 1929; Bliss 1933). The term later was adopted by Ingetraut Dahlberg, another major researcher in the field and the first president of the International Society for Knowledge Organization (ISKO). In 1989, the ISKO was organized from an existing German association, for the purpose of emphasizing conceptual aspects (as opposed to automated statistical procedures) and building an international community around this idea. The term "knowledge organization" now has gained a wide acceptance in literature and conferences on the topic, and serves as the best umbrella to connect the variety of approaches and experiences in the field (Dahlberg 1993).

Some have observed that the word "knowledge" could be just a more fashionable way to denote what commonly is called "information." The latter term probably is more appropriate when discussing it as a general phenomenon that can be found not only in human culture, but also in genomes, animal behavior, and mechanical devices. Some authors and university departments also label their own work as "information organization," a term that basically is synonymous with knowledge organization. The latter is the prevailing term, therefore overall it should be preferred (Hjørland 2012). One additional connotation carried by the word "knowledge" is that it does not deal only with raw, isolated factual data that can be retrieved (or not retrieved) by some mechanism. Rather, each term used to index or search information is part of the larger system of what mankind knows and records in its information resources. This implies that the whole system of knowledge should be represented in a general framework, in which each concept has a place and is connected with others. Therefore knowledge organization is both a technical and a cultural enterprise.

Of course, the details of the framework are debated according to the views of different knowledge organizers. This is part of the game, so to speak: Having to refer to a single authority providing one final, ultimate knowledge organization system would be a disquieting situation. The term "knowledge" can be used differently in different cultures and evolves over time; so it is natural that systems reflecting it evolve as well. Some authors emphasize that systems only reflect mainstream culture (Olson 2002), suggesting that no system can claim to be absolute or perfect. This clearly is true, as knowledge organization is not an exact science. General principles commonly acknowledged after decades and centuries of research do exist, however, and there clearly are systems which are more consistent and effective than others. Because the purposes here are of a practical nature, the focus is on these general criteria rather than individual systems discussed from critical sociological or philosophical viewpoints.

DIMENSIONS OF KNOWLEDGE

Knowledge is a combination of models that try to represent the real world to make humans better aware of the world and better able to manage it for their purposes. Such representation reproduces the structure of knowledge objects by using different elements of an intellectual nature. That is, the network and properties of relationships between the external phenomena are mapped as carefully as possible to a corresponding network of the concepts identifying them.

To Popper (1972) and Lorenz (1973), this intellectual form of knowledge is but one among several. Indeed, biological "knowledge" also reproduces the properties and relationships of an organism's environment using DNA segments as new units. For example, horse genes guiding the development of a flat hoof are a form of knowledge of the flatness of the steppe. In the same way, mental knowledge reproduces the properties and relationships of an individual's environment by using his or her mind's perceptions as units. Verbal knowledge shared between individuals does the same by using words as units. Cultural knowledge recorded in documents does it by using memes (ideas transmitted in a culture) as units. The shape of the network is kept more or less the same through each of these levels—it is isomorphic, although its material basis is completely different in each case (Gnoli and Ridi 2014).

Of course, reproduction does not mean identity. Instead, each model is in some way a simplified idealization of its modeled objects. What then must be considered are the "steps from the world to the classifier" (Vickery 2008).

- Reality manifests itself in certain phenomena.
- Phenomena are experienced by someone's mind.
- Such personal knowledge is recorded in an information resource (also called a document), that is, in any material carrier enabling it to be conserved and transmitted to other individuals.
- The information resource is identified as relevant by some institution, which produces a synthetic formulation of its subject matter that becomes part of an index of all subjects.

The resulting subject heading does refer to the original phenomena—but only indirectly, through the whole sequence of steps. The existing network of relationships is reduced at each step to a new model, and the subject index acquires each time one additional "dimension" (Gnoli 2012). Let us follow this path through each of the involved dimensions.

- (α) reality
- (β) phenomena [ontology]
- (γ) perspectives [epistemology]
- (δ) carriers [bibliology]
- (ε) collections [library science, museology, etc.]
- (ζ) users [sociology]

The ideal reference of knowledge is reality as it is in itself (α). This original source can correspond to what Kant called "the thing in itself" or the "noumenon." Reality in itself, however, is only indirectly attainable by humans, through the intermediation of their human senses and minds. Rather, what actually is known are phenomena (β), which is reality as perceived by humans through various experiences and means (also described as "data" by some authors). For example, humans can perceive a limited range of electromagnetic radiations in the form of what is called visible light. Additional tools enable us to learn about a broader range, including infrared and ultraviolet radiations. These radiations belong to the phenomena being the object of knowledge. We cannot know which fraction of the noumenon (α) still is unknown—or will always be so—although knowledge does progress in discovering more and more parts and properties of the noumenon (α). As the sciences develop, the organization of available information must be content to deal with what currently is in the phenomenon (β).

The nature and types of existing phenomena are the objects of ontology, the branch of philosophy concerned with what exists. Thus, the first dimension of what must be organized is ontological. In other words, information organization must reflect the properties of the known phenomena. If tigers are a phenomenon sharing more properties with lions than with starfish, for example, then this should be reflected in the systems.

Conversely, ontology is not the only relevant dimension. Indeed, when communicated by humans, knowledge also implies a particular perspective (γ) under which phenomena are considered and discussed. Extending the tiger example, they can be examined as a component in the jungle ecology, as part of Indian folk traditions, or as a metaphor for strength in the history of advertising. They might be discussed by a contemporary zoologist or by a medieval alchemist. They could be treated in academic studies or in comics for children. All these factors make a difference when indexing and searching information on tigers. This forms the epistemological dimension of knowledge, including all sorts of perspectives under which the information at hand is presented (methodological, theoretical, ideological, disciplinary, applied, functional), either overtly or implicitly. This dimension is variously accounted for in the existing systems. For example, most bibliographic classifications use disciplinary perspective as the primary principle of subdivision. So tigers fall under completely different classes according to how they are treated by zoologists, by veterinary surgeons, or by ethnographers. On the other hand, in a thesaurus "tigers" can be an entry that is independent of any particular perspective but the entry can be freely combined with other phenomena, for example "tigers—use in traditional medicine—India."

Carriers (δ) add one further dimension to knowledge. The same topic (tigers in Indian traditional medicine) can be recorded and enjoyed as a handmade draft, as a printed book, as a movie, or as a museum diorama; an information resource on tigers could be written in various languages; it could be available in various sizes, durations, and formats. Although not the most important component in the subject content of a document, this dimension must be taken into account to store, find, and use the knowledge it contains.

Institutions dealing with documents—such as archives, libraries, museums, and galleries—gather them according to particular aims and available resources. Each piece of knowledge thus is kept alongside others that are collected by a particular institution. Individual owners can even play an authorial role in collecting a particular set of information resources documents and organizing them according to their own interests (Feinberg 2011). For example, a tiger diorama can be displayed at the museum in the context of a hall devoted to presenting the ecology of tropical regions. This is yet another dimension (ε) that could be relevant in knowledge organization.

The last dimension can be said to be the dimension of users (ζ), in that each individual user interprets and uses the same knowledge—presented under the same perspective in the same carrier and collection—in different ways, according to his or her own previous knowledge, personal interests, and immediate needs. In a sense, taking care of this is not the task of knowledge institutions, as they must offer the same knowledge to all their users, leaving them free to make any use of it. The optimal correspondence of the collection with the particular needs of each individual user, however, is promoted by what in libraries and information centers is known as reference services, aimed at helping users to find their way in the vastness of the available collections.

Thus, if using the example of subject headings (discussed in more detail below)—a type of knowledge organization system which represents actual phenomena in the world—then all the dimensions described above, from actual phenomena to headings representing them, are included. The heading "tigers," which is part of the subject headings, is not the same thing as the common word "tigers," which, in turn, is not the same as a tiger itself. Identifying the different dimensions should help us to be aware of the complexity implied in a single subject heading. Some systems compress more than one dimension into pre-established headings; for example, disciplinary knowledge organization systems assuming that tigers are part of either zoology or ethnography. Other systems, such as that recommended by the León Manifesto (ISKO Italia 2007), offer a more explicit distinction between phenomena, perspectives, carriers, and collections.

A LONG-STANDING ENTERPRISE

Although its modern name only arose in the twentieth century, knowledge organization can be said to be as old as human thought itself. Indeed, any accumulation of notions and ideas must be structured and expressed in precise terms to be exploited and communicated to subsequent users. In the words of philosopher Herbert Spencer, "Science is organized knowledge" (Columbia World of Quotations 1996).

One of the most ancient classical texts of Chinese culture, the *I Ching*, proposed a worldview based on a hierarchical knowledge organization system. According to the *I Ching*, the ultimate reality consists of two basic elements, called "Heaven" and "Earth," which can be split respectively into "Softness" and "Hardness," and into "Yin" and "Yang." These, in turn, can be split into eight elements (i.e., Water, Fire, Soil), which can be split until 64 more detailed concepts are identified. At each division, the two subclasses are represented by a horizontal line, either continuous or interrupted in the middle; the set of all their combinations is an interesting binary graphical notation.

Western thinkers also have paid attention to the organization of knowledge. Aristotle and his scholars produced a classical systematization of disciplines; each discipline is discussed in one of Aristotle's books, and presented in canonical order. The discipline of metaphysics took from this sequence its very name, literally meaning "what comes after—or beyond—the natural sciences."

Medieval universities organized their teachings into sets of three plus four disciplines, called the "Trivium" and the "Quadrivium." Botanists such as Gesner and Linné, who needed to organize the vast corpus of information on plants that was coming from all over the world, devised the first detailed taxonomies. Encyclopedists organized works based on networks of cross references between entries. Philosophers such as Bacon, and later Ampère and Comte, introduced ordered lists of all the modern sciences. These then are used by librarians as the basis for classification systems—aimed at organizing the ever-growing mass of published books and articles.

This very brief history shows that knowledge organization always has been present in many aspects of life. Although knowledge storage and retrieval have acquired a special relevance in our information-dominated era, their technical sides also are connected to the wider organization of the cultural life of an entire civilization. Not only do information databases need conceptual structure, but so do museum displays and artworks galleries with their guided paths; zoological and botanical gardens with their descriptive signs; curricula in universities; chapters in handbooks; departments and offices in governments and in companies; shelves in stores; and the directories and websites that refer to *all* of them. The more we examine the notion of knowledge organization, the more it appears to permeate many parts of society.

THE LAYERS FORMING KNOWLEDGE ORGANIZATION

The field that has come to be known as knowledge organization is developed every day through research, experimentation, conferences, and publications. If looking at the program for a professional or scientific meeting, or the index of a journal devoted to knowledge organization, at first the apparent heterogeneity of the topics addressed can seem puzzling. Indeed, there are many sides of and many approaches to knowledge organization that can be discussed, ranging from very abstract speculations to very practical problems. Are they really all part of the same enterprise?

To find a way through it, it can be useful to model the field as composed of several layers:

- Knowledge organization theory;
- Knowledge organization systems;
- Knowledge organization representation; and
- Knowledge organization applications.

Each of these layers can be addressed by different professionals with different aims in mind; however, they all are needed to collectively yield good fruit. Not only is it necessary to study and develop all the layers, but they all also must be properly connected to each other. For example, sound theories must be reflected in actual knowledge organization systems. These, in turn, must be represented in formats expressing their conceptual structures carefully and without any loss of information. The represented structures must be known and applied in the appropriate situations by information professionals, rather than be replaced by solutions that do not account for the problems implied in them.

"Theories" provide philosophical foundations upon which knowledge organization can be based. Indeed, every system rests on philosophical assumptions, regardless of whether they are explicit. Not all philosophy, however, is relevant for the purposes of organizing information: The most interesting theories are those dealing with categories of things and of ideas, and producing their systematic arrangement.

In the last few decades, knowledge organizers have examined various theories in the philosophy of science—especially those not constrained to a single science, but able to present the different sciences as parts of some general framework. Bacon's distinction between the sciences of memory (history), those of imagination (literature and the arts), and those of reason (natural and social sciences) is known to have inspired the sequence of main classes in the Dewey Decimal Classification. More recently, Eleanor Rosch's theory of prototypes has been very relevant in exploring the bases on which concepts can be identified and connected to each other, suggesting that clear-cut definitions of essential properties as in Aristotle's logic can be inadequate for providing a rationale for fuzzy categories used in everyday life. Jason Farradane's relational indexing is based on psychological theories identifying four fundamental types of relationships, and has selected them as the basic way to combine concepts.

All these theories are of an epistemological nature, that is, they pertain to the way humans are able to know the world (dimension γ) and consequently organize its knowledge. A complementary family of theories is ontological, describing which basic types of things exist in the external world and how they relate to each other (dimension β). Theories include:

- General systems theory, which states that any phenomenon can be modeled as a system with component parts, a structure, and an environment;
- Integrative levels theory, which states that phenomena can be grouped into levels of increasing organization; and
- Evolutionary emergentism, which states that new phenomena and successive ontical (referring to reality; compare with "ontological" which refers to the study of reality) levels emerge from simpler, pre-existing ones. Each level, although based on the levels below it, behaves in its own special ways, variously described as "levels of being" (Nicolai Hartmann) or "fundamental aspects" (Herman Dooyeweerd).

Systems such as the Bliss Classification or the Information Coding Classification (discussed below)—which present items in a graduated sequence of increasingly sophisticated entities—often are based on these types of theories.

Such theories on how knowledge should be organized are embedded more or less explicitly in actual knowledge organization systems. That is, conceptual schemes—consisting of schedules of terms, symbols, and relations connecting them—can be used as tools to subject index the knowledge content of information resources and to arrange them in consistent and useful ways. As shown in the next section, there is a wide variety of systems with different names and features, although all try to serve the basic need of managing knowledge by subject.

For centuries, these systems have been represented in drafted or printed forms as lists and diagrams. They often use visualization metaphors like the Medieval "*scala naturae*" (a ladder of increasingly complex classes of phenomena) or the hierarchical trees of disciplines and subdisciplines common in the Modern Age to introduce and organize encyclopedic works; more recent metaphors include "nets" and "webs" (Weingart 2013).

With the advent of the digital age, KOSs now can be stored and represented in digital formats, exchanged through the Internet, and provided in the same formats as the very contents indexed by them. This presents the possibility of automatically producing new associations, or even inferring new knowledge as the result of logical procedures. This visionary perspective of the Semantic Web would remain an unfulfilled dream, however, if KOSs were not expressed in some standard form that actually can be shared and reused in a consistent manner. Such a process only has started in the past few years, with the development of markup formats like SKOS and OWL, which are reviewed in Chapter 3 of this book.

Lastly, the systems thus structured and represented must be applied to the organization of particular collections of documents.

- A library pastes subject-representing classmarks on its books and arranges them on the shelves accordingly.
- A digital repository assigns subject-representing categories (the term usually used in repositories) or tags to its documents to make them browsable and retrievable.
- A bibliography lists classes and controlled terms with its records.
- A museum or a botanical garden builds its halls and planting beds according to the conceptual plan of what will be displayed.
- A website organizes the architecture of its pages, menus, and displays to help its users navigate its contents in some systematic way.
- Relevant objects of a territory are labeled with appropriate metadata to make them appear in a geographic information system so that anyone passing by them and using a car navigation system or a smartphone can find their way and learn about various attractions.

Dealing with the layer of applications often means having to adapt the adamantine consistency of conceptual schemes to the constraints of the actual situation. For example, oversized books might have to be moved to a shelf away from standard-sized books on the same topic; microfilms or videocassettes must be kept close to the machines that enable people to use them, regardless of their subject; the skeleton of a dinosaur might need a hall separate from that where the fossils of smaller organisms are kept; terminology and visualization in a website menu must be understandable to the majority of users, not always matching their conceptually rigorous forms. The actual implementations can differ in various details according to their context. Still, if a rigorous KOS structure was not the basis, it would not be possible to achieve the same degree of effectiveness, or to integrate local resources into larger networks of knowledge sources.

TYPES OF KOSs

As discussed, all KOSs are tools used to summarize knowledge contained in information resources into short statements that can be used to index and retrieve them within large collections (Lancaster 2003). Their particular features can vary widely, however, including such diverse systems as keywords, folksonomies, subject headings lists, thesauri, taxonomies, classifications, and ontologies. The next section surveys these types of systems—in order from the most simple to the most complex—which enables a progressive introduction to some of their major features.

Titles

The most immediate form of summarization of a text in natural language (sometimes complemented or replaced by images, raw data, or other media) is by a phrase also expressed in natural language—sometimes called a "subject statement"—such as, "[this resource is about] wolf diet in the Apennines as affected by wild ungulates abundance."

This type of phrase might be the title of the resource itself—this is especially common in scientific papers or in the long titles of old books, such as Hume's *A Treatise of Human Nature: Being an Attempt to Introduce the Experimental Method of Reasoning into Moral Subjects.* Titles then can be considered the simplest form of KOSs, as they summarize some key concepts of the resource contents. Modern books often have shorter metaphorical titles and include a more faithful description of their content in a subtitle. In the case of fiction works, the title is even less reliable as a summary of contents. The novel *The Name of the Rose*, for example, deals neither with gardening nor with onomastics.

Keywords and Tags

It then is clear that a more objective system is required to index the subject matter of information resources. Another simple approach is selecting some words—perhaps taking them from the title itself, or from titles of sections—which are especially representative of the contents. These are called "keywords" and can be associated (in alphabetical order or in no particular order) to a work, to help in its retrieval from within a collection (Foskett 1996). The practice is common for scientific papers; authors usually are asked by the publisher to provide some keywords, together with a title and an abstract for the article. There is not any special rule or guideline on how to choose keywords other than using common sense. Having keywords is better than having nothing, especially when searching in very large collections for which no one could afford the work of providing more rigorous index terms.

A similar situation is found in Web repositories of photographs, videos, blog posts, or bookmark links (as in the pioneer case of Del.icio.us) that are freely uploaded by their authors. As the collections quickly reach millions of items, the only hope for providing some index terms for them is to ask authors or the subsequent users of the same resources to assign "tags" for them—which basically are another form of keywords.

The system of tagging contributed by all users has become known as a "folksonomy," a taxonomy cumulatively developed by end users themselves, rather than by information professionals. Users of the collection then can search and retrieve all resources tagged with a given word, and navigate among those sharing one or more tags. Folksonomies offer several advantages. They are economical, as they grow due to volunteer work, thus providing an important example of crowdsourcing; they are methodological, as tags tend to reflect the actual everyday language of users, rather than some abstract convention that could result in limiting its use to an élite of academic experts. For example, a video showing wolves probably would be tagged as "wolf" or "wolves" rather than as "*Canidae*" or some other less-familiar scientific name.

Conversely, because tagging is left to the goodwill and whimsy of users, it suffers from several consistency problems. Resources might lack a relevant tag, for example, or have too few or too many. Tags cannot reflect contents in objective ways, as they often refer to the personal viewpoints of the person doing the tagging (e.g., grandma, beautiful, to-read) and might not be useful to other users. They might be too generic (e.g., places, pet) or be written using word forms, spellings, or synonyms different from those adopted by other users.

The result is that, although tags do help users to retrieve interesting items, tags cannot ensure a complete and consistent control of all items potentially available in the collection. Although users will find some things, they always will miss something else. Several studies and experiments have been performed to improve folksonomies with more refined principles or to integrate them with more powerful KOSs, such as classification schemes (Golub, Lykke, and Tudhope 2014). These approaches obviously tend to produce better results, but they also require users to spend more time and mental effort with indexing—something that only a small fraction is willing to do in everyday use of Internet resources.

Subject Headings Lists and Terminologies

These problems illustrate the next needed step, which is making the KOS a controlled vocabulary. A controlled vocabulary is a system that does not just use any word of natural language, but uses only words corresponding with a set of lexical and morphological rules (Foskett 1996). These become more than just words, they become "terms"—each corresponding to a concept as modeled by the KOS. This also means that some combinations of several words, such as "pet therapy," could work as a single term because they refer to a single concept. In the same way, words such as articles, conjunctions, or conjugated verbal forms are not terms. The rules for controlled vocabularies prescribe that only nouns in their plural form ("wolves"), or gerunds count: This is another way to reduce scattering of the same concept under different terms.

If a set of synonyms exists for the same concept then only one preferred term is chosen. The non-preferred terms are recorded only as entries for cross-references to the preferred terms in the subject headings list ("*x*, see *y*"). Related concepts also can be provided as a suggestion to indexers and users ("*x*, see also *y*").

For many decades, libraries have developed sets of rules to produce subject headings for their catalogues. The most widely known of them are the Library of Congress Subject Headings (LCSH), produced by the U.S.

Library of Congress (LOC) and used for its collections and for many other libraries that import bibliographic records from it. The subject headings can be found in the records of many library catalogs online, and also have been used to index digital resources in such projects as the "Librarians' Internet Index."

Because they are verbal rather than presented in symbolic form, subject headings lists depend on their particular language. Although LOC subject headings form the most widespread verbal KOS in the English-speaking world, similar systems exist for other languages, including Schlagwortnormdatei (SWD) for German, Répertoire d'autorité-matière encyclopédique et alphabétique unifié (RAMEAU) for French, and Nuovo Soggettario for Italian. Some now have been mapped into a unified, interlinguistic framework called Multilingual Access to Subjects (MACS).

Subject headings can be formed with either a single term or a combination of terms (which most often is the case) to fully represent the subject statement. Subject indexing systems provide syntactical rules to combine terms in optimal and consistent sequences. The first cited term should be a noun representing the focus of the information resource ("base theme"), followed by its modifiers, its relationships with other concepts, and, finally, the specifications of place, time, and literary form: wolves—diet—influence of ungulate abundance—Apennines—surveys.

Rules for the citation order of terms are important to ensure consistency in grouping and alphabetical presentation of subject headings. Such syntactical principles (Craven 1986) usually are shared by most verbal indexing systems. Since the 1970s they have been formulated in highly sophisticated ways in systems based on a relational structure and on facet analysis, such as the British Preserved Context Indexing System (PRECIS), French Syntagmatic Organization Language (Syntol), Indian Postulate-Based Permuted Subject Indexing (POPSI), and the Italian Research Group on Subject Indexing (GRIS) Guide.

Guidelines for subject indexing have been published by a working group of the International Federation of Library Associations and Institutions (IFLA) (Yahns 2012). A high-level abstract model of subject data is the IFLA's *Functional Requirements for Subject Authority Data* (FRSAD), formalizing the relationships between a resource, its subject ("*thema*"), and the representation of this by verbal labels ("*nomen*") (Zeng, Žumer, and Salaba 2011).

A different group that also is dealing with controlled terms is the linguistics community. These scholars specialize in terminologies, glossaries, and dictionaries for particular domains, especially technical ones in which many novel terms not reported in general dictionaries are included—sometimes accompanied by definitions and descriptions—to serve the needs of specialized communication (Cabré 1998). Some international standards deal with how to develop and maintain such terminological resources (ISO 704:2009,

Terminology work, Principles and methods; ISO 1087-1:2000, Terminology work, Vocabulary, part 1: Theory and application; ISO 22274: 2013, Systems to manage terminology, knowledge and content).

Thesauri

"See" and "see also" references used in subject headings only account for synonyms or strictly related terms. The concepts expressed in vocabularies, however, are connected in a much more complex semantic network which can be made more explicit to lead users to the most appropriate term for their search, and to explore the KOS and find other relevant connections. These functionalities are provided by another type of controlled vocabulary, "retrieval thesauri," which takes its Latin name from encyclopedic works of the past, especially from Peter Mark Roget's *Thesaurus* first published in 1852.

As semantic relationships are innumerable (Green 2008), retrieval thesauri (as opposed to the general *Roget's Thesaurus*) focus only on a limited set of basic semantic relationships, which follow the recommendations of international standards published or updated in recent years (ISO 25964, Thesauri and Interoperability with Other Vocabularies, Part 1 (2011): Thesauri for Information Retrieval, and Part 2 (2013): Interoperability with Other Vocabularies; IFLA Guidelines for Multilingual Thesauri, 2009). "See also" cross references are expressed here as related terms (RT). Further, they are integrated with hierarchical relationships: the broader term (BT) relationship, and its inverse, narrower term (NT). A thesaurus entry thus consists of a preferred term followed by its non-preferred synonyms ("used for," "UF"), its broader term(s), its narrower terms, and its related terms. The following is an example of this structure.

Cats

UF *Felis catus*

BT *Felids*

NT Persian cats

NT Siamese cats

RT *ailurophilia*

RT cat litter

Experience demonstrates that even this limited number of basic relationships enables thesauri to provide an effective structure to model a domain of knowledge.

Managing a greater number of relationships would make the thesaurus more rich and expressive, but also would make it very complex. Indeed, only a minority of thesauri do so, for example, by making the basic relationships more specific: BT/NTs are further distinguished based on genus/species, whole/part, and class/instance relationships; RTs are further distinguished based on any type of associative relationship such as action/agent, object/discipline.

Every term in a thesaurus has at least one broader term. A term can have more than one, however, and thesauri incorporating these are called "polyhierarchical" thesauri. Each BT, in turn, has a BT until a "top term" (TT) is reached. The set of all BT/NT relationships under a top term thus ideally forms a hierarchical tree of concepts. The tree also can be represented explicitly if the thesaurus is presented in a systematic arrangement supplementing the standard alphabetical order. Top terms are very general concepts, such as "persons," "activities," or "places," and sometimes are called the "facets" of the thesaurus. Terms from different facets often are combined in the indexing phase into faceted subject strings.

Most thesauri only cover a special domain of knowledge, as they tend to be very detailed. If no thesaurus is available for a particular domain, information professionals might want to develop one, following the ISO standards (Broughton 2006; Soergel 1974). Covered domains, however, also can be very broad and can encompass several disciplines or subdisciplines, such as the well-established "Art and Architecture Thesaurus" (AAT) (*see* Harpring 2010). Some tools that originally were developed only as subject headings lists now incorporate hierarchical relationships and term identifiers. This is the case of both LCSH and the Italian "Nuovo Soggettario," which now can be described as general thesauri.

Thesauri usually account for common nouns and do not include the names of individual people, organizations, conferences, or places (proper nouns). These names, however, also must be controlled and recorded. Lists of these terms can be found in encyclopedias (either general or domain-specific) and in such authority lists as VIAF (Virtual International Authority File), mainly used for bibliographical purposes, or FOAF (Friend of a Friend), used in the Semantic Web. A related issue is that of geographical names, as they are very numerous and often have variants, synonyms, or homographs (e.g., Dublin, Ireland, and Dublin, Ohio); controlled lists of geographical proper names addressing these needs often are referred to as "gazetteers."

Other general sources of controlled terminology and relationships come from linguistic databases. The best known of them is WordNet, a freely available and reusable collection of nouns, verbs, adjectives, and adverbs grouped into sets of synonyms (synsets) and connected by hierarchical relationships.

Taxonomies

Hierarchical trees are a very natural and common way of organizing knowledge. Indeed, they also are found in less-formalized structures outside information science. Scientists use hierarchical trees to organize the names of chemical compounds, climates, soils, plants, animals, languages, traditional tales, musical instruments, religious movements, and many other objects of study. The corresponding sciences thus include a systematic branch (e.g., systematic zoology, typological linguistics), and experts in the subjects often develop sophisticated principles that should be considered as part of knowledge organization theory (although the research communities still tend to be separate). This especially is true in the case of biological sciences, in which systematic problems addressed in past centuries currently are debated by the opposing schools of phenetic taxonomy (emphasizing morphological diversity), cladistic taxonomy (emphasizing the sequence of evolutionary branching), and phylogenetic taxonomy (which seeks a balance of both).

The systems produced by such systematic branches of the sciences often are called taxonomies or classifications. In the context of information science, "taxonomy" usually refers to a hierarchical tree of phenomena that are the object of study (e.g., animals, languages), and "classification" most often organizes disciplinary approaches studying them (e.g., zoology, linguistics) and their subdivisions. The word "taxonomy" also is popular among knowledge managers modeling the information outputs of organizations (Lambe 2007), and information architects working on website structures or a catalogue of products to sell (e.g., wines, flowers, cars). The hierarchical trees of these taxonomies usually are not very formalized; they simply consist of a set of categories and their subcategories—what is important is just the label by which a category of items is described, as users should quickly grasp its meaning while browsing the website menus. This means taxonomies are not very helpful in searching for an unknown or unfamiliar term, or in navigating to explore related concepts.

Classification Schemes

In libraries, bibliographic classification schemes (Foskett 1996) typically have been based on a set of traditional disciplines which are grouped by criteria of either an epistemological nature (such as Bacon's mentioned tripartition into disciplines of reason, imagination, and memory) or an ontological nature (in the definition of H. E. Bliss, disciplines of increasing specialization which deal with increasingly organized phenomena: from physics and chemistry through biology and psychology, then sociology and the humanities).

An epistemological approach is at the origin of the Dewey Decimal Classification. First published by Melvil Dewey in 1876, the DDC is updated regularly and currently is in its twenty-third edition, published by the Online Computer Library Center (OCLC). The title word "decimal" suggests a basic feature of the system and of bibliographic classifications in general:

Classes and subclasses are identified by a symbol composed of a series of digits, but also include letters and other symbols in other classification schemes. The symbols work just like decimal numbers—the more digits added the more specific the represented subject becomes.

Such symbolic notation provides a basic functionality of classification schemes. Unlike in verbal systems, symbolic classes are not listed alphabetically, as that would make the order dependent on the contingency of the vocabulary and the order would change according to languages. Rather, classes are ordered systematically by subjects. This enables users to easily explore the structure of the whole system and to navigate from more general to more specific classes. The order is recorded in notation, as symbols are chosen in such ways to produce the most effective sequences (Broughton 2004; Mills 1960). A complex tree (or even network) of concepts thus is translated into a linear sequence, which can be reflected in the arrangement of books on shelves or of browsable records in an online information service. Notation is especially well suited for exploitation in digital applications. For example, it can be truncated to automatically retrieve all records assigned to a given class and all its subclasses.

Other major general classification schemes include the Universal Decimal Classification (UDC). Created by Paul Otlet, the UDC is based on the DDC but features more devices to combine concepts through several relationships. Then there is the Library of Congress Classification (LCC), which is based on the holdings of the U.S. Library of Congress; the Chinese Library Classification (CLC) providing for this large part of the world; the Bliss Bibliographic Classification (BC), featuring a main class order well founded on philosophical considerations; and the Colon Classification (CC).

The CC is of great theoretical importance, as it first introduced the powerful technique of facet analysis (pioneered by J. O. Kaiser and others) on a wide scale. In "faceted classifications," such as CC and BC2—the second edition of BC—classes not only are divided into subclasses, but also are articulated in a set of facets allowing for the optional specification of their attributes. Facets usually belong to a set of general categories, for instance those already found in thesauri, such as parts, properties, processes, operations, agents, space, and time. Classmarks then can be built by combining concepts taken from various facets according to their standard citation order, allowing for a more flexible and accurate representation of subjects. As a result, users can search for a class and its subclasses, and also for all combinations of a given facet with different basic classes. This flexibility is even greater in freely faceted classifications, such as the experimental Integrative Levels Classification (ILC), in which facets enable combination of any concept with any other, irrespective of any basic disciplinary class.

The ultimate option for freedom of combination is simply to allow for the juxtaposition of each class with any other from a different part of the schedules, in what classification literature calls a "phase relationship." Typical phase relationships include the influence of a subject on another, comparison between two of them, or one subject considered under the bias of another. Some systems allow these relationships to be made explicit, although in many cases only an unspecified connection is expressed, as in UDC 34:2 "law in relation to religion." The DDC traditionally prescribes assigning a resource to a single class; however, in the practice of online databases, often an effective solution is to assign the same resource to several DDC classes freely juxtaposed. From the syntactical viewpoint this works just like tags in folksonomies, although it provides additional information concerning the hierarchical position of each subject within the KOS.

Special classifications also exist for non-textual resources. An important example is IconClass, a KOS of subjects represented in visual works, such as paintings or photographs. These are divided into categories including religious, natural, human, and abstract, then are further subdivided. Protocols for cataloguing audio or video recordings, for example, in ethnographic research and documentation, often include their own classifications.

Ontologies

Computer science is yet another community that has addressed knowledge organization, although it uses different terminology from that provided above. Application of classical logic to research on artificial intelligence and automated reasoning has produced KOSs where the definition of classes and their relationships with other classes are formalized in rigorous ways to be used by both machines and humans (Sowa 1984). These are called ontologies, after the branch of philosophy devoted to the kinds of existing entities, as they usually are inspired by a realistic worldview.

As in classification schemes, the basic structures of ontologies are hierarchical trees, here represented as relationships of the type "A is a B," that are functionally equivalent to BT/NT in thesauri or to additional characters in classification notation. Other relationships are less frequently represented, although syntax allows for defining any of them according to the purposes at hand. For example, Ranganathan's theory of facets recently has been received as a useful enrichment of the structure of facets (Giunchiglia, Dutta, and Maltese 2009).

To ensure consistency in automated processing, ontologies include formal constraints; for example, specifying that the arguments of a relationship must have a certain cardinality (i.e., must be single, multiple, or null) or must be taken from a certain range (e.g., be a proper noun of place, or a date in a standard format).

Ontologies are used to model complex knowledge networks in technological domains (e.g., management of an airport), and now increasingly are used to model large knowledge bases accessible through the Internet. Hence, these also must be represented in interoperable formats (*see* Chapter 3).

How to Choose an Appropriate KOS

As discussed in the previous section, a wide variety of KOS types and implementations is provided in the literature. Although some are mainly the product of theoretical research, other types of KOS already have been applied to many collections across the world. Despite their differences, there clearly is a core set of principles shared by most of them, suggesting that what is important are the principles applied rather than the particular KOS adopted. In principle, anyone can develop a new KOS for his or her own purposes, provided that these consolidated principles are followed. This sometimes occurs in projects aimed at organizing and making collections of resources available in libraries, museums, text archives, audiovisual archives, museums, websites, or any other institution storing knowledge.

Although developing one's own KOS has the advantage of adaptability to the particular situation, it also demands significant resources in terms of expertise and time. Further, a collection organized by a local KOS will have much more difficulty in being connected to other collections organized by different KOSs—an opportunity that is more and more important in the developing context of the global data network.

This suggests that adopting an existent KOS, even if it does not correspond perfectly to the particular situation, brings advantages of another nature. Although it might not be possible to build a perfectly satisfying KOS, in attempting to do so we should consider that creating an imperfect KOS still is better than having no way to organize resources and make them findable and usable in today's linked world.

Local needs can be better satisfied if a KOS is available for the very domain of knowledge in which we are operating. Indeed, a KOS focusing on a particular domain often is more detailed and accurate in modeling knowledge produced by its scholars and information providers. Most thesauri, taxonomies, and ontologies are domain-specific. There also are special classification schemes and subject headings, such as the Mathematics Subject Classification (MSC), the Medical Subject Headings (MeSH), and the *Journal of Economic Literature* (JEL) scheme.

Conversely, adopting a universal system offers advantages in terms of international interoperability. Even if the structure of some DDC classes is outdated or not detailed enough, it still is useful for connecting local data with those of millions of libraries around the world that use the same KOS. Domain ontologies—no matter how efficient in modeling their field of knowledge—often must be connected to other domain ontologies.

There are two alternative strategies used to perform this connection. One is KOS-to-KOS mapping, which is developing tables of correspondence between the elements of a system and the equivalent elements of another system (keeping in mind that equivalence often is an approximation, as the underlying conceptual structures often imply semantic differences). The other strategy is to connect domain-specific KOSs to a more general, shared framework that can act as a bridge between local KOSs. This is the impetus for the recent development of some general ontologies, such as Cyc, Basic Formal Ontology (BFO), General Formal Ontology (GFO), Suggested Upper Merged Ontology (SUMO), Descriptive Ontology for Linguistic and Cognitive Engineering (DOLCE), and Universal Knowledge Core (UKC). They offer a framework of ontological categories such as entities, attributes, processes, and places that can be used as a mapping backbone through which the particular concepts of domain ontologies can be reconnected.

At a more general level, knowledge managers might wonder which type of KOS best suits their needs. As shown in this chapter, there is a gradation in sophistication from simple keywords and term lists to the complex networked semantic structures of faceted classifications and ontologies. There also are major differences between the numerous instances of a certain type of KOS, which also should be taken into account. Terminology registries could help find and identify the most appropriate KOSs (Golub et al. 2014).

It is important to be aware that this increase in semantic richness also means an increase in economical resources needed to learn, apply, and manage them. The choice of the right KOS type thus depends on the extent, purposes, and resources of each information project. A KOS does provide added value to any collection, therefore the more KOSs included the better. At the same time, they should be selected according to the actual possibilities and constraints of the specific situation.

SUMMARY

Although tools aimed at indexing information by subject have taken different names over time, a useful general term for them is "knowledge organization systems." Knowledge can be described as the totality of information available to humans as it is connected in meaningful ways through a network of relationships. It involves several dimensions, including the real phenomena observed and studied; the different perspectives by which these are addressed and discussed; the carriers in which their treatment is recorded and transmitted; the collections of information resources that are selected and kept by such institutions as libraries, archives, or museums; and their end users. Although phenomena are the ultimate reference, each of the dimensions also contributes to knowledge organization.

The basic problems of knowledge organization have been addressed by philosophers and scientists since antiquity, although specialized techniques for detailed organization have been developed in libraries and documentation centers in the last couple centuries. Techniques include theoretical principles for ordering and relating concepts, the systems themselves in which such principles are implemented, formats to represent and to share the systems, and the practice of applying them to actual collections of information resources.

There exist various KOS types of increasing refinement and complexity. These include simple keywords and tags, controlled subject headings lists and terminologies, thesauri and taxonomies, hierarchical relationships, classification systems providing a notation for systematic arrangement, and highly formalized ontologies. Each system has pros and cons and can be most useful for certain applications.

This brief review of systems for knowledge organization clearly is not sufficient for instructing readers on how to use each of them—particularly considering that only some of the most widespread systems are mentioned. To perform knowledge organization, one must identify an appropriate KOS, obtain a copy of its full schedules and manual, and learn about its details. Some are such complex and rich tools that their application is not just a clerical job but also an art—one that only can be learned progressively with practical experience. The choice of the KOS most appropriate to the present needs depends both on its intrinsic qualities (such as completeness, consistency, or flexibility in compounding concepts) and on its availability in an appropriate number of languages and formats. The latter makes it more suitable as a conceptual bridge between a local collection and the rest of information resources available in the wider global network. This implies technical issues that are addressed in Chapter 3.

CHAPTER REVIEW

1. What is the division of knowledge organization systems in this chapter based upon?
2. What are some other ways of grouping knowledge organization systems?
3. Describe a knowledge organization system that is ideal for your needs.
4. Describe a knowledge organization system ideal for use by most people.
5. What would be the most common use of the knowledge organization system described in #4 above?

GLOSSARY

Classification scheme: A KOS type consisting of schedules of concepts arranged systematically, by means of a symbolic notation, based on hierarchies of classes and their subclasses and possibly on additional specifications (e.g., common auxiliaries, facets).

Controlled vocabulary: A KOS type consisting of standardized selected terms. Although often used as if synonymous to KOS in the context of networked information, it more properly should refer only to verbal systems such as thesauri and subject headings lists.

Facet: An attribute of a class specifying it according to a general category, such as "Material," "Process," "Agent," "Place," and "Time." In the context of thesauri, the set of terms belonging to such general categories.

Hierarchical relationship: The relationship between a concept and a broader concept to which it belongs (or, conversely, to the latter and its narrower concepts). It can be further distinguished into genus-species, whole-part, or class-individual.

Keyword: A word in natural language selected as representative of the content of an information resource, without any particular formal control.

Knowledge organization system (KOS): Any tool for indexing and arranging information resources based on their subject matter, spanning from simple lists of keywords to highly complex ontologies.

Ontology: A KOS type consisting of a network of classes, their attributes, and their relationships, expressed in a formal language including logical restrictions, making it suitable to be used in automated applications. It takes its name from a branch of philosophy.

Subject heading: An entry in an index of information resources. Consists of a verbal phrase taken from a controlled list of terms, possibly combined with other terms, and rendered in some standard citation order.

Tag: A keyword added freely by an author or user of a networked service to index a resource.

Taxonomy: A KOS type consisting of a hierarchical tree of classes, usually expressed by verbal labels and referring to actual objects of study or discussion rather than to any fields of knowledge studying them.

Term: A phrase consisting of one or more words that have been identified as a preferred (or a non-preferred) label for a concept.

Thesaurus: A KOS type consisting of controlled terms connected by hierarchical (BT-NT), associative (RT), and lexical (UF) relationships.

REFERENCES

Bliss, Henry E. 1933. *The Organization of Knowledge in Libraries.* New York: Wilson.

Bliss, Henry E. 1929. *The Organization of Knowledge and the System of the Sciences.* New York: Holt.

Broughton, Vanda. 2006. *Essential Thesaurus Construction.* London: Facet.

Broughton, Vanda. 2004. *Essential Classification.* London: Facet.

Cabré, M. Teresa. 1998. *La Terminologie: Théorie, Méthode et Applications.* Ottawa: Presses de l'Université d'Ottawa.

Columbia World of Quotations. 1996. Columbia University Press. Accessed August 28, 2014. http://quotes.dictionary.com /Science_is_organized_knowledge.

Craven, Timothy C. 1986. *String Indexing.* Orlando: Academic Press.

Dahlberg, Ingetraut. 1993. "Knowledge Organization: Its Scope and Possibilities." *Knowledge Organization* 55 (4): 211–22.

Feinberg, Melanie. 2011. "How Information Systems Communicate as Documents: The Concept of Authorial Voice." *Journal of Documentation* 67 (6): 1015–37.

Foskett, Anthony C. 1996. *The Subject Approach to Information*. 5th ed. London: Library Association.

Fugmann, Robert. 1993. *Subject Analysis and Indexing: Theoretical Foundation and Practical Advice*. Frankfurt am Main: Index Verlag.

Giunchiglia, Fausto, Biswanath Dutta, and Vincenzo Maltese. 2009. "Faceted Lightweight Ontologies." In *Conceptual Modeling: Foundations and Applications*, edited by Alex Borgida Vinay Chaudhri, Paolo Giorgini, and Eric Yu. Berlin, Heidelberg: Springer.

Gnoli, Claudio. 2012. "Metadata about What? Distinguishing Between Ontic, Epistemic, and Documental Dimensions in Knowledge Organization." *Knowledge Organization* 39 (4): 268–75.

Gnoli, Claudio, and Riccardo Ridi. 2014. "Unified Theory of Information, Hypertextuality and Levels of Reality." *Journal of Documentation* 70 (3): 443–60.

Golub, Koraljka, Marianne Lykke, and Douglas Tudhope. 2014. "Enhancing Social Tagging with Automated Keywords from the Dewey Decimal Classification." *Journal of Documentation* 70 (5): 801–824.

Golub, Koraljka, Douglas Tudhope, Marcia Zeng, and Maja Žumer. 2014. "Terminology Registries for Knowledge Organization Systems—Functionality, Use, and Attributes." *Journal of the American Society for Information Science and Technology* [forthcoming].

Green, Rebecca. 2008. "Relationships in Knowledge Organization." *Knowledge Organization* 35 (2–3): 150–59.

Harpring, Patricia. 2010. *Introduction to Controlled Vocabularies: Terminology for Art, Architecture, and Other Cultural Works*. Online ed. J. Paul Getty Trust. Accessed August 28, 2014. http://www.getty.edu/research/publications/electronic_publications /intro_controlled_vocab/.

Hjørland, Birger. 2012. "Information Organization = Knowledge Organization?" In *Categories, Contexts and Relations in Knowledge Organization: Proceedings of the Twelfth International ISKO Conference*, edited by A. Neelameghan and K.S. Raghavan, 8–14. Würzburg: Ergon.

ISKO Italia. 2007. "The León Manifesto." *Knowledge Organization* 34 (1): 6–8.

Lambe, Patrick. 2007. *Organizing Knowledge: Taxonomies, Knowledge and Organization Effectiveness*. Oxford: Chandos.

Lancaster, Frederick Wilfred. 2003. *Indexing and Abstracting in Theory and Practice*. 3rd ed. London: Facet.

Lorenz, Konrad Z. 1977. *Behind the Mirror: A Search for a Natural History of Human Knowledge*. New York: Harcourt Brace Jovanovich.

Mills, Jack A. 1960. *Modern Outline of Library Classification*. London: Chapman & Hall.

Olson, Hope A. 2002. *The Power to Name: Locating the Limits of Subject Representation in Libraries*. Dordrecht: Kluwer.

Popper, Karl R. 1972. *Objective Knowledge: An Evolutionary Approach*. Oxford: Clarendon.

Soergel, Dagobert. 1974. *Indexing Languages and Thesauri: Construction and Maintenance*. Los Angeles: Melville.

Sowa, John F.1984. *Conceptual Structures: Information Processing in Mind and Machine*. Reading, PA: Addison-Wesley.

Vickery, Brian C. 2008. "The Structure of Subject Classifications for Document Retrieval." Republ. ISKO Italia. Accessed August 28, 2014. http://www.iskoi.org/ilc/vickery.php.

Weingart, Scott B. 2013. "From Trees to Webs: Uprooting Knowledge through Visualization." In *Classification and Visualisation: Interfaces to Knowledge: Proceedings of the International UDC Seminar 2013,* edited by Aida Slavic, Almila Akdag Salah, and Sylvie Davies. Würzburg: Ergon, 43–57.

Yahns, Yvonne ed. 2012.*Guidelines for Subject Access in National Bibliographies*. Berlin, München: De Gruyter Saur.

Zeng, Marcia Lei, Maja Žumer, and Athena Salaba, eds. 2011. *Functional Requirements for Subject Authority Data (FRSAD): A Conceptual Model*. Berlin, München: De Gruyter-Saur.

3

Technological Standards

MAJOR QUESTIONS

- Why are standards needed for representing a knowledge organization system?
- How do the different standards compare to one another?
- Which protocols, APIs, and querying languages exist for accessing various data from a knowledge organization system?
- What are terminology registries and how can they be used?

INTRODUCTION

In general, standards ensure consistency, reliability, and quality. There are several types of standards related to a knowledge organization system (KOS) (Tudhope, Koch, and Heery 2006), including those for design and construction of a KOS; technological standards for the representation and interchange of a KOS in the digital environment, and for programmatic access (because many Web services are based on a KOS). The standards ensure that each KOS is represented in the same format and structure which, in turn, enables the KOS to be presented, organized, browsed, and searched in an interoperable and easy manner. For instance, the standards might enable cross-domain searching by subject of information systems held by libraries, archives, museums, or of any other interdisciplinary information systems that use KOSs. Thus, the Finnish ONKI project for museums (ONKI Ontology Service 2014) enables integrated search of dozens of KOSs by first formatting them in a standard representation. If KOSs applied are multilingual such as, for example, the EUROVOC thesaurus (the multilingual thesaurus maintained by the Publications Office of the European Union) or the Universal Decimal Classification (UDC) scheme, then the standards also can ensure cross-language searching. Using a standard format for representing various KOSs also can support easier mapping between them, as exemplified by Isaac et al. (2009). Other applications for a standardized KOS include (semi-)automated subject indexing and tagging, and KOS management software.

This chapter first discusses standards for the design and construction of a KOS as related to standards for representation and interchange, and then explains underlying Web standards such as XML (Extensible Markup Language) and RDF (Resource Description Framework). It further examines standards for representation and interchange of a KOS. It also examines protocols, query languages, and application programming interfaces (APIs) for accessing KOS concepts and their elements. The chapter then considers identification of KOSs and their elements in the context of Linked Data, and briefly overviews terminology registries that are important for both human use and machine-to-machine communication and access. The chapter ends with conclusions and reflective questions for the reader, and lastly includes a glossary of terms.

STANDARDS FOR DESIGN AND CONSTRUCTION OF KOSs

Standards for the design and construction of a KOS largely are restricted to thesauri (rather than other types of KOS). Dextre Clarke and Zeng (2011) reflect on the history of thesauri since their emergence in the 1960s, including standardization by the International Organization for Standardization (ISO) in 1974 (ISO 2788, International Organization for Standardization 1974) and a number of national standards. In its most recent form, which dates from 2011, the standard is published as ISO 25964 (International Organization for Standardization 2011; 2013a), Thesauri and interoperability with other vocabularies. It comprises two parts, Part 1: Thesauri for information retrieval, from 2011, and Part 2: Interoperability with other vocabularies, from 2013. This reflects an evolution from thesauri design and construction only, toward interoperability between thesauri and other KOS types.

Part 1 of ISO 25964 (Thesauri for information retrieval) covers monolingual and multilingual thesauri for indexing and information retrieval. Compared to previous standards it is very strict in differentiating between terms and concepts; indeed, the broader terms (BT), narrower terms (NT), and related terms (RT) relations are defined as between concepts, not terms. Such strict guidelines are a requisite for the data model to enable easy implementation by computers, preserve consistency in thesaurus construction and mapping, ensure interoperability across KOSs, and enhance KOS development, management, and exchange (Dextre Clarke and Zeng 2011). Moreover, Part

1 provides functional requirements for thesaurus management software, a data model, and an XML schema for exchange of data between thesauri. The data model and the XML schema are described in more detail below.

Part 2 of ISO 25964 (Interoperability with other vocabularies, ISO 25964-2), published in 2013, provides models and guidelines for mapping between thesauri and the following knowledge organization systems: classification schemes, file plans (classification schemes used for records management), taxonomies, subject heading schemes, ontologies, terminologies, name authority lists, and synonym rings (sets of terms considered equivalent and which are used in retrieval). Chapter 2 includes definitions of other knowledge organization systems. Recommended types of mapping are based on the three major thesaurus relationship types: equivalence, hierarchical, and associative. Mapping with ontologies is not recommended, as ontologies are defined as formalized representations of a domain of knowledge used for inferencing. The level to which ontologies serve information-retrieval purposes is restricted to those defining structural elements of a KOS (e.g., facets) whereby the KOS "populates" those elements (e.g., provides values for the facets). Some other authors define ontologies more flexibly to include any RDF graph which is not a pure data set, that is, it uses RDFS (RDF Schema) or OWL (Web Ontology Language) elements, both of which standards allow expressing more complex relationships between elements than pure RDF does (see the following section on RDF).

Other widely used instances of KOSs are those considered to be the standard in their user community (Dextre Clarke 2011). The world's most widely used classification scheme is the Dewey Decimal Classification (DDC). First published in the United States in 1876, it is now in its twenty-third edition—despite criticisms about its inconsistencies and tendency toward bias. Similarly, the Universal Decimal Classification (UDC) can be considered a national standard in countries where it is predominantly used (e.g., Spain, Croatia).

For subject headings languages, the situation is similar—subject headings languages primarily are guided by the U.S. Library of Congress Subject Headings (LCSH), the most widely used subject headings system, although international guidelines do exist, such as the IFLA (International Federation of Library Associations and Institutions), *Principles Underlying Subject Heading Languages* (Lopes and Beall 1999).

UNDERLYING WEB STANDARDS: XML AND RDF

Before discussing standards for coding and the exchange of a KOS in particular, it is important to understand the technological standards on which they are based. The most viable Web standards are based on XML and RDF, the latter in particular if the KOS will be integrated into the Semantic Web.

The Web as it is today already uses XML, whereas the Semantic Web requires RDF. Used together XML and RDF will bridge both infrastructures.

Extensible Markup Language is an encoding scheme developed by the World Wide Web Consortium (2013a). Its beginnings go back to SGML (Standard Generalized Markup Language, ISO 8879) (International Organization for Standardization 1986), which was developed for structuring and tagging text in electronic publishing. At the time, SGML was rather complex to implement for many applications, thus the simplicity of HTML and its readability by both machine and human users gave it a widespread popularity. In 1996, XML was developed for the high-level structuring of information resources in a manner simpler than that of SGML. It also allows for readability by both machines and human users, as does HTML. Today, XML is used widely in various applications exchanging data on the Web and beyond. It is maintained by the World Wide Web Consortium, therefore its usage on the Web and compliance to other Web standards is ensured. Many Web standards and specifications rely on XML as a base format.

To ensure the interoperability and the exchange of XML files and their content, it is necessary to define each element and its tags, as different information resources use the same tags to refer to different concepts. Definitions of all tags and their prescribed usage, attributes, and hierarchy are provided in DTDs (Document Type Definitions) in SGML. Today, however, an XML schema—which is more powerful—is used more commonly for this purpose. In the XML schema, an XML namespace (xmlns) element is provided to ensure that the information source uses unique identification for the tags included. The identifier is a URI (Uniform Resource Identifier), which could be a Uniform Resource Name (URN) or a Uniform Resource Locator (URL).

The two XML instances shown below, for example, each define the meaning of the term "leopard" using a different namespace prefix (a or b) and associated URI. Therefore, if the word "leopard" is used in an XML document, its prefix a: or b: shows the document user which meaning is attributed, either the animal (defined at http://id.loc.gov/authorities/subjects/sh85076038) or the military tank (defined at http://id.loc.gov/authorities/subjects/sh85076032).

```
<a:leopard xmlns:a="http://id.loc.gov/authorities/subjects/sh85076038">
    <a:name>Leopard (Panthera pardus)</a:name>
    <a:family>Felidae</a:family>
</a:leopard>
<b:leopard xmlns:b="http://id.loc.gov/authorities/subjects/sh85076032">
    <b:name>Leopard (tank)</b:name>
    <b:type>main battle tank</b:type>
</b:leopard>
```

An XML file looks similar to an HTML file in that angle brackets are used to define a tag and its attributes, < > representing an opening tag, and </> a closing tag; the content to be tagged is placed between the two tags. The XML extract below, for example, is from the AGROVOC agricultural thesaurus. It defines the concept of "banks," with "financial institutions" as a broader term, various types of banks as the narrower terms, and "banking" as a related term. The tags and the text are readable by a human user. The first line defines the element type (KOSItem) with a unique identification number, and the line following defines "banks" as an instance of the element type. In a complete XML file, all the other terms would be defined as instances of the element type including their unique identification numbers.

```
<KOSItem id="812">
    <preferredlabel>banks</preferredlabel>
    <broaderterm>financial institutions</broaderterm>
    <narrowerterm>agricultural banks</narrowerterm>
    <narrowerterm>cooperative banks</narrowerterm>
    <narrowerterm>development banks</narrowerterm>
    <relatedterm>banking</relatedterm>
</KOSItem>
```

The syntax of XML is stricter than that of HTML. All tags must have a closing tag, tags must be properly nested, and capitalization denotes a different tag; these features help ensure consistency. An XML document is tested for both its syntax (in a Web browser) and its conformance to a given XML schema (in software referred to as XML editors or dedicated XML validators).

A document coded in XML is easy to present in a Web browser in any preferred manner using a style sheet for XML called XSTL (Extensible Stylesheet Language). An added advantage is that an XSLT has a rather powerful querying functionality, ensuring that only certain content is presented in the preferred manner.

The RDF, also developed and maintained by the World Wide Web Consortium since the late 1990s, specifies the meaning of content in greater detail. It could be considered the data model of the Semantic Web because all data that are part of the Semantic Web are represented, transmitted, and queried as RDF data (the World Wide Web Consortium 2004). An RDF requires that predicates—which are the equivalent of XML attributes—be globally uniquely identified; XML permits the same attribute to have different meanings in local applications. The URIs for RDF classes and properties then can be the subjects of what are known as "triples" in the RDF community, giving definitions and scope notes of those classes and properties for use by Semantic Web applications. The RDF uses the form of subject, predicate, and object statements—similar to statement forms in English grammar. The subject is a resource being described, and the predicate states the relationship of the subject with the object. Objects can either refer to other things (i.e., the URI of a thing) or be literals. Triples include Web URIs, unlike for XML in which the documents tend to be self-contained instead of having data mandatorily linked.

For example, by using RDF it is possible to specify that the resource, in this case a concept at http://skos.um.es/unescothes/C01194 (subject), belongs to the UNESCO thesaurus (for which the namespaces "unesco" is defined as having the following URI: http://skos.um.es/unescothes/), and that it has a label (predicate) "education" (object), that it has a related term (another predicate) with the URI http://skos.um.es/unescothes/C02240 (another object). The related term has a Web URI, and the "rdf:resource" attribute is best used to indicate this.

```
<rdf:RDF
    xmlns:rdf="http://www.w3.org/1999/02/22-rdf-syntax-ns#"
    xmlns:unesco="http://skos.um.es/unescothes/">
    <rdf:Description rdf:about="http://skos.um.es/unescothes/C01194">
        <unesco:label>education</unesco:label>
        <unesco:related rdf:resource="http://skos.um.es/unescothes/
          C02240/">
    </rdf:Description>
</rdf:RDF>
```

The RDF enables semantic reasoning. For example, say that there are two attributes "author name" and "pseudonym of the author name," and the mapping triple "'pseudonym of the author name'—(is) sub-property of—'author.'" Then, when a data triple exists "This resource—(has) pseudonym of the author name—'Mark Twain,'" someone reasoning semantically could deduce that "This resource—(has) author—'Mark Twain'" (analogous to an example from http://managemetadata.com/blog/2012/05/12/using-the-sub-property-ladder/).

A standardized format for ontologies which builds on RDF is OWL. A standardized format for the information-retrieval KOS that relies on RDF is SKOS (Simple Knowledge Organization System).

Extensible Markup Language serves as the most frequently used carrier serialization of RDF data. Other serializations used commonly are Notation3 (N3), which is a representation of RDF models designed to be more readable by humans; and Turtle, a subset of N3 which is more human-readable than XML and often is chosen for the purpose of exemplifying

RDF data. XML and N3 are serializations of the native RDF graph, which are intended to be completely interchangeable. The previous example rendered in N3 would be written as shown below.

```
@prefix unesco: <http://skos.um.es/unescothes/>.
@prefix rdf: <http://www.w3.org/1999/02/22-rdf-syntax-ns#>.
unesco:C01194 unesco:label "education";
unesco:related unesco:C02240.
```

Or in expanded N3 with unclustered triples clearly separated, as shown below.

```
@prefix unesco: <http://skos.um.es/unescothes/>.
@prefix rdf: <http://www.w3.org/1999/02/22-rdf-syntax-ns#>.
unesco:C01194 unesco:label "education".
unesco:C01194 unesco:related unesco:C02240.
```

The two triples in full expanded N3 format would read as follows.

```
<http://skos.um.es/unescothes/C01194> <http://skos.um.es/unescothes/label>
  "education".
<http://skos.um.es/unescothes/C01194> http://skos.um.es/unescothes/related
<http://skos.um.es/unescothes/C02240>.
```

Other formats in which RDF data can be represented include JSON (JavaScript Object Notation), a standard based on JavaScript, and JSON-LD (JavaScript Object Notation for Linked Data) which is used to transport Linked Data using JSON. Like XML, JSON is a syntax for storing and exchanging data; however, JSON representations are shorter, easier to understand, and easier to parse.

STANDARDS FOR REPRESENTATION AND INTERCHANGE OF KOSs

ISO 2709

International standard "ISO 2709, Information and documentation—Format for information exchange," is the standard for the representation and exchange of bibliographic and related data in a machine-readable form (International Organization for Standardization 2008a). Its origins go back to the 1960s and to the U.S. Library of Congress; its latest version is from 2008. The ISO 2709 format directs the format required for records to be exchangeable. It follows cataloging standards and, to a certain degree, mimics the paper catalog cards it replaced. As such, the standard could be made more flexible for the wider digital environment.

Two major instances of ISO 2709 are used today, MARC 21 (MAchine Readable Cataloging 21) (Library of Congress 2013a) and UNIMARC (UNIversal MAchine Readable Cataloging) (International Federation of Library Associations and Institutions 2013). MARC 21 is predominantly used in the United States and Canada and supports five parts of a record's bibliographic data that are used to describe the library material; the authoritative forms of names for persons, organizations, meetings, titles, and subjects; holdings data; community information; and classification data. UNIMARC is used worldwide, including in a number of European countries, countries in North Africa, Japan, Russia, and China.

Any ISO 2709 record comprises three main sections:

1. A label, which tells the system how to read a particular record. The label is a 24-character string that identifies the record and contains coded details about the record.
2. A directory, which serves as an index to the location of fields and contains information about the fields.
3. Fields and their subfields, which contain all the values. For example, in MARC 21 bibliographic format, fields starting with number 6 are subject-access fields (Library of Congress 2005). In the following instance, an information resource titled *The Essentials of Art History* by George M. Cohen (LCCN permalink http://lccn.loc.gov/98068782) has been assigned a subject heading *Art—History—Juvenile literature*, coded in field 650 for Subject Added Entry-Topical Term, where subfield "a" contains a topical term, subfield "x" contains a general subdivision, and subfield "v" is for a form subdivision. Two indicators are possible in this field. In the example below, the first indicator is not provided (_), and the second indicator "0" shows that the source of the subject-added entry is the Library of Congress Subject Headings (LCSH).

```
650   _0 |a Art |x History |v Juvenile literature
```

Subject headings and classification numbers used in bibliographic records are verified against corresponding authority records. Authorities for subject headings contain the authorized forms of subject headings and references to their synonyms (unauthorized headings) and related headings. Each record represents one heading. Similarly, each record in the classification data authorities represents one classification number and the information related to it.

In MARC 21, for example, an authority record for art history in juvenile literature (http://lccn.loc.gov/sh2009115831) when viewed in MARC

21 comprises 13 lines of code. The most relevant line is that starting with 150, which represents a field used for topical headings. Subfields are the same as those in the bibliographic field for subject-added entries, 650. As described above: subfield "a" indicates a topical term (Art), subfield "x" is the general subdivision (History), and subfield "v" is form subdivision (Juvenile literature).

```
000  00466cz a2200169n 450
001  7886599
005  20110729162053.0
008  090512|| anannbabn |n ana
010  __ |a sh2009115831
035  __ |a (DLC)425589
035  __ |a (DLC)sh2009115831
040  __ |a DLC |b eng |c DLC
150  __ |a Art |x History |v Juvenile literature
667  __ |a Record generated for validation purposes.
670  __ |a Work cat.: Discovering art history, c1997
```

The first line (starting with 000) is a leader and tells how long the record is, whether the record has been corrected or revised (c), whether it is an authority record (z), and other details. The second line (starting with 001) is a control number. The third line (starting with 005) is the date and time of the latest transaction. The fourth line (starting with 008) provides a number of details about the record, such as whether it contains subheadings and which standards (if any) are applied. The line starting with 010 contains the Library of Congress control number. Lines starting with 035 are system control numbers. The line starting with 040 provides details about cataloging, such as the cataloging agency (a), language of cataloging (b), and transcribing agency (c). The line starting with 667 is a field for including a general note not intended for the public. The line starting with 670 indicates the source from which the data has been taken.

MARC 21 also provides the following subfields in field 150.

- #b: Topical term following geographic name entry element,
- #y: Chronological subdivision, and
- #z: Geographic subdivision.

In UNIMARC, for authorities' format (International Federation of Library Associations and Institutions 2009) similar options are available using different codes for fields and subfields. For example, for topical subject or subject category field 250 is used. Available subfields are:

- #n for subject category code,
- #m for subject category subdivision code,
- #j for form subdivision,
- #x for topical subdivision or subject category subdivision text,
- #y for geographical subdivision, and
- #z for chronological subdivision.

The record example given above for art history also lists the Library of Congress Classification number in the 050 field, subfield #a, as N5305. There are several other fields related to classification numbers from other classification systems. When a bibliographic record is created, in MARC 21 format, the classification number is verified against the authority file. The two best-known schemes coded in MARC 21 are Dewey Decimal Classification (DDC) and Library of Congress Classification (LCC). The MARC 21 format for classification data was based on the Library of Congress Classification schedules (Beall and Mitchell 2010). In its introduction, however, the LC Classification Schedule (Library of Congress 2006) claims that data elements were designed to be applicable to any classification scheme, wherever possible. When DDC was converted from a proprietary format to the MARC 21 format in 2009, however, both formats for classification and for authority data had to be used: MARC 21 format for classification data to represent schedules, tables, and manual, and MARC 21 format for authority data for the Relative Index and mapped terminology. This conversion also resulted in the need to improve other MARC 21 formats to enhance access to classification data presented in the two formats (Beall and Mitchell 2010).

In MARC 21 format for classification data, the classification scheme is identified in field 084 (Classification Scheme and Edition), subfield #a (Classification scheme code). The information indicating that the record is a classification record is provided by code #w (Classification data) in Leader/06, Type of record. Three types of classification records can be identified, the first being the schedule record in which field 153 (Classification Number) contains a classification number or span from the schedule itself, including a number which has been built from applying "add" instructions. A classification data record must contain at least 154 General Explanatory Index Term fields, or the following three fields: 008 Fixed-Length Data Elements, 084 Classification Scheme and Edition, and 153 Classification Number Fixed.

Although UNIMARC for classification data currently is being developed (International Federation of Library Associations and Institutions 2000), UNIMARC for authorities also provides within itself fields for classification data, including 675 for UDC, 676 for DDC, 680 for LCC, and 686 for other classification numbers. Subfields are provided to indicate class number or range of numbers (a and b), and explanatory terms (c) as well as to indicate the edition of the classification system used and similar information.

ISO 2709 in XML

To allow for a more flexible and extensible format than MARC 21 and UNIMARC, initiatives are underway to convert records to XML. The U.S. Library of Congress has implemented XML-based versions of MARC 21 (Library of Congress 2012a) referred to as MARCXML, MODS, and MADS, which are described below. UNIMARC conversion to XML has been conducted at a level of experimentation (BookMARC 2004). An ISO standard also has been drafted to provide an XML schema, an extension to ISO 2709, called ISO 25577: MarcXchange (International Organization for Standardization 2006).

MARCXML is a straightforward coding of MARC formats with XML. It consists of <datafield> and <subfield> elements and their values, corresponding to fields and subfields of MARC 21 formats. For example, the LCSH heading from the previous MARC 21 example is coded in MARCXML as shown below (http://id.loc.gov/authorities/subjects /sh2009115831.marcxml.xml).

```
<marcxml:record>
    <marcxml:leader>00374nz a2200133n 4500</marcxml:leader>
    <marcxml:controlfield tag="001">sh2009115831</marcxml:controlfield>
    <marcxml:controlfield tag="003">DLC</marcxml:controlfield>
    <marcxml:controlfield tag="005">20090512090445.0</marcxml:
    controlfield>
    <marcxml:controlfield tag="008">090512|| anannbabn |n ana
    </marcxml:controlfield>
    <marcxml:datafield tag="010" ind1=" " ind2=" ">
        <marcxml:subfield code="a">sh2009115831</marcxml:subfield>
    </marcxml:datafield>
    <marcxml:datafield tag="040" ind1=" " ind2=" ">
        <marcxml:subfield code="a">DLC</marcxml:subfield>
        <marcxml:subfield code="b">eng</marcxml:subfield>
        <marcxml:subfield code="c">DLC</marcxml:subfield>
    </marcxml:datafield>
    <marcxml:datafield tag="150" ind1=" " ind2=" ">
        <marcxml:subfield code="a">Art</marcxml:subfield>
        <marcxml:subfield code="x">History</marcxml:subfield>
        <marcxml:subfield code="v">Juvenile literature</marcxml:subfield>
        </marcxml:datafield>
    <marcxml:datafield tag="667" ind1=" " ind2=" ">
        <marcxml:subfield code="a">Record generated for validation
        purposes.</marcxml:subfield>
```

```
        </marcxml:datafield><marcxml:datafield tag="670" ind1=" " ind2=" ">
            <marcxml:subfield code="a">Work cat.: Discovering art history, c1997
            </marcxml:subfield>
        </marcxml:datafield>
    </marcxml:record>
```


A more advanced transition to XML and the wider digital infrastructure is MADS (Metadata Authority Description Schema) (Library of Congress 2013b), which uses named elements rather than direct codes from MARC. It is an XML schema for MARC 21 authorities including subject headings and classification data. For example, the LCSH heading in the previous example is coded in MADS as follows (http://id.loc.gov/authorities/subjects/sh2009115831.madsxml.xml).


```
<mads:mads version="2.0" xsi:schemaLocation="http://www.loc.gov/mads/v2
http://www.loc.gov/standards/mads/mads-2-0.xsd">
    <mads:authority>
        <mads:topic authority="lcsh">Art</mads:topic>
        <mads:topic>History</mads:topic>
        <mads:genre>Juvenile literature</mads:genre>
    </mads:authority>
    <mads:note type="nonpublic">Record generated for validation
    purposes</mads:note>
    <mads:note type="source">Work cat.: Discovering art history, c1997
    </mads:note>
    <mads:identifier type="lccn">sh2009115831</mads:identifier>
    <mads:recordInfo>
        <mads:recordOrigin>Converted from MARCXML to MADS
        version 2.0 (Revision 2.10)</mads:recordOrigin>
        <mads:recordContentSource authority="marcorg">DLC
        </mads:recordContentSource>
        <mads:recordChangeDate encod-
        ing="iso8601">20090512090445.0</
        mads:recordChangeDate>
        <mads:recordIdentifier source="DLC">sh2009115831
        </mads:recordIdentifier>
        <mads:languageOfCataloging>
            <mads:languageTerm authority="iso639-
            2b"type="code">eng</mads:languageTerm>
        </mads:languageOfCataloging>
    </mads:recordInfo>
</mads:mads>
```

Notice that field 150 from the MARC 21 record is coded as <mads:-authority>, with subfields "a" and "x" as <mads:topic>, and subfield "v" as <mads:genre>. (For a complete list of elements, see Library of Congress 2012b.)

MARCXML and MADS for authorities are implemented by the Library of Congress as part of the "LC Linked Data Service: Authorities and Vocabularies" (Library of Congress 2014). In the service, retrieved classification records could be viewed in MADS, and subject headings records are available in both MADS and MARCXML. MADS is made available in XML, in RDF/XML, as well as in JSON and N3. The RDF/XML output of a MADS record has to use blank nodes, however, which means that the triples cannot be disaggregated for use in global Semantic Web applications. In this service, records also are made available in SKOS (additional details are given below).

Metadata Object Description Schema (MODS) is a new metadata encoding schema largely based on MARC bibliographic format. Like MADS, it uses language-based tags rather than numbers and symbols for fields and subfields. Its aim is to be simpler than MARC so that wider communities outside of library professionals can understand it, yet complex enough to cover all the aspects, unlike Dublin Core metadata (Dublin Core Metadata Initiative 2012a) which are the most simple.

Dublin Core was created in 1995 as a Web-oriented simpler metadata set, in contrast to the complex standards such as ISO 2709. The Dublin Core Metadata Element Set (DCMES) comprises fifteen basic elements. Over time, extensions to these elements started being developed for applications requiring more attention to detail, such as Dublin Core Metadata Initiative Terms (DCMI Terms) and various application profiles. The basic fifteen elements serve as the common backbone for metadata elements applicable in many metadata contexts, at the same time allowing for finer detail through DCMI Terms and application profiles. Application profiles are based on the Dublin Core Abstract Model which supports representing "record" structures in RDF, and prescribes KOSs from which values can be taken—known as Vocabulary Encoding Schemes (Dublin Core Metadata Initiative 2012b).

XML Schema of ISO 25964

As discussed at the start of this chapter, the ISO 25964 standard for thesauri prescribes both how to build a thesaurus and how to represent it in a machine-readable manner to ensure greater interoperability with other KOSs and with other applications for a variety of purposes. The standard thus provides an abstract data model for the exchange of thesauri or parts of them (National Information Standards Organization 2014), as well as its XML Schema (National Information Standards Organization 2011).

The data model is presented as a UML (Unified Modeling Language) diagram; a tabular data version also is available. The model sets out five major UML classes to which other classes in the thesaurus are assigned as associated classes. Each class has various attributes. Following Dublin Core naming conventions, names of the classes are represented in "UpperCamelCase" (no spaces between words and each word starting with a capital letter), and attributes in "lowerCamelCase" (no spaces between words and each word except the first starting with a capital letter). Below is the list of five main classes, together with some of the associated attributes (listed in parentheses).

- Thesaurus, referring to the thesaurus as a whole.
- ThesaurusArray, referring to an array of sibling concepts forming part of the thesaurus.
- ThesaurusConcept, referring to a concept that is a member of the thesaurus.
- ThesaurusTerm, referring to a term in the thesaurus by which a concept could be sought.
- Note, referring to a piece of text giving additional information about the term or concept to which it is linked.

The associated XML schema specifies the root element as ISO25964Interchange. Top-level elements all are classes from the data model, apart from "Thesaurus," which is set to contain three flat lists representing the classes ThesaurusConcept, ConceptGroup, and ThesaurusArray. Using identifiers to link all the elements, rather than a structure of hierarchies (as used by the ADL thesaurus format discussed below), avoids the need for repetition of polyhierarchical concepts and also enables only parts of thesauri to be exchanged.

SKOS

Simple Knowledge Organization System (SKOS) is a format for representing, sharing, and exchanging KOSs, developed and maintained by the World Wide Web Consortium (W3C) since 2005. It became a W3C recommendation in 2009. Although developed in the context of the Semantic Web, its major purpose is not to serve as a formal knowledge representation language like OWL is (discussed below), but to allow for sharing and linking KOSs via the (Semantic) Web. Such modeling at a relatively superficial level accommodates a broader range of KOS types and supports their wider exchange, and is done at the cost of stripping it of possibilities for more powerful reasoning (Dextre Clarke 2011). A detailed overview of the development that led to its current state, its comparison to OWL, including pointers for future revision is given in a recent paper by T. Baker et al. (2013).

Like ISO 25964 and its British predecessor BS 8723-2, the SKOS data model is based on concepts rather than terms. In *SKOS Primer* (Isaac and Summers 2009) a distinction is made between basic SKOS and advanced SKOS. Basic SKOS provides for unique identification of concepts with URIs, labeling of terms in one or more languages, notes for concepts, and the linking of concepts with relationships of hierarchy, equivalence, and relatedness. Advanced SKOS additionally supports mapping across KOSs and grouping concepts. Simple Knowledge Organization System eXtension for Labels (SKOS-XL) Namespace Document provides additional support for describing and linking labels (e.g., ability to state that IFLA is an acronym of the International Federation of Library Associations and Institutions) (Miles and Bechhofer 2009). Similarly, it is possible to provide SKOS extensions for advanced features of KOSs to accommodate specific needs, such as establishing finer distinctions between hierarchical relationships, generic, partitive, and instantial (known as BTG/NTG, BTP/NTP, BTI/NTI, respectively) (Dextre Clarke 2011).

An example of a thesaurus made available in SKOS is the UNESCO thesaurus (United Nations Educational, Scientific and Cultural Organization 2010). Each concept is made available both in HTML and in SKOS. For example, the concept of artists in English in HTML as available at http://skos.um.es/unescothes/C00266/html, is as follows.

Artists (http://skos.um.es/unescothes/C00266)

Microthesauri

  MT 3.45 Art

Used for (non-descriptors)

  UF Graphic designers

  UF Photographers

Narrower terms

  NT Architects

  NT Film makers

  NT Painters

  NT Performers

  NT Sculptors

  NT Theatre directors

  NT Women artists

Related terms

  RT Cultural personnel

  RT Occupations

The same concept of artists is presented in SKOS at http://skos.um.es/unescothes/C00266/rdfxml as follows (only English terms extracted). Note that, instead of "topConceptOf," it would have been better to use "skos:broader," as "topConceptOf" was introduced to SKOS for technical reasons (Antoine Isaac, personal communication).

```
    <rdf:RDF>
        <skos:Concept rdf:about="http://skos.um.es/unescothes/C00266">
        <skos:prefLabel xml:lang="en">Artists</skos:prefLabel>
        <skos:inScheme rdf:resource="http://skos.um.es/unescothes/CS000"/>
        <skos:topConceptOf rdf:resource="http://skos.um.es/unescothes/CS000"/>
        <skos:narrower rdf:resource="http://skos.um.es/unescothes/C00215"/>
        <skos:narrower rdf:resource="http://skos.um.es/unescothes/C01520"/>
        <skos:narrower rdf:resource="http://skos.um.es/unescothes/C02878"/>
        <skos:narrower rdf:resource="http://skos.um.es/unescothes/C02941"/>
        <skos:narrower rdf:resource="http://skos.um.es/unescothes/C03568"/>
        <skos:narrower rdf:resource="http://skos.um.es/unescothes/C04042"/>
        <skos:narrower rdf:resource="http://skos.um.es/unescothes/C04335"/>
        <skos:related rdf:resource="http://skos.um.es/unescothes/C00904"/>
        <skos:related rdf:resource="http://skos.um.es/unescothes/C02796"/>
        <skos:altLabel xml:lang="en">Graphic designers</skos:altLabel>
        <skos:altLabel xml:lang="en">Photographers</skos:altLabel>
    </skos:Concept>
</rdf:RDF>
```

The SKOS representations of the UNESCO thesaurus are available in several carrying formats, XML/RDF, JSON, N3, and Turtle. This illustrates the possibility of creating multiple formats to support a wider number of applications.

The SKOS data model is mostly compatible with the above-described ISO 25964 data model. It does not, however, cover use of arrays (groups of sibling concepts, which are two or more concepts with the same immediate broader concept), concept groups (concepts grouped using a classification structure), compound equivalence (one term or concept in one context is represented by two or more terms or concepts in another context), version history, custom extensions, or specific properties of concepts, terms, notes, and thesaurus (Tudhope 2012). A detailed correspondence between the two data models is provided by International Organization for Standardization TC46/SC9/WG8 Working Group and Isaac (2012).

The SKOS initially was developed for thesauri, but different types of KOSs, including classification schemes, taxonomies, and folksonomies can be accommodated subject to a level of creative adjustments. Summers et al. (2008) describe, for example, a technique for converting Library of Congress Subject Headings (LCSH) in MARCXML to SKOS, suggesting solutions that are not provided for by SKOS, such as subheadings and dates related to record creation and update, and an associated LC classification number. A significant amount of information is lost for subheadings; MARC allows for distinction between facets such as historical, geographical, and form and SKOS does not. Therefore all the subheadings and the main heading must be flattened into a literal, and the resulting string cannot be parsed to recover the subheadings. For the example given above, SKOS code would be just one line.

```
<skos:prefLabel xml:lang="en">Art—History—Juvenile literature</skos:prefLabel>
```

All subheadings thus are joined into one string and are not searchable or retrievable, and cannot be mapped. Similarly, Gnoli et al. (2011) found that several structural elements of a freely faceted classification scheme could not be represented in a full way with SKOS, and would require special extensions. This all is a consequence of SKOS initially being developed for thesauri which do not use precoordination.

Summers et al. (2008) suggest that the SKOS be extended with subclasses of "skos:Concept" such as "lcsh:TopicalConcept," "lcsh:GeographicConcept," "lcsh:GenreConcept," and "lcsh:ChronologicalConcept." Also, the LCSH use creation and last modification date of the record, and related LC classification number, which SKOS cannot include. The authors suggest that these be converted into the Dublin Core standard as "dcterms:lcc," "dcterms:created," "dcterms:modified," and then imported into the SKOS record. This also is an instance of RDF that allows for the flexibility of importing other elements from, for instance, RDFS (RDF Schema) and Dublin Core. The implementation at the LC Linked Data Service: Authorities and Vocabularies (Library of Congress 2014) seems to use the "Change Set" schema (Tunnicliffe and Davis 2009) rather than Dublin Core for dates nested within the note on changes (skos:changeNote). The example above also provides an attribute (xml:lang="en") which is recommended by SKOS to denote the language of the concept. Moreover, the use of the language tag is built into all RDF literals. More recently, MADS/RDF which accommodates precoordination has been mapped to SKOS, thus covering the need for keeping precoordination (Library of Congress 2012c).

Related to this idea is the handling of multilingual SKOS. One approach is to use a separate SKOS vocabulary for each language—using only terms from that language—leading to separate URIs. Another approach is to use the language attribute within a single URI. The former is suitable for KOSs which are developed independently, for example, and the latter for KOSs which contain internal translations of labels.

Similarly, although it was possible to represent UDC summaries in SKOS as RDF/XML and Linked Data (Universal Decimal Classification Consortium 2014), the whole of the UDC—including more than 70,000 classes and more than 13,000 superseded numbers—is now planned to be converted to SKOS, but devices must be devised to deal with linking superseded numbers with their new versions because SKOS does not support this function (Aida Slavić, personal communication). Attempts to create a SKOS format for DDC have resulted in suggestions to extend SKOS to appropriately accommodate for classification systems in general (Panzer and Zeng 2009).

Many KOSs have been published as SKOS and more efforts are underway. As of May 2013, 39 major efforts are listed at the W3C SKOS dataset Wiki (World Wide Web Consortium 2014). Among others, these include the Library of Congress Linked Data Service (Library of Congress 2014) which made available the large and widely used LCSH, the Thesaurus for Graphic Materials, and other KOSs maintained by the Library of Congress. OCLC's FAST (Faceted Application of Subject Terminology), a subject headings language derived from LCSH, was released as SKOS and Linked Data in 2011, and also provides mappings to LCSH.

Other major examples of KOSs include AGROVOC, an agricultural thesaurus published by the Food and Agriculture Organization of the United Nations and available in 22 languages (Food and Agriculture Organization of the United Nations 2013); GEMET (General Multilingual Environmental Thesaurus) available in 28 languages (European Environment Agency 2010); EUROVOC, the European Union multilingual thesaurus in all EU languages (European Union 2014b); the Government of Canada Core Subject Thesaurus (Government of Canada 2014); and the Web NDL Authorities of National Diet Library of Japan (National Diet Library 2011) in Japanese, which offers about one million authority records as RDF triples, with each record represented in SKOS as well as other formats. Today, SKOS also is used by Europeana, the European Community Digital Library.

In a review of SKOS on the Web (Manaf, Bechofer, and Stevens 2012), 478 KOSs have been identified as available in SKOS, although almost one third of them are simple term lists—therefore they do not apply SKOS semantic relations—and many do not use SKOS lexical labels for preferred and non-preferred terms ("skos:prefLabel," "skos:altLabel"). Many other projects to make existing KOSs available in SKOS are underway. As was done for UDC, certain editions and languages of DDC also have been converted into SKOS and Linked Data (OCLC 2014). Representations are made in RDF, in XHTML, and RDFa (Resource Description Framework in Attributes). RDFa is a W3C recommendation broadening RDF with extensions for attributes to support embedding rich metadata within Web information resources.

An example of the importance of interoperability is given by Isaac et al. (2009). This research set up and tested a system for enhancing subject indexing of books at the National Library of the Netherlands (KB). It suggests subject terms from the same or a different KOS already available in subject indexes of Dutch public libraries for the same book. KB uses the Brinkman general subject thesaurus, and the public libraries use the Biblion general thesaurus. The KOSs first were formatted in SKOS, and then automated mapping was conducted. The researchers predict that conversion of other KOSs to SKOS would enable their seamless integration into the automated mapping prototype, as well as allow for further services and inclusion of various other collections.

All the advantages of SKOS as a standard for presentation, access, and the interoperability of the KOS on the Web will not be realized unless the SKOS version of KOS is valid and properly formatted. Suominen and Mader (2014) assessed 24 SKOS-formatted KOSs made available on the Web based on 26 criteria against which the researchers could analyze them algorithmically. The criteria included, for example, the validity of URIs (which can be syntactical, semantic (such as registered URI schemes), and functional (such as dereferenceability of HTTP URIs)); whether language tags specifying the language of the represented content are provided; whether there are concepts which are neither top concepts nor have links to any other concepts (orphan concepts); that there is no more than one preferred term for each concept; that mapping is consistent (e.g., two terms cannot be both an exact match and a related match); presence of surrounding whitespaces which, although permitted by SKOS, could cause problems when exact string matching is performed. They found that each of the 24 KOSs had one or more problems. Upon automatically applying a set of corrections, they reduced the problems significantly. The tools used are available as open source.

Representation Standards for Ontologies

Ontologies are considered to be a special type of KOS, designed to be rather formalized to allow for reasoning, logical inferencing, and artificial intelligence applications. As noted, some define ontologies more flexibly to include any RDF graph which is not a pure data set—it uses RDFS or OWL elements.

Special representation standards for ontologies have been developed. Web Ontology Language is a standard used for representing ontologies in RDF, with the ultimate purpose of ontologies becoming interoperable with other components of the Web and playing a major role in the Semantic Web. The OWL format reflects the complexity and detailed elaboration required by ontologies. This is why it is best used for ontologies only, rather than for other types of KOSs, although some researchers suggested that OWL also can be used to represent some relationships that are not covered adequately by SKOS (Zeng, Panzer, and Salaba 2010). One of the largest initiatives is the Finnish ONKI SKOS server (Semantic Computing Research Group 2012) which retains ontologies in the OWL format, as well as other KOSs in the SKOS format.

OWL has been developed and maintained by W3C, which declared the first version of OWL as a W3C recommendation in 2004, and replaced it in 2009 with OWL 2 (W3C OWL Working Group 2012). OWL 2 contains minor changes and introductions as compared to the first version, and maintains backward compatibility. OWL has three sublanguages: OWL Lite, OWL DL (which includes OWL Lite), and OWL Full (which includes OWL DL). OWL 2 also includes three profiles for specific application purposes: OWL 2 EL which is aimed at very large ontologies for which computational performance is a priority over expressing elaborate detail; OWL 2 QL, used when the priority is to support querying of ontologies based on relational databases; and OWL 2 RL, which is similar to OWL QL but querying must be operated on RDF triples, which then could allow for more advanced reasoning than OWL 2 RL.

The OWL data consist of classes, subclasses, their instances (called individuals), and properties. It builds on RDF Schemas (RDFS), a framework for describing application-specific classes based on RDF. Classes denote sets of individuals, and properties relate individuals to other information such as other individuals or literal values. Each property has a URI, which has a crucial value in the context of RDF and Linked Data. All these characteristics allow for more advanced logical inferencing as compared to simply coding content in XML. A brief example is given for mammals as a class, with monotremes and marsupials as its subclasses.

```
<owl:Class rdf:about="http://en.wikipedia.org/wiki/Mammal">
    <rdfs:label>Mammal</rdfs:label>
    <rdfs:comment>The class of mammals.</rdfs:comment>
</owl:Class>
<owl:Class rdf:about="http://en.wikipedia.org/wiki/Monotreme">
    <rdfs:subClassOf rdf:resource="http://en.wikipedia.org/wiki/Mammal"/>
    <rdfs:label>Monotreme</rdfs:label>
    <rdfs:comment>Monotremes are primitive egg-laying mammals.</rdfs:comment>
</owl:Class>
<owl:Class rdf:about="http://en.wikipedia.org/wiki/Marsupial">
    <rdfs:subClassOf rdf:resource="http://en.wikipedia.org/wiki/Mammal"/>
    <rdfs:label>Marsupial</rdfs:label>
    <rdfs:comment>Marsupials are another group of mammals; their young are
    born in an extremely immature state; most female marsupials have pouches.</
    rdfs:comment>
</owl:Class>
```

Open Biological and Biomedical Ontologies (OBO), developed by the OBO Foundry, is another format used to represent ontologies. OBO Foundry is a registry of freely available ontologies in the domain of biology and biomedicine (The Open Biological and Biomedical Foundry 2014). BioPortal

(National Center for Biomedical Ontology 2014), a prominent example of ontology registries, holds ontologies in either OWL or OBO formats.

Other KOS Representation Formats

Several other formats which are applied to a lesser extent are briefly reviewed in this section. ZThes is a specification for thesauri representation, access, and navigation. It derived from ISO 2788 (International Organization for Standardization 1974) and ANSI/NISO Z39.19 (National Information Standards Organization 2005). ZThes originally aimed to support the exchange of thesauri data as part of the Z39.50 protocol which allows for standardized and multi-catalog search and the retrieval of MARC records. ZThes development continued, so it also supports the SRU protocol (Search/Retrieval via URL, a successor of Z39.50 for the Web environment) which enables cross-searching of library catalogs and other databases. These search requests simply are encoded in URLs and sent to servers; results are returned in XML.

In the ZThes model (ZThes Working Group 2006a) a thesaurus is represented as a database of interlinked terms. In contrast to SKOS which, like ISO 25964, bases its structure on concepts which then are represented by terms, ZThes uses terms as primary elements. Terms in one thesaurus could link to other thesauri. Both preferred and non-preferred terms are represented by a record in the database. Each record contains information such as a unique identifier for the term as well as various notes and elements describing related terms. There also could be a special record that provides information about the thesaurus in general, similar to a catalog record (e.g., publisher, edition, year of publication). The latest ZThes XML Schema is version 1.0 from 2006 (Zthes working group 2006b). ZThes specifications have not been used widely: KOSs which had been made available using ZThes specifications—such as AGROVOC, EUROVOC, UDC, DDC, and UNESCO thesaurus—now are available in SKOS and are accessible using other protocols. Attempts to have the specifications adopted as a British Standard Institute recommendation were unsuccessful (Mike Taylor, personal communication).

The ADL thesaurus protocol format (Janée 2009a) was developed from 2001 to 2002 for the geospatial Alexandria Digital Library, one of the earliest digital libraries (in existence since 1994). Like ZThes, the thesaurus model follows ANSI/NISO Z39.19. The definition of the model is specified in an XML schema, and eight XML elements are used (Janée, Ikeda, and Hill 2009):

- Properties, which describe the thesaurus and supported queries;
- Term, which briefly describes the term by its name and preferred usage;
- Term description, which more fully describes the term, its immediate relationships to other terms, and notes;

- Extended, allowing any thesaurus-specific format to also be applied;
- List, which is a list of zero or more terms;
- Hierarchy, which describes the hierarchy of terms broader or narrower than a starting preferred term;
- Error, which reports an error made by the code or by human description; and
- Response, which is the response from a thesaurus service.

In this format, the hierarchy is indicated by nesting the XML elements—which was shown to be unneeded in XML Schema of ISO 25964.

Based on ANSI/NISO Z39.19, yet another RDF/XML representation format was designed. The California Natural Resources Agency developed it as part of the California Environmental Resources Evaluation System (CERES) (California Natural Resources Agency [s.a.]).

The Vocabulary Definition Exchange (VDEX), defined by IMS Global Learning Consortium, Inc., is an XML-based standard proposed for marking up KOSs in the e-learning domain to support the KOS interchange in the domain (IMS Global Learning Consortium 2004). Although complex KOSs are supported to a limited extent, IMS makes extensive use of VDEX for the KOSs associated with other IMS specifications. For example, the IMS Learning Information Services 2.0 specification has more than 20 VDEX-defined vocabularies (IMS Global Learning Consortium 2014). Other implementations include projects such as Scottish Doctors, in which VDEX was used as a format for representing learning outcomes, although the outcomes also are available in ZThes (The Scottish Doctor Project 2011).

An XML-based representation standard for Topic Maps is defined by ISO/IEC 13250-3:2013 (International Organization for Standardization 2013c); the data model is defined in ISO/IEC 13250-2 (International Organization for Standardization 2006). Topic Maps focus on the visualization of relationships between concepts as a graph. They are similar to RDF and are considered to be a form of the Semantic Web technology. As compared to RDF, Topic Maps allow for a greater expressivity of semantic relations than do triplets of RDF, because Topic Maps allow any number of relationships between any number of nodes (see Chapter 2 for more details on Topic Maps).

Based on Topic Maps, XFML (eXchangeable Faceted Metadata Language) (Van Dijck 2003)—an open XML format for faceted taxonomies—was developed in 2002 and 2003. Several years later its author wrote that "it was an interesting experiment . . . but I now don't think there's demand for a format to exchange faceted data, and it hasn't been used much" (Van Dijck 2007).

Other Related Standards

In the field of computational and applied linguistics, ISO Technical Committee 37 works on the standardization of principles, methods, and applications relating to terminology and other language and content resources. These standards in many ways are related to KOS standards, but they focus more on word senses, uses of terms, and types of synonyms. Unlike KOS, standards which focus on concepts versus terms, linguistic standards often distinguish between concepts, terms, and their lexicalizations as strings (Tudhope, Koch, and Heery 2006).

Subcommittees 3 and 4 seem most related to the present topic, with the former defining standards for systems to manage terminology, knowledge, and content, and the latter defining standards for language resource management. ISO/TC 37 claims to liaise with the IFLA (International Federation of Library Associations) and the ISKO (International Society for Knowledge Organization).

ISO/TC 37 SC/3 released several standards. ISO 16642:2003 Computer applications in terminology—Terminological markup framework (International Organization for Standardization 2003) defines a standardized framework for representing terminological data to make data in language resources exchangeable and applicable for use by linguists and across applications. Its model for describing terminological markup languages (TMLs) is expressed in RDF/XML. The standard is implemented by the TermSciences terminology portal (TermSciences 2014) which provides integrated access to specialist vocabularies, dictionaries, and thesauri aiming to share other terminological sources and to promote the portal's use among various communities. The portal showed that the standard supports organizing by concepts, associating terms with them, and expressing other relationships (Khayari et al. 2002).

A closely related standard is ISO 12620:2009 Terminology and other language and content resources—Specification of data categories and management of a Data Category Registry for language resources (International Organization for Standardization 2009). The standard supports the exchange, interchange, and reuse of existing terminology resources. These two standards (ISO 16642:2003 and ISO 12620:2009) enable the exchange, interchange, and reuse of existing terminology resources and provide the baseline for work of ISO TC37 SC4 (Language resource management) focusing on the interchange of metadata encodings and linguistic annotation (Khayari et al. 2002).

There is also ISO 30042:2008 Systems to manage terminology, knowledge, and content—TermBase eXchange (TBX), an XML-based format for interchange of terminological data (International Organization for Standardization 2008b). A standard on the management of terminological management systems exists as well: ISO 26162:2012 Systems to manage terminology, knowledge and content—Design, implementation and maintenance of terminology management systems (International Organization for Standardization 2012).

ISO 22274:2013 Systems to manage terminology, knowledge and content—Concept-related aspects for developing and internationalizing classification systems (International Organization for Standardization 2013b), provides advice on how to design classification systems in contexts of different linguistic environments. Its scope is defined to include guidelines and requirements for making internationally accepted terminological principles for classification systems, and workflow and administrative considerations to support worldwide use. This standard does not seem to have been aligned with thesauri standards or the library and information science community, despite the fact that its governing committee, TC 37, lists liaisons with IFLA and ISKO.

PROTOCOLS, APIs, QUERYING LANGUAGES

An application programming interface (API) is a specification for how software components should interact with each other, usually specific for a given technology. An API can be based on protocols such as HTTP (Hypertext Transfer Protocol) to enable communication between software components across the Web. APIs for KOSs are needed to support Web services based upon them, such as querying and browsing a KOS. Protocols and APIs designed specifically for KOSs could offer more powerful exploitation of KOS characteristics, and general-purpose APIs could facilitate interoperability and integration with other tools or functionalities.

Common APIs for general Web services use HTTP protocol's methods GET and POST (HTTP GET, HTTP POST), lightweight, and URL-based REpresentational State Transfer (REST), Simple Object Access Protocol (SOAP) that requires an XML wrapper, and URL-based Remote Procedure Call (RPC) taking various formats such as XML and JSON (referred to as XML-RPC and JSON-RPC respectively). For Linked Data, at present HTTP content negotiation and Simple Protocol and RDF Query Language (SPARQL) can be used. HTTP content negotiation allows de-referencing for RDF representations, which is a type of common API for Linked Data. What is returned as a de-reference is under the control of the host application. SPARQL is a query language, allowing specification of what triples are to be retrieved. There also is a common API for RDF data, but is under the control of the consuming application. The Linked Data API (Reynolds et al. 2014) also has been developed.

Web services for KOSs relying on common APIs include the following examples.

- OCLC uses REST for some of its experimental (as of July 2013) Web services such as an auto-complete searching of FAST subject headings, returning authorized headings and "see also" headings (OCLC 2012b), and linking the top three levels of Dewey as Linked Data resources (OCLC 2010b).
- Leibniz Information Centre for Economics, publishing the STW Thesaurus for Economics, provides experimental economics terminology and authority

Web services (Leibniz Information Centre for Economics 2013) also following REST design principles.

- AGROVOC has made Web services accessible via SOAP (Food and Agriculture Organization of the United Nations 2014), as did the USGS Biocomplexity Thesaurus (U.S. Geological Survey 2012).
- NERC (BODC) Data Grid's Vocabulary Server provides access both by SOAP and REST (British Oceanographic Data Centre 2014), and the Explicator Project uses XML-RPC in its vocabulary search Web service (Explicator Project 2009).
- Getty Web services allow access via SOAP and HTTP protocols (the latter using GET and POST methods) (J. Paul Getty Trust 2011).

A general query language and protocol used for accessing and querying RDF is SPARQL (World Wide Web Consortium 2013b, now in version 1.1 from 2013). Thus, KOSs that have been represented in RDF can be queried using SPARQL. For example, the UNESCO thesaurus has an interface available in SPARQL for its SKOS version (Sánchez 2013). SPARQL, however, has limitations when used for KOSs. Wielemaker et al. (2008) and Van der Meij, Isaac, and Zinn (2010) show that SPARQL queries are insufficient to address a KOS search appropriately, although new developments could alleviate these issues.

For XML documents there is XSLT, a programming language for XML transformations. To a limited extent, XSLT also can be used as a query language. Otherwise, a query language that can be used for XML documents is XQuery.

The Z39.50 protocol (ISO 23950 [International Organization for Standardization 1988]) allows for standardized and multi-catalog search and retrieval of MARC records. The protocol supports very complex queries, and this functionality is preserved in its Web-adjusted descendants, SRU (Search and Retrieve via URL) and SRW (Search and Retrieve via Web service).

A simplified version of the Z39.50 protocol model—adjusted for performing searches and the required communication between a client and server in the Web environment—was defined by the OASIS Search Web Services initiative (OASIS 2013). This model is a basis for three specific protocols: OpenSearch, SRU1.2, and the revised specification SRU2.0 (DeWitt [s.a.]). The model is designed for unstructured documents and therefore supports simpler querying. SRU is based on XML and, as such, supports complex and more advanced querying functions than does OpenSearch, similar to what Z39.50 supported in the non-Web environment. It allows usage of the REST API and of SOAP protocol; the latter SRU also is referred to as SRW. The SRU uses its own Boolean query language—Contextual Query Language (Library of Congress 2013c). CQL also can be defined for specific implementations as a special set (e.g., the ZThes Thesaurus

Context Set for CQL). An example of SRU usage is OCLC's WorldCat Identities (2010c) which provides personal, corporate, and subject-based identities (e.g., writers, authors, characters, corporations, horses, ships) based on information in WorldCat, for which it uses the SRU protocol. Another OCLC service in its experimental stage (as of July 2013) uses SRU (as well as REST) to search for authority data by keywords and retrieve FAST authority records (OCLC 2012c).

The following are examples of KOS-specific APIs. The ADL Gazetteer and Thesaurus Protocols (Janée 2009a; Janée 2009b) were developed in 2001–2002 for the geospatial Alexandria Digital Library. Protocols are needed when consulting more than one KOS at a time. The two protocols also can complement one another—for example, if gazetteer place names have been categorized by feature type (e.g., regions, administrative areas, manmade features, physiographic features), then the set of all features can be made available via the thesaurus protocol (Greg Janée 2013, personal communication). The thesaurus protocol supports five Web services:

- Retrieving the information about the thesaurus in general;
- Using a list of preferred and non-preferred terms;
- Querying the thesaurus by term (based on phrase, part of term, and regular expression matching with optional stemming and spelling correction);
- Retrieving broader terms up to a specified number of steps; and
- Retrieving narrower terms up to a specified number of steps.

In 2006, Janée revisited the gazetteer protocol in relation to five use cases and indicated the need for multiple protocols and multiple KOSs which would serve a range of use cases and functionalities.

Another gazetteer protocol is the OGC (Open Geospatial Consortium) Gazetteer Protocol, which is based on the ISO 19112 standard model for gazetteer data. It is interoperable with other OGC standards and, as such, is more complex than ADL gazetteer protocol (Hill 2006). Unlock (Edina 2013) is a gazetteer service which offers access based on REST and uses its own API.

The ZThes API has been made available both for Z39.50 and for SRU. The ZThes 0.5 API has been employed by several thesaurus Web projects, including BECTA Vocabulary Service (Knowledge Integration Ltd. 2013). Binding and Tudhope (2004) reviewed several protocols and APIs for KOS and concluded that more experience in real use situations is necessary for further evolution.

IDENTIFICATION OF KOSs AND THEIR ELEMENTS

The Semantic Web and Linked Data require that resources be identified with URIs; Linked Data recommends that these be resolvable HTTP

(HyperText Transfer Protocol) URLs (Uniform Resource Locators). A URL is a type of URI—a string of characters—used to identify a resource location, for example, a file path on a computer or HTTP for interacting with Web resources.

Every KOS, its concepts, its terms, and its relationships must be uniquely and persistently identifiable to ensure its reuse and long-term access by humans and software agents for various purposes (Tudhope, Koch, and Heery 2006). A later report from 2009 (Golub and Tudhope) recommends investigating the addition of identifiers to a freely available KOS which is widely used, as well as educating KOS providers on the importance of supplying identifiers.

One of the main benefits of the SKOS is that it provides a model to publish KOSs as Linked Data. The SKOS uses URIs to identify the KOS and its concepts. The start page of the UNESCO Thesaurus (http://skos.um.es/unescothes/CS000/html) in its SKOS representation, for example, identifies the thesaurus with the same HTTP URL (http://skos.um.es/unescothes/CS000/) in the first of the two lines given below.

```
<skos:ConceptScheme rdf:about="http://skos.um.es/unescothes/CS000">
<skos:prefLabel xml:lang="en">UNESCO Thesaurus</skos:prefLabel>
```

The concepts themselves also are given HTTP URLs as unique identifiers.

```
<skos:Concept rdf:about="http://skos.um.es/unescothes/C00266">
<skos:prefLabel xml:lang="en">Artists</skos:prefLabel>
```

The Library of Congress uses the unique identifier of MARC catalog records, its LCCN (Library of Congress Control Numbers). As part of the Linked Data initiative, the Library of Congress has converted the LCCN of authorities (subject headings, classification, names) into HTTP URLs. In LCSH, for example LCCN sh85026719, the identifier for the concept of "classification" is made a permanent URL by pending the LCCN to the base http://id.loc.gov/authorities/subjects/sh85026719.html. The Linked Data records also include an info URI scheme identifier "info:lc/authorities/sh85026719," part of a previous effort for creating identifiers. The LCSH as Linked Data allow both machine-readable and human-friendly access, as do many Linked Data efforts, which is de-referencing based on HTTP content negotiation. For a given URI, a Web browser is presented a user-friendly labeled display, but computer programs might choose one of the machine-readable formats (e.g., RDF/XML, N-Triples, JSON).

Library of Congress Subject Headings as Linked Data also include in their records mappings to German and French subject headings (SWD and RAMEAU, respectively) which also have been made available as Linked Data, and mappings have been completed in a project (Van der Meij, Isaac, and Zinn 2010). For example, for "subrogation" as an LCSH concept available at http://id.loc.gov/authorities/subjects/sh85129525.html#concept, exact matching to one French subject heading and close matching to two German subject headings are provided. These are examples of how isolated data sets can be integrated using Linked Data and HTTP URLs. Summers et al. (2008) additionally suggest other external data sets to link to LCSH:

- GeoNames (GeoNames 2013) and the CIA World Fact Book (Research Group Data and Web Science at the University of Mannheim 2014) for geographic headings.
- The RDF BookMashup, which integrates information about books, their authors, and reviews, from sources like Amazon and Google (Bizer and Gauß 2009) for links to items that prompted creating an LCSH concept.
- DBpedia (DBpedia 2014), which is comprised of data from Wikipedia structured in RDF and Linked Data.

TERMINOLOGY REGISTRIES

"Terminology registries" is a term used to refer to a type of catalog of KOSs or KOS-based services for human inspection and machine-based access. These registries are important today with so many KOSs available in various domains, as well as their numerous (potential) applications. The registries provide descriptions of KOSs (e.g., the commercial Taxonomy Warehouse, in existence since 2001; and Taxo Bank, a more recent effort) and also can include the KOSs themselves (e.g., ONKI, BioPortal for ontologies) as well as various services based upon them, for example, the Library of Congress Linked Data Service: Authorities and Vocabularies. Other types of potential applications could include query expansion, mapping, subject indexing and classifying, translating user terms into controlled terms, and disambiguation of terms representing concepts. In total, potential functionality of terminology registries in general includes: acquisition, creation, and modification of a KOS; publication of a KOS; access, search, and discovery of a KOS; use of a KOS; and archiving and preservation of a KOS.

A detailed overview of the state of terminology registries plus use cases, functionalities, and suggested metadata is given in Golub et al. (2014). In providing the descriptions of KOSs, the paper proposes that metadata should be made available both for human inspection and for machine-to-machine access. Descriptions would include the following core attributes: Title, Identifier, Description, Type (of KOS), Language, Creator, Contact, Rights, Publisher, Format, Date (created or issued), Date (updated), Subject, Relation (to other KOS), Sample (a relation), Supporting doc (a relation), Used by (a relation).

The following are recommended as additional attributes: Frequency of Update, Audience, Size (of vocabulary), and Service offered. If providing

KOSs themselves, then standards previously described in this chapter should be used—those based on RDF, including SKOS and OWL, would ensure interoperability within the (Semantic) Web. These recommendations are a result of a combined approach, an examination of existing registries and potential use cases, together with the work done as part of development of the Dublin Core Application Profile for KOSs resources.

Related is ADMS (Asset Description Metadata Schema) (European Union 2014a), a metadata schema intended for publishers of semantics-related standards which include KOSs to describe them. It was developed by the EU's Interoperability Solutions for European Public Administrations (ISA) Programme of the European Commission. The latest version (1.0) was released in 2012. The metadata elements include: Name, Alternative Name (alternative name for the asset), Date of Creation, Date of Last Modification, Description, Identifier (which is a URL), and Version. Of the KOS types available as of July 2013, the European Commission's catalog of semantic assets—which is a type of terminology registry (see the section on terminology registries, below)—includes thesauri, ontologies, and code lists of KOS types, which are described using ADMS. The thesauri include GEMET (GEneral Multilingual Environmental Thesaurus), EuroVoc, and AGROVOC. The W3C also is working on making the registry into a formal specification, and RDF/XML and Turtle representations of vocabulary used are available.

SUMMARY

The chapter discusses technological standards for the representation and the interchange of knowledge organization systems in the digital environment, and for programmatic access to KOSs as Web services. These standards ensure that KOSs are represented in the same format and structure which, in turn, enables all the KOSs that are structured in the same standard to be presented, organized, browsed, and searched in an interoperable and easy manner.

Standards for design and construction of KOSs largely are restricted to thesauri rather than other types of KOSs. The latest ISO 25964 standard (Thesauri and Interoperability with Other Vocabularies) incorporates a data model and guidelines for mapping between thesauri and other KOS types, using the three major types of semantic relationships in thesauri (equivalence, hierarchical, associative) as the basis for mapping.

The most viable standards today in relation to the Web should be based on XML and on RDF. XML enables the self-defining of elements and their names; at the same time it requires structuring according to strict principles. The flexibility and strictness of XML have made it a widespread and good-quality representation standard. It also is much easier for human users to understand because it uses language labels rather than codes such as ISO

2709. Further, XML ensures widespread use, compatibility, and exchange with other metadata. Examples could include searching across repositories applying the Open Archives Initiative Protocol for Metadata Harvesting (OAI-PMH), searching library catalogs via the Web applying the SRU (search and retrieval via URL) protocol, and easy potential integration with other XML-based applications in the Web. Also, through application of XSLT style sheets, the content of XML documents can be displayed in any manner that the end user prefers.

The RDF provides a great specification of detail, allowing for logical inferencing, which is important in particular for the realization of a vision for a truly semantic Web. It also requires predicates (which are the equivalent of XML attributes) to be globally uniquely identified, unlike XML which allows the same attribute to be used with different meanings in local applications. It can be considered as the data model of the Semantic Web—all data that are part of the Semantic Web are represented, transmitted, and queried as RDF data.

The most prominent standard not based on XML or RDF is the ISO 2709 format. Two similar versions of it exist: MARC 21 and UNIMARC. Each has a bibliographic and an authorities format—the former allowing searching of bibliographic records based on a variety of fields including classification and subject headings, and the latter supporting KOS-like subject headings and classification systems. The two MARC 21 authorities' formats for subject headings and for classification data are based on the Library of Congress Subject Headings and the Library of Congress Classification. As such, they might not readily accommodate for features specific to other subject headings and classification systems, as shown in the DDC example. The UNIMARC classification data format still is in development.

To allow for a more flexible and extensible format than MARC 21 and UNIMARC, initiatives have taken place to convert them to XML. The most concrete and perhaps the best-quality example is MADS (Metadata Authority Description Schema), an XML schema for MARC 21 authorities including subject headings and classification data, and using human-readable names of elements in place of MARC numerical codes and symbols.

SKOS is the most prominent example of RDF/XML-based standards for representing a KOS. The SKOS data model is based on concepts rather than terms, in line with the ISO 25964 standard. The concepts each are associated with a URI. There are several aspects of ISO 25964, however, which SKOS does not presently support. Additionally, SKOS initially was developed for thesauri. Other types of KOSs can be accommodated, but are subject to a level of creative adjustments. Many KOSs have been published as SKOS and other efforts are underway.

Regarding other standards, the most recent (2013) XML-based format for representation and interchange of KOSs is the ISO 25964 standard's XML Schema. It primarily is intended to provide interoperability for thesauri across applications and with other KOSs. For ontologies there are dedicated formats (such as OWL) which reflect the complexity and elaboration in the detail required by other formats for representing KOSs.

APIs for KOSs are needed to support Web services such as querying and browsing a KOS. Protocols allow communication between KOSs across applications. Protocols and APIs designed specifically for KOSs could offer more powerful exploitation of KOS characteristics, and the general-purpose protocols and APIs could facilitate interoperability and integration with other tools or functionalities. There exist many examples of Web services for KOSs that are based on general APIs and protocols, such as REST and SOAP. For querying XML documents there is XQuery, although XSLTs also could be used, with some limitations. For querying RDF there is SPARQL, but it is less appropriate for querying KOSs—which has been documented in literature. Of traditionally library-specific protocols, examples of using SRU for KOSs exist. SKOS API also is in use. Many application-specific APIs exist for KOS.

Every KOS, its concepts, terms, and relationships must be uniquely and persistently identifiable to ensure their reuse and long-term access by both human users and software agents. The Linked Data initiative helps promote this. A prominent example is LC Linked Data Service for LCSH—each authorized subject heading has a URL that is available both for machine-readable and human-friendly access. For a given URI, a Web browser is presented with a user-friendly labeled display, and computer programs could choose one of machine-readable formats (e.g., RDF/XML, N-Triples, JSON). Additionally, LCSH records provide URLs to mapped concepts in French and in German subject headings, thus demonstrating the potential of applying HTTP URLs to each concept and making isolated data sets integrated on the Web.

Terminology registries are a type of catalog of KOSs and KOS-based services, made available for human inspection and machine-based access. The metadata for KOS also should be made available both for human inspection and for machine-to-machine access. Potential functionality of terminology registries in general is composed of acquisition, creation, and modification of a KOS; publication of a KOS; access, search, and discovery of a KOS; use of a KOS; and archiving and preservation of a KOS.

CHAPTER REVIEW

1. How does XML compare to HTML?
2. Why are RDF and HTTP URLs important?
3. How does SKOS compare to OWL?
4. What, if any, improvements would you like to see in the APIs you have used?
5. What do you think the uptake of all the discussed standards will be?
6. Are terminology registries needed? Why or why not?
7. What are the barriers to linking all terminologies together (i.e., issues of scale and culture)?

GLOSSARY

API (Application Programming Interface): Specifications of how software components should interact with each other, usually specific to a given technology.

HTTP URL (HyperText Transfer Protocol Uniform Resource Locator): A type of URI (Uniform Resource Identifier); a string of characters used to identify a resource location using HTTP for interacting with Web resources.

ISO 2709: The international standard for the representation and exchange of bibliographic and related data in a machine-readable form, the most common instances being MARC 21 (MAchine Readable Cataloging 21) and UNIMARC (UNIversal MAchine Readable Cataloging).

MADS (Metadata Authority Description Schema): A schema which uses named elements to represent MARC 21 in XML.

MARC 21 (MAchine Readable Cataloging 21): One of major instances of ISO 2709.

MARCXML: A straightforward coding of MARC formats with XML.

MODS (Metadata Object Description Schema): A new metadata encoding schema largely based on MARC bibliographic format. Aimed to be simpler than MARC, so that communities beyond library professionals can understand it, yet complex enough to cover all the needed aspects.

OWL (Web Ontology Language): An RDF element set for representing ontologies.

RDF (Resource Description Framework): The data model of the Semantic Web; it uses the form of subject, predicate, and object statements similar to statements in English grammar, known as "triples," which support semantic reasoning. It requires the predicates to be globally uniquely identified.

SKOS (Simple Knowledge Organization Systems): An RDF element set for representing, sharing, and exchanging KOSs.

SPARQL (Simple Protocol And RDF Query Language): A query language for RDF.

SRU (Search/Retrieve via URL): A descendant of Z39.50 in the Web environment, preserving the functionality of supporting very complex queries.

Terminology registries: Catalog of KOSs and KOS-based services, for human inspection and machine-based access, which also can include the KOSs themselves.

UNIMARC (UNIversal MAchine Readable Cataloging): One of the major instances of ISO 2709.

XML (Extensible Markup Language): An encoding scheme for high-level structuring of documents that also allows for readability by both machines and human users.

Z39.50: Protocol which allows for standardized and multi-catalog search and retrieval of MARC records (i.e., mostly library databases).

REFERENCES

Baker, Thomas, Sean Bechhofer, Antoine Isaac, Alistair Miles, Guus Schreiber, and Ed Summers. 2013. "Key Choices in the Design of Simple Knowledge Organization System (SKOS)." *Web Semantics: Science, Services and Agents on the World Wide Web* 20: 35–49.

Beall, Julianne, and Joan Mitchell. 2010. "History of the Representation of the DDC in the MARC Classification Format." *Cataloging & Classification Quarterly* 48 (1): 48–63.

Binding, Ceri, and Douglas Tudhope. 2004. "KOS at Your Service: Programmatic Access to Knowledge Organisation Systems." *Journal of Digital Information* 4 (4). Accessed September 3, 2014. http://journals.tdl.org/jodi/article/view/110/109.

Bizer, Chris, and Tobias Gauß. 2009. "RDF Book Mashup: Serving RDF Descriptions of Your Books." Accessed August 28, 2014. http://www4.wiwiss.fu-berlin.de/bizer/bookmashup/.

BookMARC. 2004. Accessed August 28, 2014. http://www.bookmarc.pt/unimarc/.

British Oceanographic Data Centre. 2014. "NERC Vocabulary Server." Last updated February 11, 2014. http://www.bodc.ac.uk/products/web_services/vocab/.

California Natural Resources Agency. [s.a.] "Thesaurus: RDF—The RDF Thesaurus Descriptor Standard." http://ceres.ca.gov/thesaurus/RDF.html.

DBpedia. 2014. Accessed August 28, 2014. http://dbpedia.org.

DeWitt, Clinton. [s.a.] "OpenSearch: 1.1: Draft 5." Accessed August 28, 2014. http://www.opensearch.org/Specifications/OpenSearch/1.1/Draft_5#Notice.

Dextre Clarke, Stella G. 2011. "Knowledge Organization System Standards." In *Encyclopedia of Library and Information Sciences*, third edition, edited by Marcia Bates: 3164–3175. http://dx.doi.org/10.1081/E-ELIS3-120044538.

Dextre Clarke, Stella G., and Marcia Lei Zeng. 2011. "From ISO 2788 to ISO 25964: The Evolution of Thesaurus Standards Towards Interoperability and Data Modelling." *Information Standards Quarterly* 23 (1): 20–26.

Dublin Core Metadata Initiative. 2012a. *Dublin Core Metadata Element Set.* Version 1.1. Accessed August 28, 2014. http://dublincore.org/documents/dces/.

Dublin Core Metadata Initiative. 2012b. *DCMI Metadata Terms: Section 4: Vocabulary Encoding Schemes.* Accessed August 28, 2014. http://dublincore.org/documents/dcmi-terms/#H4.

Edina. *Unlock.* 2013. http://unlock.edina.ac.uk.

European Environment Agency. 2010.*GEMET Thesaurus.* Accessed August 28, 2014. http://eionet.europa.eu/gemet.

European Union. 2014a. "Asset Description Metadata Schema (ADMS)." Last updated February 20, 2014. http://joinup.ec.europa.eu/asset/adms/.

European Union. 2014b. *EuroVoc: Multilingual Thesaurus of the European Union.* http://eurovoc.europa.eu/.

Explicator Project. 2009. *Suggestion Server.* Accessed August 28, 2014. http://explicator.dcs.gla.ac.uk/Vocabularies/suggestionServer.html.

Food and Agriculture Organization of the United Nations. 2014. "AIMS: Agricultural Information Management Standards: Web Services." http://aims.fao.org/standards/agrovoc/webservices.

Food and Agriculture Organization of the United Nations. 2013. *AGROVOC.* Accessed August 28, 2014. http://aims.fao.org/standards/agrovoc.

GeoNames. 2013. Accessed August 28, 2014. http://geonames.org.

Gnoli, Claudio, Tom Pullmann, Philippe Cousson, Gabriele Merli, and Rick Szostak. 2011. "Representing the Structural Elements of a Freely Faceted Classification." In *Classification and Ontology: Formal Approaches and Access to Knowledge: Proceedings of the International UDC Seminar 2011*, edited by Aida Slavic and Edgardo Civallero, 193–206. Würzburg: Ergon.

Golub, Koraljka, and Douglas Tudhope. 2009. "Terminology Registry Scoping Study (TRSS): Final Report." Accessed August 28, 2014. http://www.jisc.ac.uk/media/documents/programmes /sharedservices/trss-report-final.pdf.

Golub, Koraljka, Douglas Tudhope, Marcia Zeng, and Maja Žumer. 2014. "Terminology Registries for Knowledge Organization Systems—Functionality, Use, and Attributes." *Journal of the Association for Information Science and Technology* 65 (9): 1901–16.

Government of Canada. 2014. "Government of Canada Core Subject Thesaurus." Accessed February 22, 2014. http://en.thesaurus.gc.ca.

IMS Global Learning Consortium. 2014. "Learning Information Services." Accessed August 28, 2014. http://www.imsglobal.org/lis/. (VDEX-defined vocabularies are listed toward the end of the page.)

IMS Global Learning Consortium. 2004. "Vocabulary Definition Exchange." Accessed August 28, 2014. http://www.imsglobal.org/vdex/.

International Federation of Library Associations and Institutions. 2013. "UNIMARC Formats and Related Documentation." Last updated August 13, 2013. http://www.ifla.org/publications/unimarc-formats-and-related-documentation.

International Federation of Library Associations and Institutions. 2009. "UNIMARC Concise Authorities Format." Accessed August 28, 2014. http://www.ifla.org/files/assets/uca/UNIMARC%20concise%20authorities%20format%20%282009%29.pdf.

International Federation of Library Associations and Institutions. 2000. "UNIMARC Classification Format." Accessed August 28, 2014. http://archive.ifla.org/VI/3/p1996-1/preface.htm.

International Organization for Standardization. 2013. *Information and Documentation—MarcXchange: ISO 25577:2013*. Geneva: International Organization for Standardization.

International Organization for Standardization. 2013a. *Information and Documentation—Thesauri and Interoperability with Other Vocabularies—Part 2: Interoperability with Other Vocabularies: ISO 25964-2:2013*. Geneva: International Organization for Standardization.

International Organization for Standardization. 2013b. *Systems to Manage Terminology, Knowledge and Content—Concept-related Aspects for Developing and Internationalizing Classification Systems: ISO 22274:2013*. Geneva: International Organization for Standardization.

International Organization for Standardization. 2013c. *Information Technology—Topic Maps—Part 3: XML syntax: ISO/IEC 13250-3:2013*. Geneva: International Organization for Standardization.

International Organization for Standardization. 2012. *Systems to Manage Terminology, Knowledge and Content—Design, Implementation and Maintenance of Terminology Management Systems: ISO 26162:2012*. Geneva: International Organization for Standardization.

International Organization for Standardization. 2011. *Information and Documentation—Thesauri and Interoperability with Other Vocabularies—Part 1: Thesauri for Information Retrieval: ISO 25964-1:2011*. Geneva: International Organization for Standardization.

International Organization for Standardization. 2009. *Terminology and Other Language and Content Resources—Specification of Data Categories and Management of a Data Category Registry for Language Resources: ISO 12620:2009*. Geneva: International Organization for Standardization.

International Organization for Standardization. 2008a. *Information and Documentation—Format for Information Exchange: ISO 2709:2008*. Geneva: International Organization for Standardization.

International Organization for Standardization. 2008b. *Systems to Manage Terminology, Knowledge and Content—TermBase eXchange (TBX): ISO 30042:2008*. Geneva: International Organization for Standardization.

International Organization for Standardization. 2006. *Information Technology—Topic Maps—Part 2: Data model: ISO/IEC 13250-2:2006*. Geneva: International Organization for Standardization.

International Organization for Standardization. 2003. *Computer Applications in Terminology—Terminological Markup Framework: ISO 16642:2003*. Geneva: International Organization for Standardization.

International Organization for Standardization. 1988. *Information and Documentation—Information Retrieval (Z39.50)—Application Service Definition and Protocol Specification: ISO 23950:1998*. Geneva: International Organization for Standardization.

International Organization for Standardization. 1986. *Information Processing—Text and Office Systems—Standard Generalized Markup Language (SGML): ISO 8879:1986*. Geneva: International Organization for Standardization.

International Organization for Standardization. 1974. *Guidelines for the Establishment and Development of Monolingual Thesauri: ISO 2788:1974*. Geneva: International Organization for Standardization.

International Organization for Standardization TC46/SC9/WG8 Working Group and Antoine Isaac. 2012. "Correspondence between ISO 25964 and SKOS/SKOS XL Models." Accessed August 28, 2014. http://www.niso.org/apps/group_public/download.php/9627/Correspondence%20ISO25964-SKOSXL-MADS-2012-10-21.pdf.

Isaac, Antoine, and Ed Summers. 2009. *SKOS Simple Knowledge Organization System Primer.* W3C Working Group Note August 18, 2009. Accessed August 28, 2014. http://www.w3.org/TR/skos-primer/.

Isaac, Antoine, Dirk Kramer, Lourens Meij, Shenghui Wang, Stefan Schlobach, and Johan Stapel. 2009. "Vocabulary Matching for Book Indexing Suggestion in

Linked Libraries—A Prototype Implementation and Evaluation." In *Proceedings of the 8th International Semantic Web Conference, October 25-29, 2009, Chantilly, VA*, edited by Abraham Bernstein, David R. Karger, Tom Heath, Lee Feigenbaum, Diana Maynard, Enrico Motta, and Krishnaprasad Thirunarayan, 843–59. Berlin, Heidelberg: Springer.

J. Paul Getty Trust. 2011. *Getty Vocabularies Web Services: User Instructions. Version 2.1.* Accessed August 28, 2014. http://www.getty.edu/research/tools/vocabularies /vocab_web_services.pdf.

Janée, Greg. "Thesaurus Protocol." 2009a. http://www.alexandria.ucsb.edu/thesaurus/protocol/.

Janée, Greg. "Gazeteer Protocol." 2009b. http://www.alexandria.ucsb.edu/gazetteer/protocol/.

Janée, Greg. 2006. "Rethinking Gazetteers and Interoperability." http://www.alexandria.ucsb.edu/~gjanee/archive/2006/gazetteer-workshop-abstract.pdf.

Janée, Greg, Satoshi Ikeda, and Linda L. Hill. 2009. "XML Formats." http://www.alexandria.ucsb.edu/thesaurus/specification.html#xml-formats.

Khayari, Majid, Stéphane Schneider, Isabelle Kramer, and Laurent Romary. 2002. "Unification of Multi-lingual Scientific Terminological Resources Using the ISO 16642 Standard: The TermSciences Initiative." Accessed August 28, 2014. http://arxiv.org/ftp/cs/papers/0604 /0604027.pdf.

Knowledge Integration Ltd. 2013. "BECTA Vocabulary Studio." Accessed August 28, 2014. http://www.k-int.com/node/24.

Leibniz Information Centre for Economics. 2013. "Web Services for Economics (beta)." Last updated November 11, 2013. http://webcl5top.rz.uni-kiel.de/beta/econ-ws/about.

Library of Congress. 2014. "LC Linked Data Service: Authorities and Vocabularies." Accessed February 22, 2014. http://id.loc.gov/.

Library of Congress. 2013a. "MARC Standards." Accessed August 28, 2014. http://www.loc.gov/marc/.

Library of Congress. 2013b. "MADS Schema & Documentation." Accessed August 28, 2014. http://www.loc.gov/standards/mads/.

Library of Congress. 2013c. "CQL: The Contextual Query Language." Accessed August 28, 2014. http://www.loc.gov/standards/sru/cql/.

Library of Congress. 2012a. "MARC21 XML Schema." Accessed August 28, 2014. http://www.loc.gov/standards/marcxml/.

Library of Congress. 2012b. "Outline of Elements and Attributes in MADS 2.0." Accessed August 28, 2014. http://www.loc.gov/standards/mads/mads-outline-2-0.html.

Library of Congress. 2012c. "MADS/RDF Primer." Accessed August 28, 2014. http://www.loc.gov/standards/mads/rdf/.

Library of Congress. 2006. "MARC 21 Classification: Introduction." Accessed August 28, 2014. http://www.loc.gov/marc/classification/cdintro.html.

Library of Congress. 2005. "MARC 21: 6XX—Subject Access Fields-General Information Bibliographic." Accessed August 28, 2014. http://www.loc.gov/marc/bibliographic/bd6xx.html.

Lopes, Maria Inês, and Julianne Beall eds. 1999. *Principles Underlying Subject Heading Languages* (SHLs). München: K.G. Saur.

Miles, Alistair, and Sean Bechhofer. 2009. "SKOS Simple Knowledge Organization System eXtension for Labels (SKOS-XL) Namespace Document: HTML Variant." August 18, 2009.

National Center for Biomedical Ontology. 2014. "Bioportal." Accessed August 28, 2014. http://bioportal.bioontology.org/.

National Diet Library. 2011. "Web NDL Authorities." Accessed August 28, 2014. http://id.ndl.go.jp/auth/ndla/.

National Information Standards Organization. 2014. "Introduction to the ISO 25964-1 Schema." Accessed August 28, 2014. http://www.niso.org/schemas/iso25964/schema-intro/#intro.

National Information Standards Organization. 2011. "ISO 25964-1 Schema. Version 1.4." Accessed August 28, 2014. http://www.niso.org/schemas/iso25964/iso25964-1_v1.4.xsd.

National Information Standards Organization. 2005. *Guidelines for the Construction, Format, and Management of Monolingual Controlled Vocabularies: ANSI/NISO Z39.19*. Baltimore: National Information Standards Organization.

OASIS. 2013. "SearchRetrieve: Part 0. Overview Version 1.0." Accessed August 28, 2014. http://docs.oasis-open.org/search-ws/searchRetrieve/v1.0/searchRetrieve-v1.0-part0-overview.html.

Online Computer Library Center, Inc. (OCLC). 2014. "Dewey Decimal Classification / Linked Data." Accessed February 22, 2014. http:// http://dewey.info/.

Online Computer Library Center, Inc. (OCLC). 2012b. "Web Services: AssignFAST." http://oclc.org/developer/services/assignfast.

Online Computer Library Center, Inc. (OCLC). 2012c. "Web Services: FAST Linked Data API." http://oclc.org/developer/services/fast-linked-data-api.

Online Computer Library Center, Inc. (OCLC). 2010b. "Web Services: Dewey Web Services." Accessed August 28, 2014. http://oclc.org/developer/services/dewey-web-services.

Online Computer Library Center, Inc. (OCLC). 2010c. "Web Services: WorldCat Identities." Accessed August 28, 2014. http://oclc.org/developer/services/worldcat-identities.

ONKI Ontology Service. 2014. "Ontology for Museum Domain." Accessed February 22, 2014. http://onki.fi/en/browser/overview/mao.

Open Biological and Biomedical Foundry. 2014. "The Open Biological and Biomedical Ontologies." Last updated February 23, 2014. http://www.obofoundry.org/.

Panzer, Michael, and Marcia Lei Zeng. 2009. "Modeling Classification Systems in SKOS: Some Challenges and Best-Practice Recommendations." In *Semantic Interoperability of Linked Data: Proceedings of the International Conference on Dublin Core and Metadata Applications*, 3–14. Accessed August 28, 2014. http://dcpapers.dublincore.org/pubs/article/view/974.

Research Group Data and Web Science at the University of Mannheim. 2014. "D2R Server for the CIA Factbook." Accessed February 22, 2014. http://www4.wiwiss.fu-berlin.de/factbook/.

Reynolds, Dave et al. 2014. "Linked Data API." Accessed February 22, 2014. http://code.google.com/p/linked-data-api/.

Sánchez, Pastor Juan Antonio. 2013. "SPARQL Endpoint: [UNESCO thesaurus]." Accessed February 22, 2014. http://skos.um.es/sparql/.

Semantic Computing Research Group. 2012. "ONKI SKOS Server." Accessed August 28, 2014. http://www.seco.tkk.fi/services/onkiskos/.

Scottish Doctor Project. 2011. "Scottish Doctor Resources." Accessed August 28, 2014. http://www.scottishdoctor.org/node.asp?id=resource.

Suominen, Osma, and Christian Mader. 2014. "Assessing and Improving the Quality of SKOS Vocabularies." *Journal on Data Semantics* 3 (1): 47–73.

Summers, Ed, Antoine Isaac, Clay Redding, and Dan Krech. 2008. "LCSH, SKOS and Linked Data." In *Proceedings of the International Conference on Dublin Core and Metadata Applications 2008,* 25–33. Accessed August 28, 2014. http://dcpapers.dublincore.org/pubs/article/view/916/912.

TermSciences. 2014. *Multidisciplinary Terminological Portal.* Accessed February 22, 2014. http://www.termsciences.fr.

Tudhope, Douglas. 2012. "Update on ISO 25964: Thesauri and Interoperability with Other Vocabularies." In *The 11th European Networked Knowledge Organization Systems (NKOS) Workshop.* Accessed August 28, 2014. https://www.comp.glam.ac.uk/pages/.../NKOS-ISO25964Update2012.ppt.

Tudhope, Douglas, Truagott Koch, and Rachael Heery. 2006. "Terminology Services and Technology: JISC State of the Art Review." Accessed August 28, 2014. http://www.ukoln.ac.uk/terminology/JISC-review2006.html.

Tunnicliffe, Sam, and Ian Davis. 2009. "Changeset." Accessed August 28, 2014. http://vocab.org/changeset/schema.html.

U.S. Geological Survey. 2012. "USGS Biocomplexity Thesaurus Web Services." Accessed August 28, 2014. http://nbii-thesaurus.ornl.gov/thesaurus/.

United Nations Educational, Scientific and Cultural Organization. 2010. "UNESCO Thesaurus." Accessed August 28, 2014. http://databases.unesco.org/thesaurus/.

Universal Decimal Classification Consortium. 2014. "UDC Summary Linked Data." Accessed February 22, 2014. http://udcdata.info/.

Van der Meij, Lourens, Antoine Isaac, and Claus Zinn. 2010. "A Web-Based Repository Service for Vocabularies and Alignments in the Cultural Heritage Domain." In *Proceedings of the 7th International Conference on the Semantic Web: Research and Applications*, edited by Lora Aroyo et al., 394–409. Berlin, Heidelberg: Springer.

Van Dijck, Peter. 2007. "eXchangeable Faceted Metadata Language." Accessed August 28, 2014. http://petervandijck.com/xfml/.

Van Dijck, Peter. 2003. "XFML Core—eXchangeable Faceted Metadata Language." Accessed August 28, 2014. http://petervandijck.com/xfml/spec/1.0.html.

Wielemaker, Jan, Michiel Hildebrand, Jacco van Ossenbruggen, and Guus Schreiber. 2008. "Thesaurus-Based Search in Large Heterogeneous Collections." In *International Semantic Web Conference*, edited by Amit Sheth, Steffen Staab, Mike Dean, Massimo Paolucci, Diana Maynard, Timothy Finin, and Krishnaprasad Thirunarayan, 695–708. Berlin, Heidelberg: Springer.

World Wide Web Consortium. 2014. "SKOS/Datasets." Last updated February 21, 2014. http://www.w3.org/2001/sw/wiki/SKOS/Datasets.

World Wide Web Consortium. 2013a. "Extensible Markup Language." Last modified October 29, 2013. http://www.w3.org/XML/.

World Wide Web Consortium. 2013b. "SPARQL 1.1 Overview." W3C Recommendation 21 March 2013. Accessed August 28, 2014. http://www.w3.org/TR/sparql11-overview/.

World Wide Web Consortium. 2009. "SKOS Simple Knowledge Organization System eXtension for Labels (SKOS-XL) Namespace Document—HTML Variant." Recommendation Edition. 2009. Accessed August 28, 2014. http://www.w3.org/TR/skos-reference/skos-xl.html.

World Wide Web Consortium. 2004. "RDF Primer." W3C Recommendation. February 10, 2004. Accessed August 28, 2014. http://www.w3.org/TR/rdf-primer/.

World Wide Web Consortium, OWL Working Group. 2012. "OWL 2 Web Ontology Language Document Overview." 2nd ed., W3C Recommendation December 11, 2012. Accessed August 28, 2014. http://www.w3.org/TR/owl2-overview/.

Zeng, Marcia Lei, Michael Panzer, and Athena Salaba. 2010. "Expressing Classification Schemes with OWL 2 Web Ontology Language." In *Proceedings of the ISKO 2010 International Conference: Paradigms and Conceptual Systems in KO*, edited by C. Gnoli and F. Mazzocchi, 356–62. Würzburg: Ergon Verlag.

Zthes Working Group. 2006a. "The Zthes Abstract Model for Thesaurus Representation." Version 1.0. Accessed August 28, 2014. http://zthes.z3950.org/model/zthes-model-1.0.html.

Zthes Working Group. 2006b. "Zthes XML Schema." Accessed August 28, 2014. http://zthes.z3950.org/schema/zthes-1.0.xsd.

4

Automated Tools for Subject Information Organization: Selected Topics

MAJOR QUESTIONS

- In what ways could bibliometrics help identify topics dealt with in an information resource?
- What major approaches to automated classification of information resources exist?
- How does machine learning work?
- How does document clustering work?

BIBLIOMETRICS AND SUBJECT REPRESENTATION (*by Fredrik Åström*)

Bibliometrics is defined as the quantitative methods for analyzing text and text representations. It has been developed within the field of library and information science (LIS)—as well as the broader disciplines of information and computer sciences, research policy, and science studies—as a set of methodologies for analyzing the content and characteristics of documents, and relationships between them.

Bibliometrics has been used to analyze structures in texts, text representations, and text collections (such as relations between texts, authors, and concepts) since the early twentieth century. As a methodology, it primarily has been applied to scientific texts. Since the 1980s, the term "informetrics" has emerged to reflect the impact of bibliometrics, not only on printed texts but also on digital information. Typically, bibliometrics has two areas of application: to evaluate research (for example, by analyzing the number of publications by an author or institution as an indicator of scientific productivity, or examining the number of citations to a publication as an indicator of scientific impact), and to map organizational structures of a research field. The latter also is of interest within the context of subject representation and knowledge organization. For an introduction and overview on bibliometrics and citation analysis in general, see De Bellis (2009).

The representation of, and the relationship among, different types of subjects can be analyzed from two different perspectives. From one perspective, subjects reflect different categories of human knowledge per se, such as knowledge about art, computers, or chemistry. From another, they act as topical descriptions, for example, of the information in a document. Both perspectives can be handled using bibliometrics.

Statistical analyses are used to identify more narrow research areas in specific fields (i.e., how a field such as physics can be divided into more specialized areas such as theoretical, nuclear, or high-energy physics), and the knowledge structure of scientific research in general. Analyses, however, also are used to cluster documents according to their subject matter. Two main strategies for identifying these structures exist: clustering different characteristics of documents and using these clusters as representations of subject categories; and using bibliometric methods to identify relations between concepts used in documents, and to determine the subject matter of a document or the relations between documents or subject areas. These perspectives and strategies can be combined in a number of different ways. The following sections analyze subject structures, first by linking documents to each other based on how they occur together in reference lists of other documents (i.e., the list of texts a scientific article or book builds upon), and then by linking concepts based on how they are used in documents.

Linking Documents: Mapping Research Fields through Document Clustering

A main line of research in bibliometrics is using bibliometric methods to identify knowledge structures through statistical analyses of texts and the relationship between texts. With the arrival of citation databases in the 1960s, indexing the references in scientific articles together with information provided by the title and author, for example, created the opportunity to identify and analyze links between documents in the form of citing-cited relations, shared references, and co-citations. These relationships are based on the references in the articles indexed in the citation databases.

Citing-cited relations describe the relationships between the indexed article and the documents in the references list of that article. Shared references describe the relationship between indexed articles and the documents in their reference lists. Co-citations describe the relationship between documents appearing together in the reference lists of the indexed articles. Early on, researchers performed analyses of the networks (i.e., sets of interlinked nodes) of scientific papers (e.g., Price 1965) and presented methods suggesting the clustering of documents based on shared references (Kessler 1963) or co-citations (Marshakova-Shaikevich 1973; Small 1973).

In 1981, White and Griffith suggested using co-citation analysis of the author as a way to map intellectual structures. The idea was to use the number of times documents by different authors appeared together in reference lists of articles as a measurement of proximity among the authors. This assumes that the more frequently authors were co-cited, the more they have in common scientifically. When performing these analyses on an aggregated level—for example, by statistically analyzing the relationships among many authors based on their co-occurrence in the reference lists of large collections of articles—it is apparent that authors form clusters that can be interpreted as different research specializations or research areas.

Co-citation has become the foremost method for analyzing the structure of—and relationships among—research fields. It is performed on different levels by analyzing relationships at the document level, author level, or journal level (McCain 1991). In these cases, the documents, authors, or journals can be understood as concept symbols, representing different research specializations or research areas (Small 1978).

As noted, the basis for the analyses is the references provided in scientific articles. By extracting the names of the cited journals from the reference lists, for example, the researcher can create an asymmetric matrix of citing-cited documents or a symmetric matrix of co-cited articles, authors, or journals. These matrices can be analyzed to identify similarities or differences among the units through a variety of statistical measurements, such as different types of cluster analyses. These relationships also can be visualized, providing a graphic representation of the relations between research areas or specializations within a field (*see* Figure 4.1).

The map provides two different representations of the relationship among the journals. One is the location of each journal relative to each other—the journals appearing closer to each other also are those being cited together more frequently (i.e., using the number of times they are co-cited as a proximity measure). The other way that relationships are represented is by the color of the network nodes representing each journal. This is based on a statistical cluster analysis of those same co-occurrence frequencies used as proximity measures.

Using these methods for clustering journals which have articles that occur together in reference lists produces a map with different groups of journals representing—in this case—different research fields. In the upper left-hand corner, we find a cluster of physiucs journals; and below those, on the lower

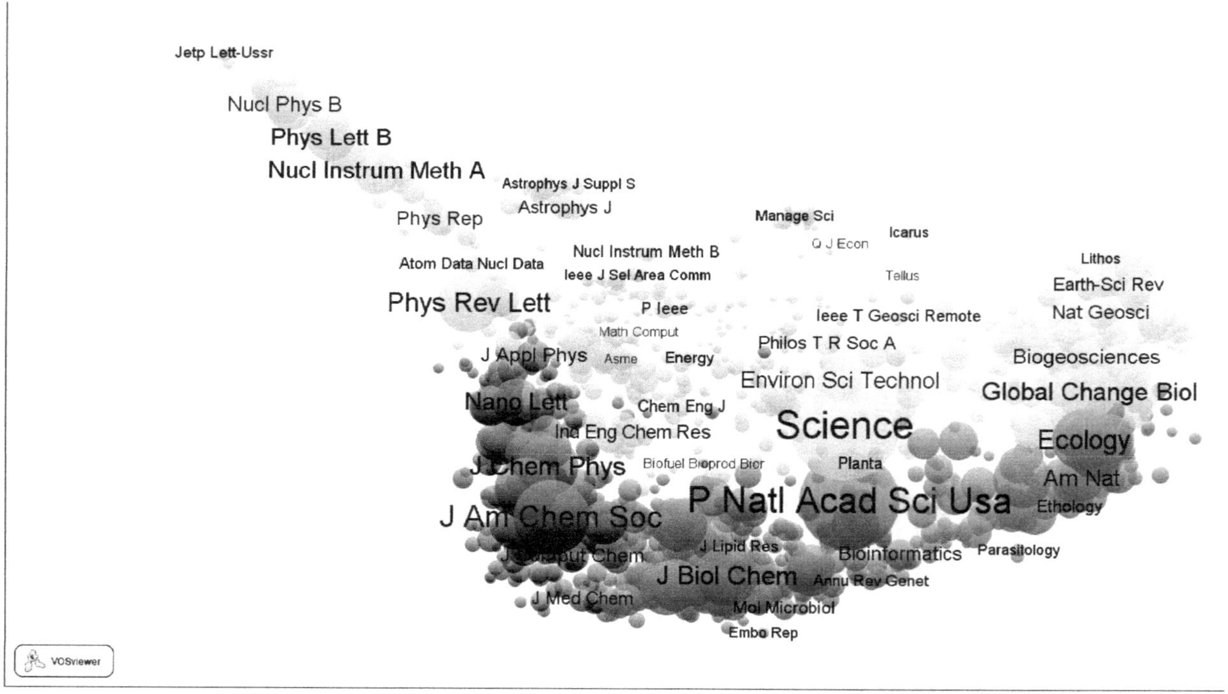

Figure 4.1. Journal co-citation map based on data from *Web of Science* (Thomson Reuters 2013a) (journal articles from the Faculties of Science and Engineering at Lund University), analyzed and visualized using the Bibexcel (Persson 2013, Bibexcel) and VOSviewer (Centre for Science and Technology Studies, VOSviewer) software. The journal names are abbreviated; for example, "P Natl Acad Sci USA" stands for *Proceedings of the National Academy of Sciences USA*; and "Phys Rev Lett" for *Physical Review Letters*.

left-hand part of the map, a cluster of chemistry journals. In the center of the map, there is a cluster of journals related to the engineering sciences. The cluster on the lower right-hand side of the map gathers journals in biology; and directly above those, a cluster of geosciences journals.This map can be interpreted as describing the relationship among different research fields. "Zooming" deeper into the map provides representations of different research areas within the fields. These clusters also represent subject categories used to describe the journals that are grouped together. This strategy is used in the *Web of Science* databases to analyze subject categories in its "Journal Citation Reports," and in the Scopus databases—both of which index references together with other metadata.

In addition to analyzing co-cited documents, there is a technique called "bibliographic coupling," in which documents are clustered based on their shared references (Kessler 1963). This method clusters the citing documents instead of the cited documents. Bibliographic coupling also is utilized for mapping research areas and—for information-retrieval purposes—for finding and ranking related documents. Documents are identified and ranked using analyses of the occurrence and number of shared references.

There are limitations to the use of these methods. One is the matter of access to—and the quality of—data, especially if seeking an all-encompassing mapping of scientific research or research areas. To perform the analyses, researchers require information about the source documents and the documents to which they refer—preferably collected in an automated manner and formatted in a way that makes it possible to identify and analyze different characteristics of the data. Bibliometric research primarily uses data from databases indexing references, such as the *Web of Science* databases (Thomson Reuters 2013a) and, more recently, Scopus (Elsevier, Scopus). These databases focus on articles in international research journals, which means that they are limited in terms of coverage of research published in other formats (e.g., books) and coverage of research published in languages other than English. Partly as a consequence of these limitations, the databases cover a great deal of research in medicine and the hard sciences, whereas social sciences and humanities are covered to a limited—possibly even a significantly limited—extent.

In terms of differences between research areas, another limitation of using bibliometrics for mapping intellectual structures and relations within and between research areas is the differences in citation structure used in different fields, and how these differences relate to one of the underlying assumptions of citation and co-citation analysis. Identifying the research areas and subject representations by using links between documents that are based on the documents' references requires assuming that the references predominantly cite other documents from within the same field. This assumption works well for some fields; for example, a high-energy physicist is likely to primarily cite other high-energy physicists. A comparative-literature scholar, however, might cite works not only from comparative literature but also from scholars in philosophy, history, psychology, and sociology—and even might include references to documents that are outside the realm of academia.

Another methodological consideration to take into account when mapping the intellectual structure of a research field is how researchers select data and what analytical techniques are used. Depending on the citation methods used in different research fields, the citation structure can differ substantially. Selecting different sets of journals to represent a research field, or choosing to perform co-citation analyses at either the author level or journal level, can result in significant variations in the research areas that appear in the maps. In addition to this problem is the issue of how to decide whether the journals selected are part of the field chosen for the analysis. If, for instance, researchers follow the subject categories of the *Web of Science*—which are based on citation-based cluster analyses—they run the risk of simply reproducing the structure of the database, rather than producing a map of the structure of the field per se.

Linking Concepts: Word Clusters for Identifying Topical Relations

Using document clustering as a basis for mapping research fields requires a knowledge of the selected field, especially for dealing with author co-citation analysis. It is important to know, for example, that the appearance of "Salton" in a co-citation map of library and information science signifies information retrieval, whereas "Garfield" is a concept symbol for bibliometrics. To identify structures in research fields in which the structures are more immediately apparent, co-word analysis is a suggested alternative to co-citation analysis. Co-word analysis consists of analyzing the structure of concepts and the relationships among words to identify different research areas within a field (Callon et al. 1983).

Figure 4.2 shows a corpus analysis performed for titles, keywords, and abstracts from research articles. The resulting map shows three concept clusters related to research evaluation: grouping concepts such as "assessment," "research output," and "h index"; analyses of structures in research using concepts such as "network," "structure," and "map"; and research and development (R&D) and innovation systems analyses, represented by examples such as "technology," "triple helix," and "patent." These three clusters correspond to three main areas of research in the bibliometrics field. This method not only identifies the main areas of interest in a research field, it also represents the conceptual structure of a field or a document.

There are, of course, problems related to the use of words or concepts instead of citations. One challenge is that language is not a stable entity; it changes both over time and over distance. Even closely related languages often use different words to mean the same thing, and use the same—or very similar—words and expressions to mean different things. Words also

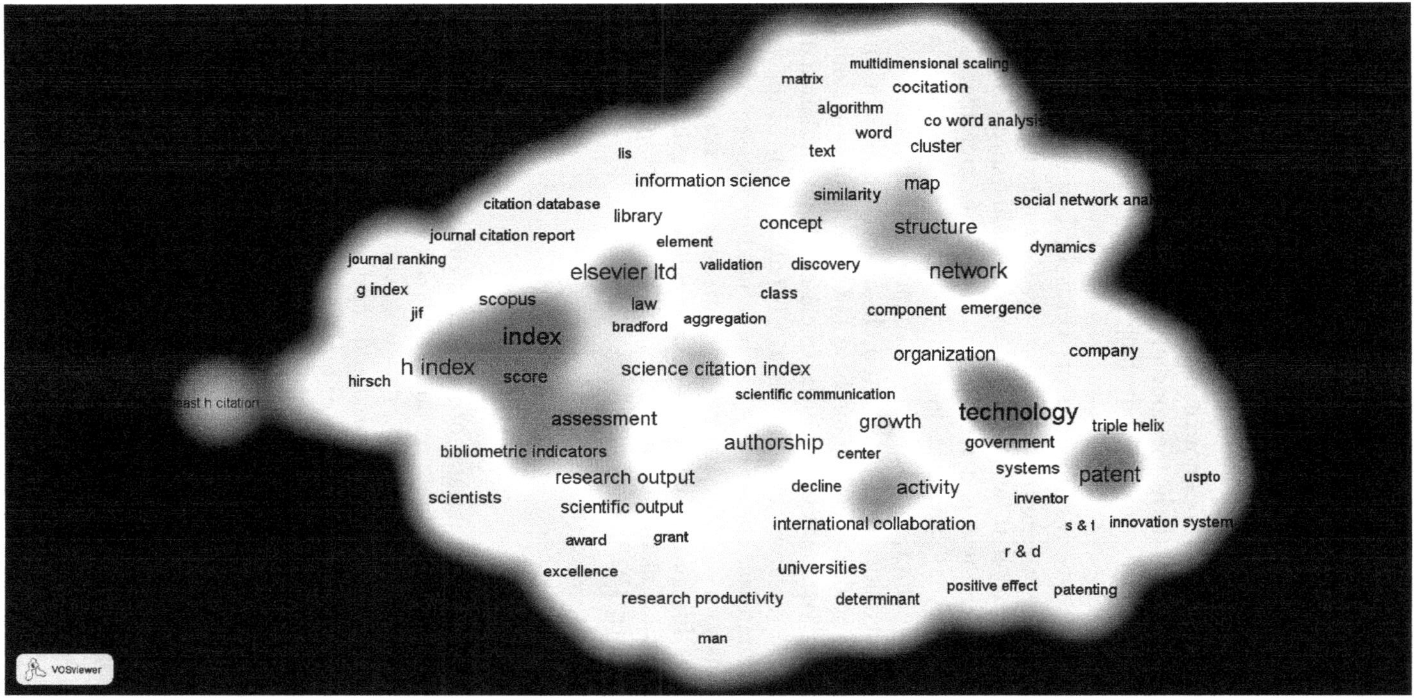

Figure 4.2. Word co-occurrence map based on data from *Web of Science* (Thomson Reuters 2013a) and journal articles (from *Scientometrics* and *Journal of Informetrics*), analyzed and visualized using "Bibexcel" (Persson 2013, Bibexcel) and "VOSviewer" software (Centre for Science and Technology Studies).

change meaning over time, or as new concepts are introduced to describe the same phenomena. For example, until 1969, "bibliometrics" was referred to as "statistical bibliography," and today the concept of "informetrics" is used more or less synonymously with "bibliometrics."

In citation analysis, however, a reference to a text by "Garfield" as a concept symbol for statistical bibliography/bibliometrics/informetrics is stable. The reference per se does not change over time, but words can change meaning over time. Similarly, the concept "discourse analysis" as used in computational linguistics means something very different in comparative literature.

A related issue involves the use of words or concepts in terms of mapping research areas—different fields use different terminologies. Also important is the extent to which a field uses a highly specialized terminology, or whether there is a tendency to use a language that is more similar to an everyday language. In fields that have a greater degree of specialized terminology, there is a better chance of finding both concepts describing the activities in the field, and clusters that represent different areas within the field. Depending on these and other issues—including the use of controlled vocabulary keywords—the use of keyword-based or conceptual maps of research fields has been debated in terms of the validity of the representations. The strategy has been used to a lesser extent than co-citation analyses over the last twenty years, but the creation of more powerful tools for automated semantic analyses has resulted in the increased use of these methods during the last decade (Klavans and Boyack 2006; Leydesdorff 1997).

Combining or Relating Co-Word/Text and Reference/Citation Analyses

Using references and citations or words and concepts to represent subject categories or for mapping research fields are not mutually exclusive strategies. Various attempts have been made to combine the methods, or to analyze to what extent concept-based and citation-based structures correspond to each other. The matching of topical structures among references and concepts has been analyzed both through investigating the retrieval performance of information searches based on one strategy or the other (*see, e.g.*, Pao and Worthen 1989), and by merging or comparing mapping and clustering analyses using the two strategies (e.g., Klavans and Boyack 2006; Yan and Ding 2012). The important question of course is: Does clustering concepts and citations result in similar structures, or does it result in different representations of a research field or a collection of documents? Another method for combining citation and concept analyses is to use conceptual analyses to name co-citation clusters (Schneider and Borlund 2004).

Data and Tools

Bibliometric research to a large extent has been driven by issues related to access to data. Although basically any collection of documents or metadata can be analyzed using bibliometric techniques, performing any larger scale studies which have enough data for robust statistical analyses requires data that is downloadable and formatted (or, at least, which can be formatted). Some work to format and standardize data is more or less unavoidable. Mistakes also are made when indexing documents and often the information in the documents is not entirely standardized. For example, an author name in a reference list can be rendered in a number of different ways. Derek J. de Solla Price can be written as "Price, DJD," as "de Solla Price, DJ," and with other variations.

Another issue related to the quality of data is the extent to which researchers can control where the information comes from and what sort of information the data source is built upon. For example, the Web of Science databases primarily include international research journals, thus excluding research published in other formats and in languages other than English. Google Scholar gathers all documents which contain a reference list that its search tools can find, thereby covering much of what is excluded from the Web of Science databases. However, Google Scholar also includes many documents that would not be considered proper research documents.

As noted, to perform citation analyses and be able to construct various citation-based links among documents requires data sources which index not only the document per se, but also the reference lists of the documents. With the exception of a few subject specific databases, this information basically is found only in two large commercial databases, Thomson Reuter's Web of Science and Elsevier's Scopus, both of which have limitations in terms of coverage (addressed above). Google Scholar also indexes references and calculates citation scores for documents, but there is an additional issue—the ability to conduct precise large-scale searches without retrieving too much redundant or irrelevant information. Yet another problem is the opportunity to access data, as the search engine returns only the first 1,000 results of a search. This severely limits opportunities to download data sources such as references and citing documents.

The data sources for conceptual analyses are more widely available, and range from commercial subject-specific bibliographic databases to institutional and subject repositories providing access to metadata and full-text documents. The issue of to what extent data is downloadable and how the data is formatted, however, remains.

There is a vast number of different tools and software for bibliometric analyses, ranging from functionalities built into databases (*see, e.g.*, the Web of Science databases), to freely available software developed by scholars in bibliometrics and computer science. For an overview of some bibliometric software, see, for example, Cobo et al. (2011). The analyses performed to provide the examples used in this chapter used Bibexcel (Persson, Danell, and Schneider 2009), which is a free toolbox for bibliometric analyses developed by the Inforsk Research Group at Umeå University in Sweden; and VOSviewer (Van Eck and Waltman 2010), a free computer program for creating and viewing bibliometric maps developed by the Centre for Science and Technology Studies (CWTS) at Leiden University in the Netherlands. Using Bibexcel, a wide range of analyses can be performed based on different types of data sets. VOSviewer is a visualization tool primarily—but not exclusively—developed for working with data from the Web of Science databases.

Bibliometrics and Information in Forms Other than Scientific Publications

The discussion of bibliometrics thus far has focused to a great extent on scholarly publications and on analyses based on data retrieved from "traditional" bibliographic data. There are, however, examples of bibliometrics that build on analyses of non-scholarly text. In 1968, five years before Small (1973) and Marshakova-Shaikevich (1973) suggested co-citation analysis as a method for mapping intellectual structures, Rosengren (1968) proposed analyzing the co-mentioning of authors of fiction literature in book reviews to reveal structures in the literary landscape. This methodology is based on the same principles as the co-citation analysis.

Since the advent of the Internet and the World Wide Web in the 1990s, much work also has been done using methods developed in bibliometrics for analyzing structures on the Web, a line of research predominately referred to as "webometrics." For an overview of webometric approaches, see Thelwall (2009). An important perspective is the analysis of Web links, the similarities between links on the Web and the references in traditional publications, and how these can be used both to analyze the impact of a document and for clustering websites and Web pages to identify topical relations and subject representations.

Obviously, there are differences between "traditional" publications and websites and Web pages, as well as between links in form of references in publications and hyperlinks on the Web. An important aspect is the dynamic nature of the Web: Links between documents, and the pages and sites per se, are not stable entities. They change over time as well as appear or disappear in ways different from traditional documents. Another aspect is the availability of data: There are tools for harvesting and analyzing Web data, such as the Webometric Analyst 2.0 (Statistical Cybermetrics Research Group, Webometric Analyst 2.0), but it is important to keep in mind that harvesting tools often depend on limitations of the search engine they are building upon, both in terms of the possibility of precision in the searches, and in terms of restrictions in number of returned hits.

In addition to using link analysis for identifying relations between documents and subject clusters, it is used for ranking documents according to the number of incoming links. Since the 1960s, researchers have ranked scientific journals according to the average number of citations per article using the Journal Impact Factor (Thomson Reuters 2013b). This method has been further developed by also taking into account the impact factor of the journals from which the citations are drawn (Pinksi and Narin 1976). Ranking search results according to the number of incoming links, as well as the "link impact" of the websites which "cite" the website being ranked, basically is the same concept as the Google PageRank algorithm (Brin and Page 1998).

AUTOMATED SUBJECT INDEXING AND CLASSIFICATION

Introduction (*by Ingo Frommholz*)

The growth of digital documents makes their manual subject indexing, often referred to in computer science as "categorization," a tedious task. The fact that these resources—be they Web pages in HTML or full texts of documents in structured or unstructured form—are available electronically, however, enables today's computers to process these resources and to perform an automated organization by subject. In particular, machine learning techniques have been successfully applied in this context.

This section therefore discusses how this type of organization can be performed by introducing the two main fields of research in these areas—automated text categorization and clustering—from a conceptual point of view. Also discussed is the relationship of categorization and clustering to a similar field, information retrieval (IR). The subsequent section acknowledges the crucial role artificial intelligence plays when classifying documents. The section therefore provides a closer look at machine learning techniques that enable the management of huge amounts of data.

Automated Text Categorization and Clustering (*by Ingo Frommholz and Muhammad Kamran Abbasi*)

Automated categorization and clustering both are means for automatically organizing documents. There is, however, a substantial difference between these two methods. "Categorization" usually requires at least one category scheme and pre-categorized documents. This means that information about these categories and their possible relationships must be present. In contrast, "clustering" does not make use of a predefined scheme. In fact, clustering is capable of proposing such a scheme automatically in a type of "bottom up" manner, by creating clusters of documents that are similar to each other in certain respects.

Automated categorization and clustering are closely related to information retrieval, which is concerned with finding relevant resources to satisfy a user's information needs (modern Web search engines are examples of applied information retrieval). Categorization is related to this task (for instance if considering the set of relevant and non-relevant documents to be two distinct categories) as well as to similar tasks such as information filtering (resources are matched against a user profile to decide whether the resource should be presented to the user). There are, of course, differences between categorization and information retrieval (Belkin and Croft 1992), but the following discussion reveals their close relationship. Clustering also borrows many ideas from information retrieval, due to the "cluster hypothesis," which states that similar documents tend to be relevant to the same information need (van Rijsbergen 1979). This made clustering an important subject of investigation in information retrieval.

The next section discusses the conceptual models underlying automated categorization and clustering, respectively. The term "document" often is used in the literature instead of "information resource," and is comprised of textual resources as well as multimedia such as music, images, and videos. Thus, herein, the term "documents" is interchangeable with the term "information resources."

Automated Text Categorization

Automated text categorization systems are designed to assign a document to one or more preexisting categories. The need for automated text categorization derives from the fact that manual classification often is not feasible and is too expensive due to the amount of resources to be classified. Automated categorization plays an important role in many applications. One of the first applications, developed more than 50 years ago, is automated subject indexing based on a controlled vocabulary (Maron 1961; Fuhr et al. 1993). Documents are automatically indexed with a given set of index terms which can be regarded as subject categories. Although, traditionally, however, text categorization means topical categorization (i.e., documents are categorized into a set of predefined topics or subjects); there also are examples of non-topical categorization. For instance, in a help desk scenario, incoming emails can be categorized by the product they refer to (a topical facet), their type (support request, gratitude, criticism), and their priority (less urgent, urgent, and very urgent could be suitable categories of non-topical facets). This would result in an automatic routing of emails to the corresponding support team member (Beckers, Frommholz, and Bönning 2009).

Automated text categorization can be classified into "hard" and "soft" (Sebastiani 2002). In "hard categorization," a binary decision is made regarding the membership of a document to the category—the document either is a member of a category or is not a member. In contrast, "soft categorization" creates a ranking of candidate categories, similar to information-retrieval systems creating a ranking of documents with respect to a given query. Soft categorization can be applied in a semi-automated classification scenario in which the user is presented with a list of possible categories from which to choose. It also can be applied when terms from a controlled vocabulary or subject headings must be automatically assigned to or suggested for a document.

Figure 4.3 presents the basic entities, functions, and processes in automated categorization. The goal is to automatically categorize documents into one or more categories described by a corresponding category scheme. The documents must be transformed into an internal, machine-processable document representation, which is done by a transformation function (α). Similar to that, categories also must be converted into a suitable category representation, which is done using another transformation function (β). Often, the category representation is based on previously categorized documents (either automated or manually categorized). Once the categories and documents are present in a machine-processable representation, a classifier (γ) performs an automatic assignment, that is, a categorization into one or more categories and facets. In addition to automatic assignments there also might exist manual assignments, defined by a function (μ) which determines the real membership of a document to one or more categories.

Manual assignments help create a category representation, but they also are important as a standard to test and evaluate automated categorization methods. Approaches applying supervised machine learning usually rely on pre-categorized documents for "training."

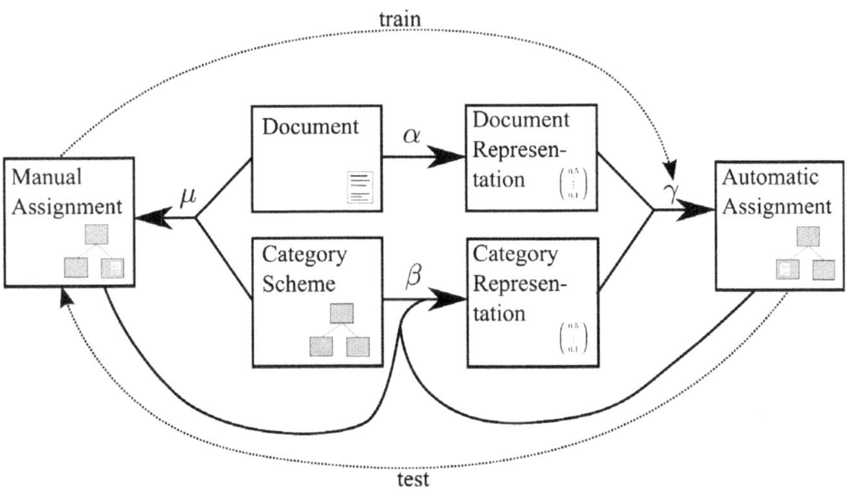

Figure 4.3. Conceptual model of automated categorization.

Document and Category Representation

To be able to process a textual resource, it must be transformed into a representation that allows categorization algorithms to perform efficiently. As noted, the transformation (α) produces a suitable representation of documents. The way this transformation is performed and its final representation depend on the actual classifier (or classification algorithm) (γ). The following section describes some basic techniques for transforming a textual document into a suitable representation (the transformation process (α)).

Although humans can perform an intellectual classification based on their interpretation of the content of a document, computers can only process symbols. This is a problem that categorization shares with information retrieval—the challenge is to get the most out of the symbols used. The process (α) of creating a document representation therefore is similar to document indexing in IR and usually is performed in three steps.

1. Tokenization, stopword elimination, and stemming
2. Term weighting
3. Representation creation

Tokenization, Stopword Elimination, and Stemming

"Tokenization" is the process of dividing the text into "tokens" or meaningful units of text. These can be single terms or words (separated by white-space characters) or phrases. All punctuation is removed. It has been shown that usually a representation as a "bag of words" (i.e., single terms) is sufficient. "Stopword elimination" means discarding terms that bear no meaning (such as "a," "the," and "is" in English). "Stemming" reduces terms to their stem base; for instance "computer," "computers," as well as the verb "computing" would be turned into "comput." This enables the grouping of terms that share the same morphological roots. Figure 4.4 shows an example of tokenization and stop word elimination. From the example text, "In theory, there is no difference between theory and practice. In practice, there is, "tokens such as "theory," "difference," and "practice" would be extracted, and "in" would be discarded as stopwords.

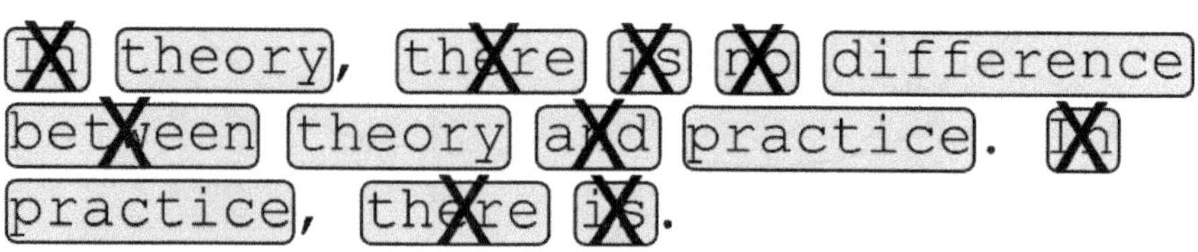

Figure 4.4. Tokenization and stopword elimination (stemming omitted).

Term Weighting

"Term weights" reflect the importance of a term. But how can a machine determine whether a term is important? Deeming every term appearing in a document as being equally important seems to be a very naive approach. A machine therefore would for instance assign binary weights: 1 if a term appears in a document and 0 if not. This simple distinction is too coarse; therefore many term-weighting approaches are based on the number of times a term occurs in a document. The approach assumes that, in a document, frequently used terms are more important than those used less frequently. In information retrieval, this led to the definition of the "term frequency" *tf(t,d)* of a term (*t*) in a document (*d*). One of the term-weighting formulas used in information retrieval is the "fractional" (*tf*).

$$tf(t,d) = \frac{occ(t,d)}{occ(t,d) + k}$$

Here *occ(t,d)* denotes the number of occurrences of the term (*t*) in the document (*d*), and (*k*) is a parameter to be determined experimentally. For instance, to take documents of different size into account, (*k*) can reflect the document length—in a Twitter "tweet," *occ(t,d)* often will be quite low, whereas in a book this value likely will be much greater. In Figure 4.4, assuming removal of stopwords and *k=1*, *tf('theory',d) =2/3 and tf('practice',d)* = *2/3* and *tf('difference', d)* = *1/2*. If *k>0* then the fractional (*tf*) yields values between 0 and 1 that can be interpreted as probabilities.

Although (*tf*) describes the importance or representativeness of a term for a document, terms themselves can be more or less informative. A term-only measure that often is applied in information retrieval is the "inverse document frequency" *idf(t)* of a term (*t*). The inverse document frequency can be computed as shown below.

$$idf(t) = \log\left(\frac{N}{n(t)}\right)$$

Here *N* is the number of documents in the collection and *n(t)* is the number of documents in which the term (*t*) can be found. Terms with a higher *idf* appear in fewer documents and are assumed to be better discriminators between documents. Terms with a low *idf* appear in many documents (think of stopwords, which usually appear in almost all documents).

There are different ways of computing *tf* and *idf* apart from the methods presented here. Other term-weighting methods have been proposed, such as BM25, language models, and divergence from randomness. Most are based on the assumptions underlying *tf* and *idf*. A thorough discussion of these models and their relationships can be found in Roelleke (2013).

The term-weighting approaches discussed thus far are widely used in automated categorization. A step beyond this is to look at additional properties that could be extracted from documents. For example, a property of a term in a document is its location (for instance, the title or abstract), or certain display characteristics (such as bold or emphasized terms in HTML documents) (Gövert, Lalmas, and Fuhr 1999). Properties such as *tf*, *idf*, and others describe documents by means of "features," and such features often are applied in the machine-learning approaches discussed in the next section.

Document and Category Representation

In many approaches documents are represented as vectors in a vector space. The nature of a vector space depends on the actual features used to describe a document. Often the vector space is a *term space* and each term represents a dimension in such a space. Documents then can be represented as vectors in the following manner. Each component (dimension) in the vector represents a term, and its value, for instance, could be given by the product of *tf* and *idf* as $tf(t,d) \times idf(t)$. Figure 4.5 shows the term space corresponding to the example text from Figure 4.4. When other features come into play (such as the location of a document), each feature is a dimension of the vector space, in which case it is termed a "feature space" (which could contain and extend the term space).

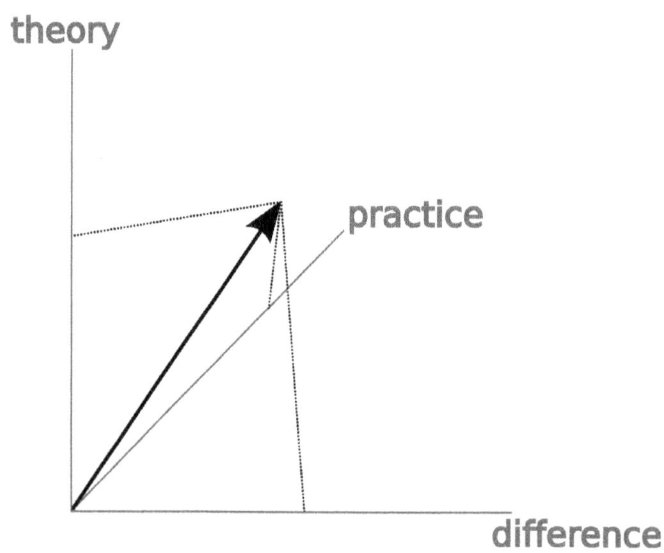

Figure 4.5. Document vector in a three-dimensional term space made of the terms "theory," "practice," and "difference."

Several approaches require a specific "category representation," which is created by the transformation (β) as shown in Figure 4.3. This representation depends on the actual classifier, but usually requires the category scheme as well as information about pre-classified documents. For example, all pre-categorized documents of a category can be merged and regarded as a single "document" for which the *tf* and *idf* values can be converted as discussed above (Klas and Fuhr 2000). Another way to represent categories is by simply viewing them as a set of documents assigned to the respective category (*see, e.g.,* Yang and Liu 1999).

Representing documents and categories as vectors introduces the problem of high dimensionality. To cope with this, "dimensionality reduction" approaches are applied. The effect of these approaches is to significantly reduce the number of dimensions of the underlying vector space, in particular if a term space is applied. Different dimensionality reduction strategies can be used, and one is to select the most promising subset of terms from the original set of terms found in the collection, for instance, based on the document frequency (Yang and Pedersen 1997). Another option is to cluster terms into groups based on their pairwise semantic relatedness, for instance using their co-occurrence in the same category (Lewis 1992; Baker and McCallum 1998; Slonim and Tishby 2001). Term clusters then are used instead of single terms. Another dimensionality reduction strategy is to utilize co-occurrences of terms in a document, as it is done in latent semantic indexing (Deerwester et al. 1990).

Automated Assignment

A "classifier" handles the actual classification of documents into the category scheme (process γ shown in Figure 4.3). Many classifiers are applying "machine learning" (ML) algorithms, discussed in more detail below. Most ML algorithms rely on a "training sample" for which the class of each object is known. Usually this training sample consists of manually assigned documents. During a "training phase" the classifier learns from the training sample about the salient features of each category. The classifier then is capable of predicting the right categories for each document.

Not every classifier utilizes traditional ML techniques; some mainly are inspired by information-retrieval techniques. Many of these are based on the well-known vector space model. Applied to automated categorization, it is assumed that each document to be categorized is represented as a vector. Further, categories are represented as one or more vectors (depending on the classifier, as shown in the examples below). The prediction of the actual categories is performed by measuring the similarity of the vectors in play. For example, in a "k-nearest-neighbor" (kNN) approach, all documents (pre-categorized and those to categorize) are represented as vectors. Vector similarity is applied to obtain a list of the *k* documents that are closest to the document to categorize (with the parameter *k* being heuristically determined). The vector similarity can be computed with the "cosine similarity"; if $\vec{a}$ and $\vec{b}$ are vectors, their similarity is computed as shown below.

$$sim(\vec{a},\vec{b}) = \cos(\theta) = \frac{\vec{a} \times \vec{b}}{|\vec{a}| \times |\vec{b}|}$$

The expression $\vec{a} \times \vec{b}$ is the dot product of the vectors, and denotes the length of a vector. The intuition behind the cosine similarity is illustrated in Figure 4.6. The closer the vectors, the higher the cosine of their angle (θ) and, hence, the greater their similarity.

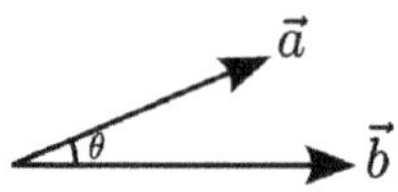

Figure 4.6 Cosine similarity.

Example: Assume we have a three-dimensional term space and the two document vectors.

$$\vec{d}_1 = \begin{pmatrix} 0.5 \\ 0.75 \\ 0.5 \end{pmatrix}; \quad \vec{d}_2 = \begin{pmatrix} 0.75 \\ 0.5 \\ 0.05 \end{pmatrix}$$

This

$$\left|\vec{d}_1\right| = \sqrt{0.5^2 + 0.75^2 + 0.5^2} \approx 1.03; \quad \left|\vec{d}_2\right| = \sqrt{0.75^2 + 0.5^2 + 0.05^2} \approx 0.902$$

and this

$$\vec{d}_1 \times \vec{d}_2 = 0.5 \times 0.75 + 0.75 \times 0.5 + 0.5 \times 0.05 = 0.775$$

results in the following.

$$sim(\vec{d}_1,\vec{d}_2) \approx \frac{0.775}{1.03 \times 0.902} \approx 0.4$$

A score for each category is calculated based on the number of documents of that category that are within the *k* nearest neighbors of the document being categorized (as shown in Figure 4.7), as well as their degree of similarity as computed above (Yang and Liu 1999; Gövert, Lalmas, and Fuhr 1999). Another option is to merge all pre-categorized documents of a category to a single document, represent it as a vector as discussed above, and create a ranking of categories based on the similarity of these vectors to the vector of the document being categorized (Klas and Fuhr 2000).

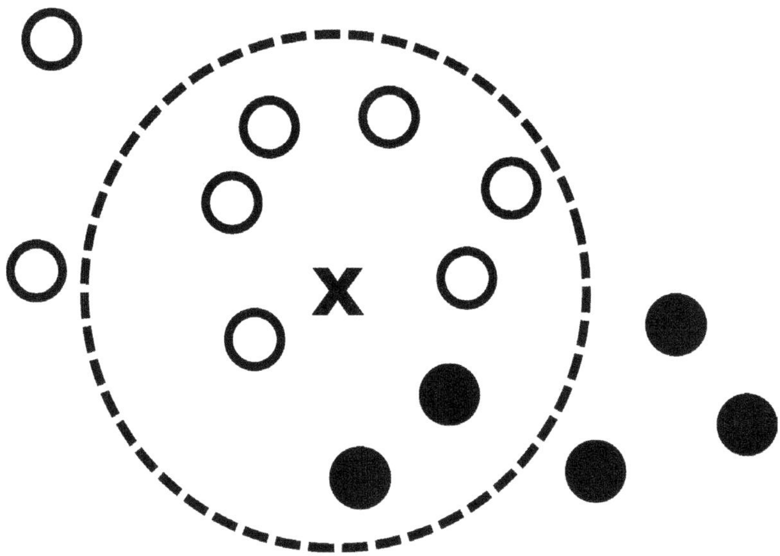

Figure 4.7. Illustration of the kNN approach. The cross represents the vector of the document being categorized and the circles are vectors of documents belonging to different categories. Vectors within the dashed circle are the 8 nearest neighbors, based on their similarity with the vector of the document being categorized.

Many real-world category schemes provide systematic hierarchies of their concepts. Examples from the Web are "Wikipedia," the "Open Directory Project," and "Yahoo!". Other examples are the classification systems introduced in Chapter 2. Such hierarchical categorization schemes provide additional information for categorization purposes, because the context of a hierarchy (for instance subcategories and supercategories) can be exploited. Utilizing the hierarchy for text categorization also poses new challenges, for instance whether documents should be assigned to the various levels of the hierarchy. Consequently, hierarchical classifiers have been proposed to make use of the hierarchy provided by the category scheme, with some reported improvements over flat classifiers (*see, e.g.*, Kosmopoulos et al. 2010; Dumais and Chen 2000; Frommholz 2001; Ceci and Malerba 2007; Mladenić and Grobelnik 2003).

Evaluation

The evaluation of automated categorization algorithms focuses on two aspects. One is "efficiency," which is concerned with the amount of computing resources (e.g., processing time, storage) needed to perform the classification tasks, and also with issues of scalability. The other is "effectiveness," which deals with the more qualitative question of how well a system is capable of making the right classification decision. To evaluate effectiveness,

Table 4.1. Contingency Table for a Category (Sebastiani 2002)

		Manual assignment	
		Yes	No
Classifier assignment	Yes	TP	FP
	No	FN	TN

the classifier's automatic assignment usually is compared to a manual assignment made by human experts. To do so, some evaluation measures must be defined. Traditional measures known from information retrieval are "precision" and "recall" (Sebastiani 2002). In automated classification, "precision" denotes the probability that if a random information resource is automatically classified under a certain category, then the decision is correct. "Recall," on the other hand, denotes the probability that if a document ought to be assigned to a certain category, then this assignment actually is performed by the automated classifier. To compute both values a contingency is designed for each category, as shown in Table 4.1.

Here, FP denotes the false positives, that is, the number of documents incorrectly assigned to the category under observation by the automated classifier. False negatives (FN) are the documents that are not assigned to the category by the classifier, but which should be according to manual assignment. True positives (TP), are all documents that are assigned to the category by both the automated classifier and the human experts. Lastly, the true negatives (TN) are documents that neither the automated classifier nor a human expert assigned to that respective category. Based on this, the precision (p) and the recall (r) of a category are defined as shown below.

$$p = \frac{TP}{TP + FP} \text{ and } r = \frac{TP}{TP + FN}$$

To obtain a recall and precision value for all categories, micro- or macroaveraging techniques can be applied (as discussed in Sebastiani 2002). Macroaveraging, for instance, takes the sum of the precision and recall values, respectively, and divides it by the number of categories.

To evaluate automated categorization approaches, suitable test collections must be provided. These collections usually consist of a category scheme and pre-categorized documents. Part of the collection is used to train the classifier, and another part is used for its evaluation. A prominent example is the Reuters corpus (Lewis et al. 2004), consisting of more than 800,000 manually classified newswire articles. Reuters provides a flat-category scheme, whereas other collections such as the Open Directory Project and Yahoo! are examples of test collections with hierarchical categories.

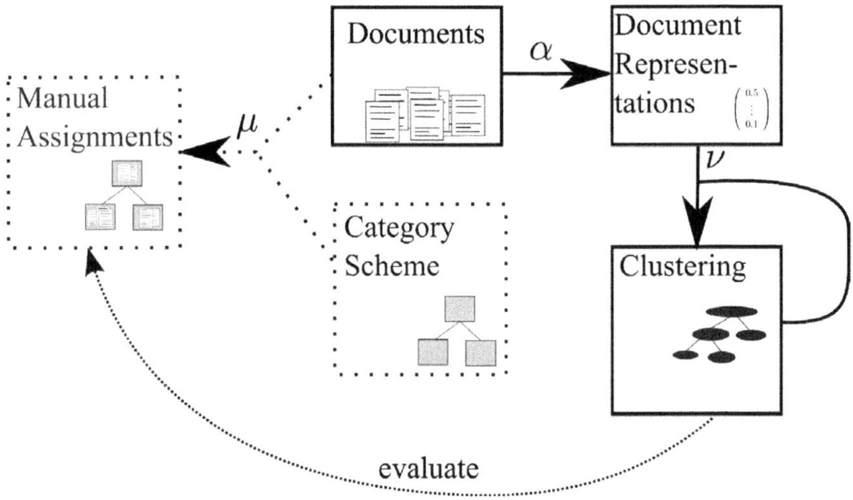

Figure 4.8. Clustering conceptual model.

Text Clustering

In the absence of a category scheme, an automated categorization of documents cannot be performed. In this case, another form of automatically organizing documents that can be used is clustering. Clustering is a type of unsupervised learning because it does not utilize pre-categorized resources. The following discusses the conceptual model of document clustering as outlined in Figure 4.8.

In contrast to categorization, clustering does not operate on a single document but rather on a set of documents. Again function α is needed to create machine-processable "document representations," which strongly depend on the chosen clustering approach. The "clustering function" (ν) organizes the resources into a set of clusters (the "clustering"). This could be an iterative process that uses an existing clustering created in a previous step. To evaluate the effectiveness of clustering approaches, an existing category scheme with manually assigned documents is often used. The following section briefly outlines the different clustering steps.

Document Representation

Similar to categorization, clustering documents must be transformed into machine-processable representations. The document representation is crucial in the clustering process and can influence the performance of the clustering algorithm (Makrehchi 2010). Many clustering approaches adopt the vector space model as described above, representing each document as a vector in a term space. The transformation function (α) used here therefore is the same as that discussed above.

Recently, a generalization of the term-based vector space representation was proposed in the context of the "optimum clustering framework" (OCF) (Fuhr et al. 2012), which is based on the cluster hypothesis. Here a document (d) is represented by the following.

$$P(R \mid d, q_i)$$

This is the probability that (d) is relevant (R) to a query (q_i). Each (q_i) then is a dimension in the vector space. By setting each (q_i) to a distinct term in the collection, the result is the classical vector space representation as described above. An OCF provides a sound theoretical framework for text clustering. Clustering algorithms measure the similarity or distance of documents in the given vector space. The assumption is that similar documents are closer to each other. The next section briefly discusses some distance measures then provides an overview of clustering algorithms.

Distance Measure

Similarity or distance measures are at the heart of a clustering algorithm. The basic idea—following the cluster hypothesis—is that the more similar or closer two document vectors are, the more likely it is that they belong to the same cluster. This is illustrated in the example in Figure 4.9. For the two terms "retrieval" and "database," a clustering algorithm can compute three clusters—one for documents about "database" only, one for those about "database" and "retrieval," and one for those about

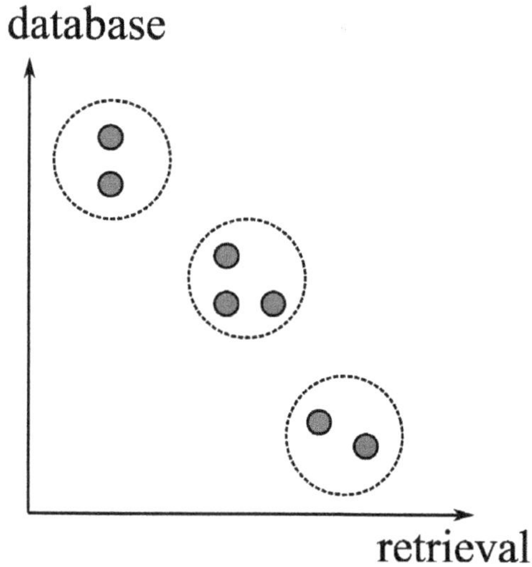

Figure 4.9. Clustering example with a two-dimensional vector space representing the terms "database" and "retrieval." Filled circles represent documents and dotted circles are clusters.

"retrieval" only. It is easy to see that documents within a cluster are closer to each other (because their vectors are similar) than those in different clusters. The choice of a distance measure depends on the document representation as well as the clustering function, and it influences the clustering quality (Huang 2008). A possible distance measure is the cosine similarity introduced above.

Clustering Functions

There are several types of document-clustering functions (*v*), as shown in Figure 4.10. The clustering approaches can be classified as hard clustering and fuzzy clustering. In hard-clustering approaches, the membership of a document to the cluster is binary (each resource can be a member of one cluster only). In contrast, in fuzzy-clustering approaches the document can belong to more than one cluster; a membership function is used to compute the degree of membership to each cluster. The hard-clustering approaches can be "partitional" or "hierarchical" and hierarchical approaches can be "divisive" or "agglomerative."

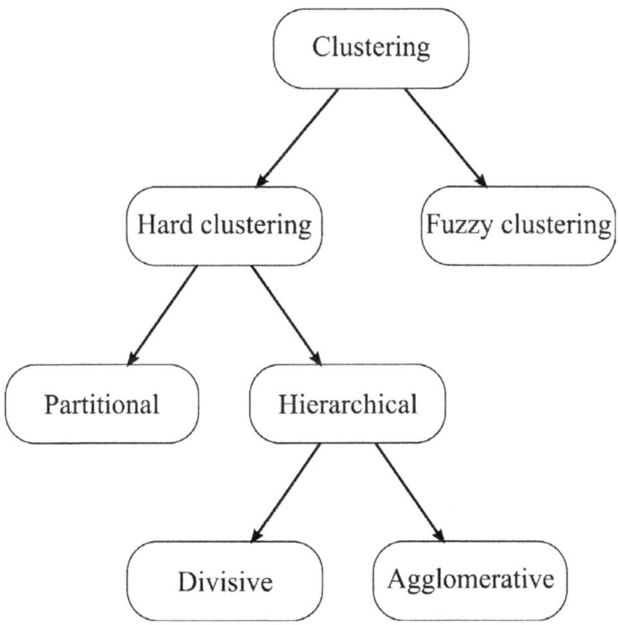

Figure 4.10. Taxonomy of clustering types (Gan, Ma, and Wu 2007).

Partitional Clustering: *k*-Means

The partition-based clustering methods divide a document collection into (*k*) partitions according to similarity/distance. One of the most prominent algorithms is *k-means*, which works iteratively (Manning, Raghavan, and

Schütze 2008). In the first phase, the algorithm chooses *k* random cluster centers (so-called centroids) and assigns each document to the nearest cluster center, creating an initial clustering. The initial cluster centers could be, for instance, (*k*) randomly chosen documents (respectively, their vectors). In subsequent phases and based on the previous clustering, the new center for each cluster is computed as the centroid of the document vectors belonging to the cluster. Each document then is assigned to the cluster represented by the nearest centroid. This process continues until it meets a defined convergence criterion. The key advantage of the *k*-means algorithm is that it converges to a (possibly local) optimum. A weakness is that usually the ideal number of clusters (*k*) is not known and only can be guessed. Varying (*k*) results in different clusters of different quality (Jain, Murty, and Flynn 1999).

Hierarchical Clustering

The two variants of the hierarchical approaches are divisive and agglomerative clustering. The "divisive algorithms" start top-down with a single cluster containing all documents. Clusters then are divided based on a given similarity/distance measure until each document finally becomes a single-element cluster composed of itself. An example of a divisive clustering algorithm is bisecting *k*-means (Savaresi et al. 2002), which utilizes a *k*-means variant as a "subroutine" to divide clusters.

"Agglomerative algorithms" are the opposite of the divisive algorithms. Each document is considered a single element cluster at first, and then the algorithm merges the clusters on the basis of given similarity/distance measures until all elements are reduced to a single cluster (bottom-up approach) or until the clustering stops based on a selected quality criterion. In a hierarchical agglomerative approach most similar clusters are merged. To compute the similarity of clusters, different strategies are used based on the similarity of the documents in the clusters under consideration. To decide which clusters to merge, agglomerative algorithms apply different cluster distance measures (*see, e.g.,* Manning, Raghavan, and Schütze 2008).

- The "single linkage" strategy takes the similarity of the two closest documents in two clusters as a measure for the cluster distance.
- "Complete linkage" means that the distance of the most distant document pair from two clusters is taken as the cluster distance measure.

Both single and complete linkage strategies base the cluster similarity on the similarity of a pair of elements from the respective cluster. This has some disadvantages, such as the effect of outliers being overemphasized. For instance, it might happen that two documents in different clusters are very far apart, whereas the remaining documents in the respective clusters are rather close. Single linkage, due to these outliers, would assume that the clusters are far away, but in reality they are not. For this reason, some additional strategies for measuring the cluster similarity have been proposed.

- "Group-average" clustering utilizes all similarities between documents, including pairs from the same cluster.
- "Centroid" clustering uses the similarity of the centroids of the respective clusters as a measure of cluster similarity.

The document clustering methods are not limited to the common approaches discussed here. Examples of other approaches explored in the clustering domain are artificial neural network-based approaches (such as self-organizing maps (Kaski et al. 1998)), genetic-algorithm based approaches (Cui, Potok, and Palathingal 2005), and model-based document clustering (Zhong 2006).

Evaluation

Clustering algorithms produce different sets of clusters when applied to different data sets and when used with different parameters and document representations. It therefore is important to validate the clustering produced with varying parameters, data, or algorithms for the quality of the clustering choices. The cluster evaluation/validity measures can be classified as "internal" and "external" (Xu and Wunsch 2008; Gan, Ma, and Wu 2007; Rokach and Maimon 2005).

"External validity measures" validate the clustering against, for instance, a category scheme with manual assignments of documents (determined by the function (μ) shown in Figure 4.8). An example of an external measure is the Rand Index (RI), which measures the number of correct decisions (Manning, Raghavan, and Schütze 2008; Rand 1971; Hubert and Arabie 1985). Another example of an external measure is based on the notion of precision (p) and recall (r) to compute what is called an "F-measure" (Manning, Raghavan, and Schütze 2008).

"Internal validity measures" evaluate the produced clustering for intra-cluster compactness and inter-cluster separability (Liu et al. 2010; Rokach and Maimon 2005). Compactness refers to the extent that documents are close to each other within a cluster (the closer the better) and separability refers to how distant two clusters are from each other (the more distant, the better). In contrast to external measures, internal validity measures do not rely on an external standard.

Further Reading

This chapter discusses automated text categorization and clustering, and provides references for further reading as appropriate. Some of these references are original papers that discuss the respective approach in depth. Others are survey articles and textbooks that provide a more thorough overview and discussion than is possible in this chapter. Sebastiani (2002) provides a comprehensive overview of text categorization; Chapter 16 and Chapter 17 of Manning, Raghavan, and Schütze (2008) provide a further overview of clustering, and Golub (2006) includes an introduction to approaches applied to Web pages.

Machine Learning on Text
(by Dunja Mladenić and Marko Grobelnik)

This chapter introduces automated categorization and clustering from a conceptual point of view and briefly outlines the processes involved. From the examination so far, it becomes clear that machine learning plays a central role in categorization and clustering. The following discusses how machine learning approaches can be utilized.

Machine learning is a research subfield of the artificial intelligence field that mainly is concerned with using computers for learning from the data or, more precisely, modeling the data with little to no human involvement. In machine learning, "learning" means any process whereby the system improves its performance based on experience. More formally, the system (i.e., a computer program) improves on task (*T*) with respect to performance metric (*P*) based on experience (*E*) (Mitchell 1997).

For instance, a goal can be to learn how to recognize handwritten terms (*T* = recognizing handwritten terms), whereby the performance is measured by the percentage of terms that are correctly recognized (*P* = percentage of terms correctly recognized) and the system is provided with a database of human-labeled images of handwritten terms (*E* = database of human-labeled images of handwritten terms). Another example is the categorization of email messages as spam or legitimate, with the goal being to achieve a high percentage of correctly classified email messages; the system is provided a database of emails in which some email messages are labeled by humans as being spam or legitimate.

Generally speaking, machine learning is about finding patterns and regularities in the data. The result is a model that could be understood as a summary or generalization of the input data (the data that was provided as evidence for the learning process). The model then can be used to explain the existing phenomena captured in the data and for predicting future situations. In principle, the model should be as simple as possible but still capture the data reasonably.

Machine-Learning Techniques

Machine-learning techniques on input typically require input data providing evidence that is used for learning, and input parameters (e.g., parameters regulating noise handling, parameters limiting size of the learned model) that enable the user to influence the learning process and properties of the model that are constructed during learning (Witten and Frank 1999). The model typically is constructed by applying an algorithm that searches the space of possible models, usually by some local optimization. The complexity of the model is determined by the language of the model.

The model, for instance, can be expressed as a decision tree. Additionally, there is a set of possible decision trees that correspond to the same data from which the learning algorithms must choose. The learning algorithm for constructing a decision tree is based on a set of examples (i.e., data providing evidence for learning) and uses local optimization so that at each step it selects the most informative attribute to be placed at a tree node. The examples then are divided based on the value of the selected attribute and the process is repeated on each subset of the examples. Each time, the process selects the most informative attribute (locally, without checking combinations of attributes steps ahead, as the search space is too big for global optimization).

Handling textual information resources using machine-learning techniques often requires assuming that a large amount of data is represented in a high-dimensional space. In the case of text, these dimensions usually are terms (so the dimensionality equals the size of vocabulary), similar to the vector space examples given in the previous section. In a typical collection it is not unusual to have hundreds of thousands of documents, each represented by the set of terms within it. Thus, there could be as many dimensions as there are different terms in the document collection—easily tens of thousands.

There are methods in machine learning that deal with reducing the dimensionality of the data and which have been successfully applied on text data (Mladenić 2007); some are discussed in the previous section. Moreover, depending on the method used for representing documents, it often is the case that documents are presented as very sparse vectors (having many 0 elements). This should be taken into account when applying machine-learning techniques.

Having a sparse representation is not unusual in the case of high-dimensional data. A whole document collection can contain 10,000 different terms, for instance, which means that without reducing the dimensionality of the data, each document is represented by a vector that has 10,000 elements (word/term weights), or one weight for each term of the vocabulary. If the term does not occur in a document, then its weight in the document representation vector is 0. The sparsity of the document vector depends on the vocabulary size and the number of different terms that a document contains. In the case of news articles, the documents can be relatively short, with each containing fewer than 500 terms. This means that each document is represented by a vector of 10,000 values (term weights), having no more than 500 non-zero elements (as it does not contain more than 500 terms, so the weights of all the other terms from the vocabulary are 0).

Learning Approaches

Depending on the input data and the goal of learning, at least three large groups of machine-learning approaches have been successfully applied on text data. These include supervised learning, semi-supervised learning, and unsupervised learning.

Supervised Learning

In "supervised learning" (also referred to as "classification" in the machine-learning community) the data is labeled. For document categorization, this means that each document is manually assigned one or more categories from a predefined set of possible categories, as is shown in Figure 4.3 (the function (μ)). One frequently used approach is a "categorization model" consisting of a collection of binary models (returning one of the two possible values, "yes" or "no"). A binary model is one that predicts for each document whether it belongs to the category. An assumption is that each of the categories contains at least one document. For each category a binary model is trained using a collection of what is referred to as positive examples (documents belonging to the category) and a set of negative examples (documents that do not belong to the category).

An example of document categorization (classifying documents by assigning one or more content categories reflecting the document content) is to use machine-learning techniques. Document categorization often uses linear models, whereby the value of (y) as a predicted category of the document is calculated as a linear combination of the feature weights (x_i) (representing terms occurring in the document) multiplied by the model parameters (a, b, c, . . .). From this a linear model is derived.

$$y = a\,x_1 + b\,x_2 + c\,x_3 + \dots$$

For instance, a simple model for categorizing news articles on the topic of "acquisition" checks the news article content (i.e., terms that occur in the document), and calculates the value of the linear function by using the learned model. Based on the training data, each term is assigned a weight; for example: 11.5, stake; 9.5, merger; 9, takeover; 9, acquire; 8, acquired, whereby a high weight indicates terms characteristic for the documents from the category, and terms characteristic for the documents but which are not from the category are assigned a negative weight. If the news article is about "acquisition," then it should contain some of the terms that have positive weight in the "acquisition" category, and few of the terms that have negative weight in the linear model.

Depending on the relationship between the categories (if any), negative examples can contain some or all of the documents belonging to the other categories. For instance, if using a hierarchy of categories such as science, computer science, artificial intelligence, or machine learning, then it is

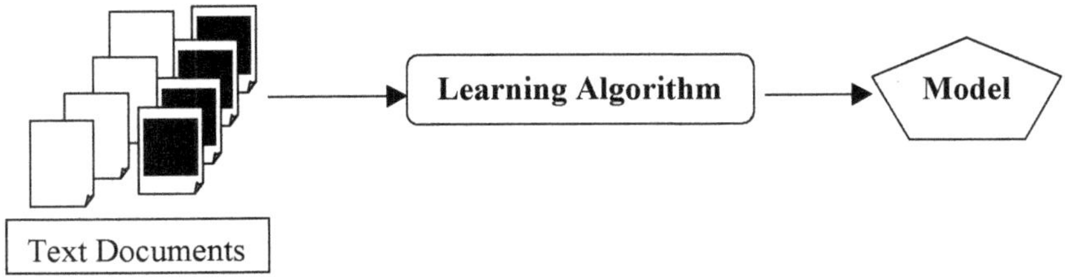

Figure 4.11. Illustration of supervised learning. Using a collection of categorized text documents (categories are denoted here as black or white), the algorithm trains a model capable of assigning a category to a new document.

advisable to take the hierarchy into account when training the model (e.g., a document about "machine learning" is not a negative example of documents about "computer science"). There exist some supervised learning algorithms capable of automatically accounting for a hierarchy of categories (Mladenić 1998, Brank, Grobelnik, and Mladenić 2007; Grobelnik, and Mladenić 2005). Figure 4.11 shows a collection of documents, each labeled by one of the two possible categories. The documents are provided as input to a machine learning algorithm. Based on the documents already categorized, a supervised learning algorithm constructs a model which generalizes the data that can be used to assign predefined categories to a new document. Note that each document can be assigned more than one label.

Semi-Supervised Learning

In "semi-supervised learning," similar to supervised learning, the goal is to train a model that can assign a category to a new example (in the present case, to a text document), but only a small part of the data is labeled and all the data is desired (not just the labeled data). When there is some labeled data and possibly a large pool of unlabeled data, the training could consider only the labeled data and ignore the unlabeled data. There are machine-learning algorithms that can use labeled as well as unlabeled data, however, and thereby obtain better performance than if using only the labeled data. The algorithms typically involve some integration through the data and retraining of the model.

First assume that the user is willing to provide labels for some small proportion of unlabeled data, in this case text documents that have not been assigned a category. A simple approach would be to randomly select some of the unlabeled documents and ask the user to label them, so that the result is a larger pool of labeled documents to be used to train (construct and generate) a model. Better results can be attained by knowing how to choose from the unlabeled documents. Use the labeled documents to train a model, then apply the model to unlabeled documents and decide which document to give to the user for labeling. The newly labeled document then is added to the pool of labeled documents and a new model is trained from this enlarged set of labeled documents. The process of selecting a document to be labeled and training the model is repeated as often as the user is willing to label documents. This type of semi-supervised learning commonly is referred to as "active learning" (analogous to active students asking questions).

Experimental results show that the classification models obtained using active learning perform better than do the models obtained by randomly selecting additional data to be labeled. In document categorization, active learning is especially helpful when the category for which the binary model is being trained (also referred to as the target category) is underrepresented in the data set. Having only a small proportion of documents that belong to a category means that, by randomly selecting documents from unlabeled data, the chance of selecting documents from the target category is low and, consequently, the model will be trained mostly based on the documents that are not from the target category. This results in a limited performance of the model.

In the case that no user is willing to provide additional labels but there still is a large pool of unlabeled data, it is possible to use a "co-training" approach (Mitchell and Blum 1997). The idea behind co-training is that two independent representations of the same data are provided, for instance images (image representation) with captions (text representation), or the text of an announcement and comments made about it. Then one model is trained for each of the data representations, and the two models are applied independently on unlabeled data to assign the labels (i.e., assign categories in case of document categorization).

Next a subset of newly labeled data for which the model is fairly certain about the label assignment is added to the pool. The two models are trained again, now on the extended set of labeled data. The process is repeated until it reaches a predefined stop criterion (e.g., a certain number of iterations). The assumption is that one model will be more confident than the other in assigning a label to different data points, so by adding newly labeled data points the models will share information and each will help.

For example, Web pages can be represented by text on the Web page itself and, alternatively, by text around hyperlinks on other Web pages pointing to the selected page. In that way one model is trained for categorization of Web pages based on the content of the page, and the other model is trained for categorization of Web pages based on the content of text around hyperlinks pointing to the Web page. It is hoped that the provided data is independent enough to result in different models that can each help in training.

Unsupervised Learning

In "unsupervised learning," there are no labels associated with the data, but some measure of similarity is provided based on how the data is grouped. This is exactly what is found in the clustering scenario discussed previously. Typically, the goal is to have data assigned to the group which is as similar as possible (high inter-cluster similarity), and have the groups be dissimilar, that is, the data points from different groups have low similarity (low intra-cluster similarity). Details are provided in the text clustering section above.

Beyond Basics

Many tasks involving text data have been addressed by machine learning techniques, either on formal (e.g., news articles) or informal (e.g., language in social media) data, as well as different natural languages and cross-lingual settings. Machine-learning techniques also have been used for the analysis of text data in combination with other types of data (e.g., images, social network data), and for handling data-intensive text streams (e.g., providing news articles from different publishing houses as they are published on the Web, and including time stamps). This section provides a very brief description of some tasks, mainly to stimulate the reader to think about other tasks and settings for which machine learning can be used on text data.

Visualization of data often is very helpful as the first step when looking at data and also as an integral part of the data analysis process. Several machine-learning methods have been proposed in visualization of text data—mostly based on finding global regularities in the data (Fayyad et al. 2002; Grobelnik and Mladenić 2002). For instance, unsupervised learning combined with multidimensional scaling used for mapping a high-dimensional data in a two-dimensional space has been applied for visualization of text documents (Fortuna, Grobelnik, and Mladenić 2005). This results in a two-dimensional map that can be shown on a computer screen. Similar documents are placed close to each other, and the map is marked by the most characteristic terms of the documents in a certain area.

Organizing a collection of documents into a taxonomy also can be performed by means of machine-learning techniques. For instance, Cimiano and Völker (2005) proposed taxonomy construction based on the extraction of entities and relations from text, and Fortuna, Grobelnik, and Mladenić (2006) proposed a semi-automatic taxonomy construction from a collection of documents. Machine-learning techniques have been used on text streams in combination with an existing document taxonomy (Grobelnik et al. 2006), whereby named entities (e.g., personal names, names of cities, company names) extracted from text are represented by a vector of terms occurring around them in the text and categorized into the taxonomy. Machine learning also has been used for extending an ontology by proposing new concepts based on news collection (Novalija and Mladenić 2013).

Automated document summarization also has been addressed by machine-learning techniques in combination with natural language processing (Leskovec, Milic-Frayling, and Grobelnik 2007). In this case, each document first is transformed into a semantic graph (a graph connecting subject-predicate-object triplets occurring in the document). The graph is used for constructing a document representation upon which supervised learning is applied to train a model assigning importance for the document summary to parts of text.

Personalized information delivery is another example in which machine-learning techniques can be used to generate a profile based on demographic data, personal preferences, and user behavior. For instance, Fortuna, Mladenić, and Grobelnik (2011) proposed user modeling with machine-learning techniques using text from Web pages that the user has accessed, user data, and semantics. Sentiment analysis using machine-learning techniques has been proposed for different tasks, including identifying the sentiment of a movie review (e.g., Pang, Lee, and Vaithyanathan 2002), blogs (e.g., Melville, Gryc, and Lawrence 2009), and multilingual informal texts (e.g., Štajner, Novalija, and Mladenić 2013). Exploratory analysis of textual data along several dimensions including topic and sentiment of the text (Trampuš et al. 2013) also is based on machine-learning techniques.

Discussion

This section provides a brief explanation of usage of machine learning on text data. It addresses some basic techniques and some advanced approaches at a fairly general level. This is by no means a complete, detailed, or technical explanation. Nevertheless, it is hoped that the section provides basic and intuitive explanation and stimulates interested readers to dig deeper.

> This is the Information Age, everybody can be informed about anything and everything. There is no secret, therefore there is no sacredness. Life is going to become an open book. When your computer is more loyal, truthful, informed and excellent than you, you will be challenged. You do not have to compete with anybody. You have to compete with yourself. (Bhajan 2000)

Given the availability of textual data and documents in general that are rapidly growing, analysis of text that can be supported by machine-learning techniques will continue to be important and valuable, not only in the research context but also in many applications—including those supporting the daily activities of many people. Machine-learning researchers actively are working to address new problems and are guided by practical opportunities and needs as well as theoretical challenges.

SUMMARY
(*including contributions by Ingo Frommholz*)

The growth of information resources that are "born" digital makes manual subject indexing a task that is impossible to achieve. Because these resources are available electronically, however, today's computers have the opportunity to process these resources and to perform an automated organization of the subject information. Although these methods have disadvantages, such as many false and missing results, they are applied in different degrees in search engines being used today. This chapter gives an overview of several approaches that can be used to automatically determine the subject of an information resource: bibliometrics, text categorization, document clustering, and machine learning on text.

Bibliometrics encompasses quantitative methods for analyzing structures in textual documents, document representations, and collections, such as author and subject relationships between documents. Bibliometrics has had two major areas of applications: evaluating research and mapping organizational structures of a research field. The latter also is of interest within the context of subject representation and knowledge organization. For example, statistical analyses can be used to identify smaller research areas in physics, such as theoretical, nuclear, or high-energy physics. This is used to inform potential use and design of KOS structures and concepts. To achieve this, documents can be analyzed based on how they occur together in reference lists or by analyzing how the concepts are used in documents. The former is referred to as co-citation analysis, and the idea is that the number of times documents by different authors appear together in reference lists of articles serves as a measurement of proximity between how close the topics dealt with by the authors are: The more frequently two authors are co-cited, the more similar their topics of research. This method also can be applied to identify research areas used by different journals in a collection, for example.

As is the case for all automated methods, however, this method does not always produce accurate reflections of fields. Humanities, social sciences, and interdisciplinary sciences scholars, for example, tend to cite outside of their own disciplines as well. It has also been shown how taking different samples of journals and articles results in producing rather different representations of research fields when applying co-citation analysis.

The second method used is co-word analysis, whereby the structure of concepts and the relationships among words are analyzed to identify different research areas within a field. An analysis can be conducted for titles, keywords, and abstracts from research articles, for example, and concept clusters are created based on the analysis. This way, not only are the main areas of interest in a research field found, but also a representation of the conceptual structure of a field or a document. Combining co-citation with co-word analysis produces both the structures of a field as well as concepts used by the various segments of the field.

Bibliometrics traditionally has been applied to research articles. Although not without problems, such as different formats of author names in different articles, publications are relatively well formatted as compared to a more recent area of bibliometric research focus: the Web. Web pages link to other pages and these links are similar to references in traditional research articles. Webometrics is a branch of bibliometrics dealing with Web pages.

The following sections deal with text categorization, document clustering, and machine learning using text. These processes are described from start to finish; from using full texts of an information resource to examining the internal representations required by the algorithm at hand. Texts first must be represented in a machine-processable form. This often is done in a sequence similar to that applied in automated indexing in information retrieval: tokenization, stopword elimination, and stemming; term weighting; and representation creation (usually given as vectors in vector space). Various heuristic principles then are applied by algorithms to calculate similarities between these representations and categories' representations, the most simple being the number of words they have in common.

Text categorization is used when a KOS structure exists into which information resources are automatically classified. If no KOS is made available then document clustering is used, whereby similar documents are grouped into clusters which then are used instead of predefined categories. Machine learning plays a central role in automated categorization and clustering as a key technique for algorithms to determine the right categories, usually based on existing, pre-categorized documents. Strategies such as supervised learning, semi-supervised learning, and unsupervised learning often are used.

Although the methods discussed here often are tailored to text documents, most of the approaches also can be applied to different, heterogeneous information resources. Multimedia documents (audio, video or images), for example, could be processed similarly by transforming them into a vector representation that instead of terms utilizes extracted physical features such as color distributions and shapes.

CHAPTER REVIEW
(*including contributions by Ingo Frommholz*)

1. What is needed to enable an information system to take advantage of bibliometrics data?
2. What are some advantages and disadvantages of document clustering in producing structures for an end user?
3. How could KOSs such as thesauri enriched with mappings to other KOSs be utilized in automated subject classification?
4. Take a small example of a text (for instance, a paragraph in this book) and consider how it can be represented as a vector.
5. Take any example of a text (for instance, an article from today's news). After reading it, think of five keywords to assign to this text (similar to what presently is known as tagging). Reflect upon why you chose these keywords. Do you think counting terms and computing term weights

(e.g.,with *tf*) is a good method to determine the most important keywords for the text? Can you think of any alternative methods a computer could apply?

6. Examine the different concepts and processes of automated categorization and clustering, respectively. What are their differences? In which case would you recommend applying a clustering algorithm? In which case would you recommend using an automated categorization algorithm?
7. Do you think automated categorization can replace assignment by a human in categorizing documents? How would you apply automated categorization?
8. Think about a supervised learning task that can be addressed by machine learning methods and involves the analysis of text data, such as categorization of email messages as spam or legitimate. Specify as many details as possible, such as what information would be provided as input, where you would get the data, and how you would ensure labeling of the data by the categories.
9. Consider a task for text data in which the large amount of information makes it difficult to obtain labels for all the data, such as descriptions of books for children that must be categorized as interesting for a particular child or a group of children of the same age or background. Think about possible ways of applying semi-supervised learning.
10. Think about tasks in your daily life that would benefit from unsupervised learning on text data. Specify some details on input data and similarity measurement.

GLOSSARY
(*by Fredrik Åström, Ingo Frommholz, Muhammad Kamran Abbasi, Dunja Mladenić, and Marko Grobelnik*)

Automated categorization: The process of automatically assigning one or more categories to a document.

Bibliographic coupling: A similarity measure describing relations between documents based on the documents sharing the same references.

Bibliographic data: Information related to a document, such as title, author, or subject.

Bibliographic database: A collection of documents represented by bibliographic data.

Bibliometrics: Quantitative/statistical analyses of texts and bibliographic data.

Category scheme: A definition of categories (e.g., category name, description) and their relationships.

Citation: A link between documents acknowledging how one document has used information from another.

Citation analysis: Analyses of references to study either relations between documents, or the impact of a document based on the number of times a document has been cited in other documents.

Citation database: A bibliographic database indexing the references in a document together with other bibliographic data.

Cited/Citing: Describing the relation between documents; a cited document occurs in the reference list of another document; the citing document is that which mentions another document in its reference list.

Classifier: An algorithms that assigns one or more categories from the category scheme to a document, based on a given document and category representation and often on previous assignments.

Cluster analysis: Methods for grouping objects based on the extent to which they share similar characteristics.

Clustering: The process of grouping similar documents into clusters (used, for instance, if there is no category scheme).

Co-citation: A similarity measure describing documents occurring together in the reference list of other documents.

Corpus: A body of work, such as a collection of texts by an author or a collection of words in a text.

Co-word analysis: A similarity measure for describing relations between documents based on the extent to which they share the same words/concepts; and for describing relations between words depending on how often they appear together in different documents.

Document representation: Internal description of a document, for instance, as a vector in a vector space, used for automated categorization and clustering, respectively.

Informetrics: Quantitative analyses of information; compared to bibliometrics, this is a broader concept because it analyzes information regardless of form, and bibliometrics is limited to text.

Institutional repository: Publication archive for an institution or a research field.

Proximity, measure of: Statistical similarities used as measurements of distance between objects in a graphic representation of relations.

Reference: The mentioning of a document in another document; acknowledging the use of information from the document being referenced.

Reference analysis: *See* citation analysis.

Scopus: A commercial database produced by Elsevier. It indexes scientific/scholarly literature (predominantly journal articles) using, for example, titles, authors, keywords, and abstracts, and indexes the reference lists of the literature.

Semi-supervised learning: Machine-learning approaches, in which labeled and unlabeled data is modeled to infer a function assigning the labels.

Supervised learning: Machine-learning approaches, in which labeled data is modeled to infer a function assigning the labels.

Unsupervised learning: Machine-learning approaches in which unlabeled data is modeled by grouping similar objects together to find a hidden structure in the data.

Web of Science: A commercial set of databases such as the Science Citation Index, Social Science Citation Index, and Arts & Humanities Citation Index; formerly known as the Institute of Scientific Information (ISI) databases. Produced by Thomson Reuters, it indexes scientific/scholarly literature (predominantly journal articles) using, for example, titles, authors, keywords, and abstracts, and also indexes the reference lists of the literature.

Webometrics: The application of bibliometric/informetric methods on datasets based on information from the World Wide Web.

REFERENCES

Baker, L. Douglas, and Andrew Kachites McCallum. 1998. "Distributional Clustering of Words for Text Classification." In *Proceedings of the 21st Annual International ACM SIGIR Conference on Research and Development in Information Retrieval*, edited by W Bruce Croft, Alistair Moffat, Cornelis J. van Rijsbergen, Ross Wilkinson, and Justin Zobel, 96–103. New York: ACM.

Beckers, Thomas, Ingo Frommholz, and Ralf Bönning. 2009. "Multi-Facet Classification of E-Mails in a Helpdesk Scenario." In *Proceedings of the GI Information Retrieval Workshop at LWA*, edited by Thomas Mandl and Ingo Frommholz. Gesellschaft für Informatik e.V.

Belkin, Nicholas J., and W. Bruce Croft. 1992. "Information Filtering and Information Retrieval: Two Sides of the Same Coin?" *Communications of the ACM* 35, 12: 29–38.

Bhajan, Yogi. 2000. "Relationships and the Information Age." In *A Year with the Master*, edited by Atma Singh Khalsa and Guruprem Kaur Khalsa, 25. New Mexico: KRI Publishing.

Brank, Janez, Marko Grobelnik, and Dunja Mladenić. 2007. "Predicting the Addition of New Concepts in a Topic Hierarchy." In *Proceedings of the 10th International Multi-Conference Information Society IS-2007*, edited by Bohenec et al., 81–85. Ljubljana, Slovenia: Jožef Stefan Institute.

Brin, Sergey, and Lawrence Page. 1998. "The Anatomy of a Large-Scale Hypertextual Web Search Engine." *Computer Networks and ISDN Systems* 30: 107–17.

Callon, Michel, Jean-Pierre Courtial, William A. Turner, and Serge Bauin. 1983. "From Translations to Problematic Networks: An Introduction to Co-Word Analysis." *Social Science Information sur les Sciences Sociales* 22 (2): 191–235.

Ceci, Michelangelo, and Donato Malerba. 2007. "Classifying Web Documents in a Hierarchy of Categories: A Comprehensive Study." *Journal of Intelligent Information Systems* 28 (1): 37–78.

Centre for Science and Technology Studies. 2013. "VOSviewer." Accessed May 27, 2013. http://www.vosviewer.com/.

Cimiano, Philipp, and Johanna Völker. 2005. "Text2Onto—A Framework for Ontology Learning and Data-Driven Change Discovery." In *Proceedings of the 10th International Conference on Applications of Natural Language to Information Systems*. Berlin-Heidelberg: Springer.

Cobo, M. J., A. G. Lopez-Herrera, E. Herrera-Viedma, and F. Herrera. 2011. "Science Mapping Software Tools: Review, Analysis, and Cooperative Study Among

Tools." *Journal of the American Society for Information Science and Technology* 62 (7): 1382–1402.

Cui, Xiaohui, Thomas E. Potok, and Paul Palathingal. 2005. "Document Clustering Using Particle Swarm Optimization." In *Proceedings 2005 IEEE Swarm Intelligence Symposium*, 185–91. IEEE.

De Bellis, Nicola. 2009. *Bibliometrics and Citation Analysis: From the Science Citation Index to Cybermetrics*. Lanham, MD: Scarecrow.

Deerwester, Scott C., Susan T. Dumais, Thomas K. Landauer, George W. Furnas, and Richard A. Harshman. 1990. "Indexing by Latent Semantic Analysis." *Journal of the American Society for Information Science* (JASIS) 41 (6): 391–407.

Dumais, Susan, and Hao Chen. 2000. "Hierarchical Classification of Web Content." In *Proceedings of the 23rd Annual International ACM SIGIR Conference on Research and Development in Information Retrieval*, 256–63. New York: ACM.

Elsevier. 2013. "Scopus." Accessed May 27, 2013. http://www.scopus.com.

Fayyad, Usama M., Andreas Wierse, and Georges G. Grinstein, eds. 2002. *Information Visualization in Data Mining and Knowledge Discovery*. Morgan Kaufmann.

Fortuna, Blaž, Dunja Mladenić, and Marko Grobelnik. 2011. "User Modeling Combining Access Logs, Page Content and Semantics." In *Proceedings of the 8th International Workshop on Information Integration on the Web—IIWeb2011 in conjunction with WWW 2011, 20th International World Wide Conference*. New York: Association for Computing Machinery.

Fortuna, Blaž, Marko Grobelnik, and Dunja Mladenić. 2006. "Semi-Automatic Data-Driven Ontology Construction System." In *Proceedings of the 9th International Multi-Conference Information Society IS-2006*, edited by Marko Bohanec et al., 223–26. Ljubljana, Slovenia: IJS.

Fortuna, Blaž, Marko Grobelnik, and Dunja Mladenić. 2005. "Visualization of Text Document Corpus." *Journal Informatica* 29: 497–502.

Frommholz, Ingo. 2001. "Categorizing Web Documents in Hierarchical Catalogues." In *Proceedings of the 23rd European Colloquium on Information Retrieval Research (ECIR)*.

Fuhr, Norbert, Marc Lechtenfeld, Benno Stein, and Tim Gollub. 2012. "The Optimum Clustering Framework: Implementing the Cluster Hypothesis." *Information Retrieval* 15 (2): 93–115.

Fuhr, Norbert, Stephan Hartmann, Gerhard Lustig, Konstadinos Tzeras, Gerhard Knorz, and Michael Schwantner. 1993. *Automatic Indexing in Operation: The Rule-Based System AIR/X for Large Subject Fields*. Technical Report, Technische Hochschule Darmstadt.

Gan, Guojun, Chaoqun Ma, and Jianhong Wu. 2007. "Data Clustering: Theory, Algorithms, and Applications." In *The ASA-SIAM Series on Statistics and Applied Probability*, Vol. 20. ASA-SIAM.

Golub, Koraljka. 2006. "Automated Subject Classification of Textual Web Documents." *Journal of Documentation* 62 (3): 350–71.

Gövert, Norbert, Mounia Lalmas, and Norbert Fuhr. 1999. "A Probabilistic Description-Oriented Approach for Categorising Web Documents." In *Proceedings of the Eighth International Conference on Information and Knowledge Management*, edited by Susan Gauch and Il-Yeol Soong, 475–82. New York: ACM.

Grobelnik, Marko, and Dunja Mladenić. 2005. "Simple Classification Into Large Topic Ontology of Web Documents." *Journal of Computing and Information Technology* 13 (4): 279–85.

Grobelnik, Marko, and D. Mladenić. 2002. "Efficient Visualization of Large Text Corpora." In *Proceedings of the Seventh TELRI Seminar.* Dubrovnik, Croatia: Institute of Linguistics, Faculty of Philosophy, University of Zagreb.

Grobelnik, Marko, Janez Brank, Dunja Mladenić, Blaž Novak, and Blaž Fortuna. 2006. "Using DMoz for Constructing Ontology from Data Stream." In *Proceedings of the 28th International Conference on Information Technology Interfaces*, 439–44. Information Technology Interfaces.

Huang, Anna. 2008. "Similarity Measures for Text Document Clustering." In *Proceedings of the Sixth New Zealand Computer Science Research Student Conference (NZCSRSC2008)*, 49–56. Christchurch, New Zealand.

Hubert, Lawrence, and Phipps Arabie. 1985. "Comparing Partitions." *Journal of Classification* 2 (1): 193–218.

Jain, Anil K., M. Narasimha Murty, and Patrick J. Flynn. 1999. "Data Clustering: A Review." *ACM Computing Surveys* (CSUR) 31 (3): 264–323.

Kaski, Samuel, Timo Honkela, Krista Lagus, and Teuvo Kohonen. 1998. "WEBSOM–Self-Organizing Maps of Document Collections." *Neurocomputing* 21 (1): 101–17.

Kessler, M. M. 1963. "Bibliographic Coupling Between Scientific Papers." *American Documentation* 14 (1): 10–25.

Klas, Claus-Peter, and Norbert Fuhr. 2000. "A New Effective Approach for Categorizing Web Documents." In *Proceedings of the 22th BCS-IRSG Colloquium on IR Research.*

Klavans, Richard, and Kevin W. Boyack. 2006. "Identifying a Better Measure of Relatedness for Mapping Science." *Journal of the American Society for Information Science and Technology* 57 (2), 251–63.

Kosmopoulos, Aris, Eric Gaussier, Georgios Paliouras, and Sujeevan Aseervatham. 2010. "The ECIR 2010 Large Scale Hierarchical Classification Workshop." In *ACM SIGIR Forum* 44 (1): 23–32.

Leskovec, Jure, Natasa Milic-Frayling, and Marko Grobelnik. 2005. "Impact of Linguistic Analysis on the Semantic Graph Coverage and Learning of Document Extracts." In *Proceedings of the 20th National Conference on Artificial Intelligence (AAAI)*, 1069–74. Menlo Park, CA: AAAI Press.

Lewis, David D. 1992. "An Evaluation of Phrasal and Clustered Representations on a Text Categorization Task." In *Proceedings of the 15th Annual International ACM SIGIR Conference on Research and Development in Information Retrieval*, 37–50. New York: ACM.

Lewis, David D., Yiming Yang, Tony G. Rose, and Fan Li. 2004. "RCV1: A New Benchmark Collection for Text Categorization Research." *The Journal of Machine Learning Research* 5: 361–97.

Leydesdorff, Loet. 1997. "Why Words and Co-Words Cannot Map the Development of the Sciences." *Journal of the American Society for Information Science* 48 (5): 418–27.

Liu, Yanchi, Zhongmou Li, Hui Xiong, Xuedong Gao, and Junjie Wu. 2010. "Understanding of Internal Clustering Validation Measures." In *Proceedings of the 10th International Conference on Data Mining*, 911–16. Los Alamitos, Washington, Tokyo: IEEE.

Manning, Christopher D., Prabhakar Raghavan, and Hinrich Schütze. 2008. *Introduction to Information Retrieval.* Cambridge University Press.

Maron, Melvin Earl. 1961. "Automatic Indexing: An Experimental Inquiry." *Journal of the ACM (JACM)* 8 (3): 404–17.

Marshakova-Shaikevich, Irena. 1973. "System of Document Connections Based on References." *Nauchno-Tekhnicheskaya Informatsiya Seriya 2-Informatsionnye Protsessy I Sistemy* 6: 3–8.

McCain, Katherine W. 1991. "Mapping Economics Through the Journal Literature: An Experiment in Journal Cocitation Analysis." *Journal of the American Society for Information Science* 42 (4): 290–96.

Melville, Prem, Wojciech Gryc, and Richard D. Lawrence. 2009. "Sentiment Analysis of Blogs by Combining Lexical Knowledge with Text Classification." In *Proceedings of the 15th ACM SIGKDD Conference*, 1275–84. New York: ACM.

Mitchell, Tom M. 1997. *Machine Learning.* New York: The McGraw-Hill Companies, Inc.

Mladenić, Dunja. 2006. "Feature Selection for Dimensionality Reduction." In *Susbspace Latent Structure and Feature Selection Techniques: Statistical and Optimisation Perspectives*, edited by Craig Saunders, Marko Grobelnik, Steve Gunn, and John Shawe-Taylor. Springer Lecture Notes in Computer Science, vol. 3940: 84–102.

Mladenić, Dunja. 1998. "Turning Yahoo into an Automatic Web-Page Classifier." In *Proceedings of the 13th European Conference on Art,* edited by Henri Prade, 473–74. Wiley & Sons.

Mladenić, Dunja, and Marko Grobelnik. 2003. "Feature Selection on Hierarchy of Web Documents." *Journal of Decision Support Systems—Web Retrieval and Mining* 35 (1): 45–87.

Novalija, Inna, and Dunja Mladenić. 2013. "Applying Semantic Technology to Business News Analysis." *Applied Artificial Intelligence* 27 (6): 520–50.

Pang, Bo, Lillian Lee, and Shivakumar Vaithyanathan. 2002. "Thumbs Up? Sentiment Classification Using Machine Learning Techniques." In *Proceedings of the Conference on Empirical Methods in Natural Language Processing*, 79–86. Stroudsburg, PA: Association for Computational Linguistics.

Pao, Miranda Lee, and Dennis B. Worthen. 1989. "Retrieval Effectiveness by Semantic and Citation Searching." *Journal of the American Society for Information Science* 40 (4): 226–35.

Persson, Olle. 2013. "Bibexcel." Accessed May 27, 2013. http://www8.umu.se/inforsk/Bibexcel/index.html.

Persson, Olle, Rickard Danell, and Jesper W. Schneider. 2009. "How to Use Bibexcel for Various Types of Bibliometric Analysis." In *Celebrating Scholarly Communication Studies: A Festschrift for Olle Persson at his 60th Birthday*, edited by Fredrik Åström, Rickard Danell, Birger Larsen, and Jesper W. Schneider, 9–24. Leuven: International Society for Scientometrics and Informetrics. Accessed May 27, 2013. http://www8.umu.se/inforsk/Bibexcel/ollepersson60.pdf.

Pinski, Gabriel, and Francis Narin. 1976. "Citation Influence for Journal Aggregates of Scientific Publications: Theory, with Application to the Literature of Physics." *Information Processing & Management* 12 (5): 297–312.

Price, Derek J. de Solla. 1965. "Networks of Scientific Papers: The Patterns of Bibliographic References Indicates the Nature of the Scientific Research Front." *Science* 149 (3683): 510–15.

Rand, William M. 1971. "Objective Criteria for the Evaluation of Clustering Methods." *Journal of the American Statistical Association* 66 (336): 846–50.

Roelleke, Thomas. 2013. *Information Retrieval Models: Foundations and Relationships*. San Rafael, CA: Morgan & Claypool.

Rokach, Lior, and Oded Maimon. 2005. "Clustering Methods." In *Data Mining and Knowledge Discovery Handbook*, 321–52. Springer US.

Rosengren, Karl Erik. 1968. *Sociological Aspects of the Literary System*. Lund: Natur och Kultur.

Savaresi, Sergio M., Daniel Boley, Sergio Bittanti, and Giovanna Gazzaniga. 2002. "Cluster Selection in Divisive Clustering Algorithms." In *Proceedings of the 2nd SIAM International Conference on Data Mining*, 299–314.

Schneider, Jesper W., and Pia Borlund. 2004. "Introduction to Bibliometrics for Construction and Maintenance of Thesauri: Methodical Considerations." *Journal of Documentation* 60 (5): 524–49.

Sebastiani, Fabrizio. 2002. "Machine Learning in Automated Text Categorization." *ACM Computing Surveys* (CSUR) 34 (1): 1–47.

Slonim, Noam, and Naftali Tishby. 2001. "The Power of Word Clusters for Text Classification." In *Proceedings of the 23rd European Colloquium on Information Retrieval Research*, 1–12.

Small, Henry G. 1978. "Cited Documents as Concept Symbols." *Social Studies of Science* 8 (3): 327-40.

Small, Henry. 1973. "Co-Citation in the Scientific Literature: A New Measure of the Relationship Between Two Documents." *Journal of the American Society for information Science* 24 (4): 265–69.

Štajner, Tadej, Inna Novalija, and Dunja Mladenić. 2013. "Informal Multilingual Multi-Domain Sentiment Analysis." *Journal Informatica* 37 (4): 373–80.

Statistical Cybermetrics Research Group. 2013. "Webometric Analyst 2.0." Accessed May 27, 2013. http://lexiurl.wlv.ac.uk/.

Thelwall, Michael. 2009. *Introduction to Webometrics: Quantitative Web Research for the Social Sciences*. San Rafael, CA: Morgan & Claypool.

Thomson Reuters. 2013a. "Web of Science." Accessed May 27, 2013. http://thomsonreuters.com/products_services/science/science_products/a-z/web_of_science/.

Thomson Reuters. 2013b. "Journal Impact Factor." Accessed May 27, 2013. http://thomsonreuters.com/products_services/science/academic/impact_factor.

Trampuš, Mitja, Flavio Fuart, Jan Berčič, Delia Rusu, Luka Stopar, and Tadej Štajner. 2013. "(i) DiversiNews—A Stream-Based, On-Line Service for Diversified News." In *Proceedings of the 16th International Multi-Conference Information Society IS-2013*, edited by Marko Bohanec et al., 184–87. Ljubljana, Slovenia: IJS.

Van Eck, Nees Jan, and Ludo Waltman. 2010. "Software Survey: VOSviewer, a Computer Program for Bibliometric Mapping." *Scientometrics* 84 (2): 523–38.

Van Rijsbergen, Cornelis J. 1979. *Information Retrieval*. London: Butterworths.

White, Howard D., and Belver C. Griffith. 1981. "Author Cocitation: A Literature Measure of Intellectual Structure." *Journal of the American Society for Information Science* 32 (3): 163–71.

Witten, Ian H., and Eibe Frank. 1999. *Data Mining: Practical Machine Learning Tools and Techniques with Java Implementations*. Morgan Kaufmann.

Xu, Rui, and Don Wunsch. 2008. *Clustering*. John Wiley & Sons.

Yan, Erjia and Ying Ding. 2012. "Scholarly Network Similarities: How Bibliographic Coupling Networks, Citation Networks, Cocitation Networks, Topical Networks, Coauthorship Networks, and Coword Networks Relate to Each Other." *Journal of the American Society for Information Science and Technology* 63 (7): 1313–26.

Yang, Yiming, and Jan O. Pedersen. 1997. "A Comparative Study on Feature Selection in Text Categorization." In *Proceedings International Conference on Machine Learning (ICML 1997)*, 412–20. ICML.

Yang, Yiming, and Xin Liu. 1999. "A Re-Examination of Text Categorization Methods." In *Proceedings of the 22nd Annual International ACM SIGIR Conference on Research and Development in Information Retrieval*, 42–49. New York: ACM.

Zhong, Shi. 2006. "Semi-Supervised Model-Based Document Clustering: A Comparative Study." *Machine Learning* 65 (1): 3–29.

5

Perspectives for the Future

MAJOR QUESTIONS

- What are similarities and differences in how library and information science and computer science approach information organization?
- Why is it important that the two disciplines join their efforts?

TWO PERSPECTIVES ON INFORMATION ORGANIZATION: COMPUTER SCIENCE AND LIBRARY AND INFORMATION SCIENCE (*by Isto Huvila and Fredrik Åström*)

Strategies for identifying the subject matter of information, for organizing information according to its intellectual content, and for making information searchable through descriptions of its topical content, have been developed since humans began using signs to communicate with each other. Anthropologists such as Douglas (1966) and Zerubavel (1991) have emphasized the cultural and social significance of categorizations, classifications, and divisions. The present endeavor relates to the management of all types of information, whether it is a matter of arranging books of similar topics in the shelves of a library, using computers to identify and decode encrypted messages between spies and their intelligence agencies, or to organize protein sequences and DNA strings.

Even if the task of organizing information seems to be a rather straightforward effort of simply putting things into a particular order, there is an abundance of possibilities to define that particular order. Different scientific and scholarly disciplines work with the issue of arranging information from different perspectives based on organizational and cultural differences between the fields. The question is explicitly or implicitly present in fields ranging from medicine to sociology, ethnology, and biosciences. At the same time, the variation points to a diversity of explicit and implicit epistemological and ontological assumptions of the nature of things and knowing. Bowker and Star (2000) and Olson (2001), for instance, have shown how this organizational work can have major consequences on not only how information is managed and found but also on how people live their lives. A prime example is found in medicine: The placing of a particular illness in a certain position in the classification of medical conditions determines the type of care a patient is likely to receive.

This section provides an overview of the basic disciplinary differences between how computer science (CS) and library and information science (LIS) perceive the issue of organizing information, and gives a glimpse into some of the theoretical underpinnings of these differences. In the following text, the terms "field" and "area" are used interchangeably to denote areas or fields of research that might or might not represent established scientific (i.e., natural sciences) or scholarly (i.e., humanities and social studies) disciplines such as mathematics, philosophy, or history. In this respect, however, both CS and LIS are both disciplines and characteristically interdisciplinary fields of research. They both have areas of convergence with such disciplines as psychology, sociology, and mathematics.

Computer science extends toward mathematical and physical sciences, statistics, and biosciences, which all incorporate areas that apply computational methods, but which also provide theoretical and practical premises for developing computational and statistical algorithms, physical and, for instance, neural approaches for computational problems such as the organization of information. Computer science usually is divided into theoretical computer sciences—which have their underpinnings in mathematics—and applied computer sciences, which have roots in the nexus of computing and various fields of natural, social, and design sciences, for instance.

Library and information science, and especially some particular branches of information science research, such as information retrieval and bibliometrics, are close to CS and computational science. Other parts of the field tend to lean more toward the social sciences and humanities, especially philosophy, linguistics, and cultural studies. The notion of LIS is itself contested, and different authors have advocated for the separation of library science (both as normative study of the methods of librarianship and as a critical study of libraries) and information science ("science and practice dealing with the effective collection, storage, retrieval, and use of information") according to Saracevic (2009). White (2011) defines LIS as an area of research that consists of "research on literature-based answering." White posits that the letter "L" in LIS is not necessary and instead is a misleading prefix that does not describe the area of research in LIS that covers the aspects of textual and literary content. Similarly, Saracevic

(2009) sees the "L" as a relic of that time when a lot of (especially human-oriented) information science research was conducted in old library schools.

In contrast, others including Estabrook (2009) and Åström (2008) highlight the significance of the institutionalization process and emphasize that LIS is a real interdisciplinary domain in the nexus of library science and information science—and of social sciences, as Estabrook adds. Even if the proponents of information science have been arguing for not including library science in the name of the field, it commonly is accepted that the broad area of information sciences partly converges with (or includes, depending on perspective) not only library science but also other fields such as archival science, museology, computer science, management, and communication.

In addition to information science, library science, and LIS, the partly synonymous terms "information studies" and "library studies" also are used, often to make an implicit reference to more a humanities-oriented understanding of the field as not being a part of the sciences. Today, there also is an increased tendency of the two fields of computer science—LIS and IS—to merge. An example of this was the forming of joint schools and departments such as the iSchools (information schools) in the United States during the late 1990s and the 2000s, where LIS and CS teaching and research organizationally are gathered into the same schools. There are distinct differences between the two fields, however, even though the boundaries between the two are sometimes far from clear.

In contrast to many other professional and scholarly disciplines which classify and organize things, the organization of information according to subject content has been, and still is, a central issue in LIS, IS, and CS. From this perspective, the tasks of CS and LIS are very similar; and there are many examples of intersections—from the exchange of ideas from one field to the other, to joint efforts between the two fields. Many areas combine CS and LIS, including:

- Database management (development of data structures and database systems),
- Information architecture (organization of how information is presented and accessed in information systems),
- Information retrieval (obtaining relevant information resources from a collection of information resources),
- Information management (organizing and administering information assets), and
- Personal information management (focusing on information held by individuals).

These different research areas themselves assume different approaches to subject access, either as a question of:

- Organizing collections (e.g., knowledge organization, automated and manual indexing, Semantic Web),
- Retrieving and organizing retrieved results in a useful manner (e.g., information retrieval, information architecture),
- Visualizing information structures (information visualization), or
- Management of information collections and processes (information management, personal information management).

Traditionally, a main distinction between the two fields has been related to what type of information they are trying to describe, arrange, and make searchable. Library and information science typically focuses on information in the form of text in physical documents such as books and articles, and often in the context of collections of documents in libraries. Computer science has dealt with information in the form of digital raw unprocessed information in automated systems. The documents and the representations of these documents in the form of bibliographic metadata traditionally handled in LIS, however, have been digitized to an increasing extent—from the computerization of indexes of scientific literature during the 1950s to today's massive availability of documents of all kinds through Google. Also important is developing strategies for an automatic identification and organization of the subject matter of documents. In LIS, even in the very early twentieth century, discussions of a widened concept of the document (information object) also include artifacts in museums and animals in zoological gardens as sources of information.

The fundamental difference between the two approaches is that, whereas CS predominantly has focused on working directly with something the discipline understands as being information, LIS traditionally emphasized documents (containing or mediating information) and metadata (i.e., information about information). Both perspectives are based on an understanding of the nature of information, which distinguishes real-world things and facts from mental representations and linguistic expressions of these things. The difference between the approaches is whether information is carried by things, thoughts, or language.

The "*objectivist*" renderings are based on an assumption that different information resources contain information and this information can be organized according to what it is. In contrast, the "*subjectivists*" suggest that different individuals assign different meanings to information resources. Even if computer science focuses on the automated processing of information and library and information science focuses on manual organization and creation of metadata, this difference suggests objectivist and subjectivist theorizing, respectively, but the division is not clear.

Earlier LIS scholarship, for example, had strong tendencies to consider expert classification and organization in highly objectivistic terms: Librarians were considered to be organizing information on an unbiased basis, and books and documents were treated as information containers, similarly to how information systems are treated in CS. Accordingly, in CS, the interest in a subjectivist idea of computer-supported information processing and organization has increased considerably since the 1980s. Further, even if it is not always explicitly acknowledged in CS, systems always are designed and built by people who make subjective prioritizations and decisions—and even allegedly "objective" algorithms are chosen by subjective individuals for particular tasks.

Another distinction between CS and LIS could be made regarding the perspective from which research on information management is conducted. CS can be said to operate from a systems perspective; developing automated methods for handling information and analyzing these systems through lab testing. LIS traditionally has operated from a human user perspective; the systems for organizing information are based on intellectual constructs emanating from a more or less philosophical perspective on the organization of different types of knowledge, and the analyses of the systems managing the information are done through end-user studies. The user perspective in CS, however, is well established through human-computer interaction research, for example. At the same time, it is argued that much research done on information-retrieval systems is performed within the realm of LIS.

The systems- versus human-oriented approaches can be traced back partly to the dichotomy of objectivist and subjectivist theorizing and to the clash of "*rationalist*" (based on the employment of reason), "*pragmatist*" (based on consideration of goals and their consequences), "*empiricist*" (based on observation and experience), and "*historicist*" (based on cultural hermeneutics) epistemologies of information organization (Hjørland 2002). The early history of library classification—until the mid-twentieth century—was characterized by rationalist aspirations of universal information organization systems and pragmatist realities of constructing useful systems for library users. Smiraglia (2002) notes that information organization began to be oriented toward empiricism and the interest in how people organize information in practice first in the mid-twentieth century. The empiricist studies were followed by a hermeneutical paradigm denoted by Hjørland (2002) as historicism and based on a qualitative hermeneutical analysis of epistemological systems rather than empirical ontology-oriented observation.

The systems perspective in CS can be traced back to a certain physical understanding of the flow of information, epitomized by Claude Shannon's (Shannon 1948) rationalist and highly influential mathematical theory of communication, often cited as information theory and applied in signal processing areas of CS. There is a long-standing philosophical dispute within the field about its epistemological basis as a rationalist branch of mathematics, a technocratic engineering discipline, or as a natural (empirical) science. Computer science approaches, however, tend to make certain claims of simultaneous controllability and empirical measurability of both *a priori* and *a posteriori* knowledge of the premises of how information is managed in the systems. Information retrieval and machine-learning approaches to information organization both are based on an assumption that it is possible to develop a computational model that corresponds with the subject access–related needs of users.

This approach is extended outside of the domain of technology in rationalist manual indexing that believes in the possibility of perfect categorizations and, for instance, posits that human-indexed collections are used as a "gold standard" to which computational indexing algorithms can be compared. In contrast, the user-oriented perspectives tend to consider information to be basically uncontrollable and existing only as *a posteriori* in the context of cognitive, socially, or culturally constructed processes of understanding and explicating the world. Information organization does not tend to follow extreme ultra-relativist forms of this latter approach that reject the existence of any shared categories. In contrast, less extreme perspectives form a basis of pragmatic manual organization of information, and the evaluation of subject access on the basis of retrieval performance and an analysis of indexing workflows. These moderate user-oriented *a posteriori* perspectives also emphasize the purpose of organizing information to make information usable (a pragmatist point of view) rather than to find the correct order (a rationalist point of view).

Yet another distinction could be made from an organizational perspective. Departments or schools of CS and LIS often are situated in distinctly different organizational contexts. Computer science schools and departments typically are located under the purview of faculties of engineering. Library and information science schools more often are associated with the social sciences and the humanities. This also reflects the distinction between the aforementioned user or systems perspectives found in LIS and CS. At the same time, there is an array of names for the schools and departments—including information studies, information science, informatics, information systems and technology, and computer science. Often these names—and the distinction between the different concepts—also vary between languages and national academic systems.

As mentioned, there is a trend toward an organizational merging of the two research fields into iSchools ("information" schools), and bringing together research and teaching in LIS and CS into joint organizational units. It might not be possible to draw direct parallels between the organizational and disciplinary convergence and the theoretical premises of information organization, but there is a shift toward approaches that attempt to bridge or bypass the subjectivist-objectivist dichotomy. Neo-pragmatism and critical realism are examples of approaches that have argued against the dualism of objective facts and subjective values. There also is much evidence of the complementary potential of the contrasting epistemological viewpoints.

A final question is whether a distinction can be made regarding literature from the two fields. Can the different types of research be identified in what has been published in CS and LIS journals? Although there are journals which distinctly belong to one field or the other, there also are many journals that do not. One example is found in the Web of Science Journal Citation Reports, which categorizes journals according to research field. Many of the journals indexed in the subject category, "Information Science and Library Science"—including journals that are considered central (L)IS journals such as the *Journal of the Association for Information Science and Technology* and *Journal of Documentation*—also are categorized as "Computer Science" journals.

The literature being used in the different fields includes work of information-retrieval researchers such as Gerard Salton and Keith van Rijsbergen—who, because of their status with regard to LIS literature, are considered LIS scholars. Both of these researchers, however, have degrees in computer science. In addition to being extremely influential upon LIS, van Rijsbergen's ideas also were central in the development of many of the search engine algorithms used on the Web. In contrast, there is much less convergence between computer science and the philosophy- or linguistics-oriented lines of information organization research.

In summary, the differences of the major approaches to information organization can be traced back to disciplinary variation. Beyond these institutionalized fields, however, it is possible to see profound theoretical differences in how information organization is conceptualized—as a computational problem, in computer science and in mathematically oriented information science; or as a philosophical problem, in humanities-oriented library and information science. Consequently, the organization of information becomes an issue that can be addressed using computers and algorithms, or a question that requires explicit human reasoning and conscious decisions regarding how things relate to each other.

THE FUTURE

This section briefly summarizes the information presented in the previous chapters. It also highlights a number of important topics to be addressed in future research on subject-based organization of information, and illustrates and emphasizes the importance of joint efforts of library and information science, computer science, and other related disciplines.

A major and all-encompassing issue is gaining an understanding of the end users and their information behavior, particularly because information-retrieval systems are built for them. There are many information-behavior models in general, and information-seeking models in particular; some are empirical and others are theoretical. It is important to investigate potential integration and generalization of these models, as well as to further contextualize them. This would enable the identification of what is still missing. The computer science approaches might complement this knowledge by providing information drawn from statistical Web analytics (e.g., which links are followed, average time spent doing what, using which keywords).

Examples of questions that still are unanswered include the following.

- When and why do various groups of end users access information systems?
- How do they use information systems?
- When do users search and when do they browse?
- Which information-seeking devices do they use and when?
- How do users interact with various types of information resources, including multimedia?
- How do people use new technologies and services?

Various user groups differ as to their needs and subsequent information-seeking behavior, and an information-retrieval system ideally should accommodate all of them. End users include, for example, different age and gender groups; people with different educational, professional, social, and cultural backgrounds; and users having specific needs, for example. In particular, some contexts (e.g., non-work contexts) and groups (e.g., children) are as yet underexplored. Additionally, most research so far has shown that many users only utilize a fraction of the information resources available, and invest little effort in searches. What effects does this produce? Can effects be improved? (In information-retrieval systems, for example, by providing search tips and help, and by integrating KOSs in the background.)

It has been shown that information behavior in general and information-seeking behavior in particular is very context dependent. Information behavior is impacted by a person's personality, age, gender, education, profession, (dis)abilities, and social and cultural circumstances; together with the type of task being performed (e.g., simple, complex, leisure, work); and the information-retrieval system used, its interface, and the technology for accessing it.

Thus, an important research topic is to further build, test, and apply triangular research methodologies on information behavior, and involve interdisciplinary cooperation. This includes human-computer interaction (HCI) (user-centered design), library and information science, and social sciences and humanities (with their methodologies, such as discourse analysis and ethnography). Studying user behavior by applying even just one of these additional disciplines or methods would provide a whole different research perspective—possibly opening brand new avenues and expanding existing knowledge.

On the Web and on the Semantic Web, there is a tendency toward integrating various formal and informal information systems—for example, various library catalogs, museum- and archival-retrieval aids, and social Web tools and services. This includes using multilingual information resources of various types and formats, and the associated challenges of how to best integrate them at technical, conceptual, and access levels. Many concepts will be hard to map or translate, for example, due to a variety of cultural and other differences. This is true even for devices such as Universal Decimal Classification which, if applied in various languages, still uses the same notation. There also will be problems of various KOSs and different indexing policies, all of which would need to be aligned in some way. Interfaces and search functionalities in different languages would have to be examined and provided appropriately for end users of different backgrounds. Again, it must be emphasized that these complex efforts would require cooperation between library and information science, computer science, and a number of other disciplines.

Knowledge organization systems are the most important device for ensuring high precision and high recall in information retrieval. It therefore is important to further explore topics including how users search and browse KOSs; how users combine them with other metadata elements; and how users perform these tasks in a variety of information systems and contexts, such as multilingual and multidisciplinary digital libraries, search engines, content-management systems, and other KOS applications. Such analysis would include the issues of multiple user groups, interfaces, and integration at various levels. Redesign aspects of the KOSs themselves also should be addressed, and should include the removal of biases, the inclusion of more end-user terms, and restructuring based on user studies and domain analysis. Thus, a triangulation of methods from different disciplines is recommended in this case as well.

Additionally, because research has shown that people generally underuse available searching and browsing devices, such as Boolean and proximity operators, truncation, and KOSs, it is important to test ways to integrate KOSs into more intelligent information systems. For example, multilingual KOSs could support multilingual searching; as the search terms could be translated automatically, the search could automatically retrieve results based on synonyms, broader terms, or related terms if few results are retrieved initially, or it could automatically narrow the search by offering narrower terms—and users would be notified of the actions performed.

The potential value of combining KOS terms and classes, social tags, and automated terms and classes in information seeking and retrieval also requires studying. A methodology framework for such an evaluation ideally also would be composed of a triangulation of methods: Evaluating indexing quality directly based on a quality standard; evaluating indexing quality through analyzing what is retrieved; and evaluating the integration of computer-assisted indexing in a workflow.

When represented in appropriate technological standards, a KOS can be used to represent and retrieve data and information resources as part of the Semantic Web. The standards ensure that KOSs represented in the same format and structure are presented, organized, browsed, and searched in an interoperable and easy manner, for both human and machine use. An important part of this information environment is finding and applying an appropriate KOS, therefore terminology registries of KOSs and of their Web services should be built and researched. Further, every KOS, its concepts, its terms, and its relationships must be uniquely and persistently identifiable to ensure its reuse and long-term access by both human users and software agents; the Linked Data initiative helps promote this. As the Semantic Web develops, its standards, technologies, and information-seeking processes are yet another significant research area that should be explored—calling for the merging of efforts across the different disciplines.

SUMMARY

The field of information retrieval (as it is referred to today) basically was restricted to the library profession until the 1950s. When it was recognized that computers could help alleviate retrieval problems, researchers from a range of academic fields, in particular computer science, began to contribute to the body of information. Library and information science is interdisciplinary, and some areas of information science research—such as information retrieval and bibliometrics—are closely related to computer science. This is why different authors have called for the separation of library science, which deals with librarianship and libraries, from information science, which focuses on information as its central concept.

Because subject-based organization of information has been a required task in both computer science and in library and information science there are many examples of intersections, such as the exchange of ideas from one discipline to the other and joint efforts between the two. Traditionally, however, major distinctions between them have existed. One is the type of information dealt with: library and information science typically focuses on information in the form of text in physical documents such as books in libraries, and computer science deals with information in the form of digital unprocessed data in automated systems. Another distinction can be made with regard to evaluation: Computer science is said to operate from a systems perspective, analyzing automated systems through lab-based methods, and library and information science traditionally has operated from a human-user perspective, evaluating the information-retrieval systems through end-user studies.

These differences are now becoming less apparent, in that library and information science deal with more than just paper-based information resources, and computer science embraces more end-user studies as part of its evaluation methodologies. Additionally, both disciplines are recognizing more of the importance of context, and the subjectivity of the concepts of "aboutness" and relevance.

Important topics for future research in subject-based organization of information include further exploration of end-user information behavior in general and information-seeking behavior in particular, in the contexts of large, integrated, multilingual, and multidisciplinary information-retrieval systems which also involve social Web and Semantic Web features and developments. KOSs need to be examined and redesigned for both existing and new applications, such as intelligent information retrieval systems of various types in which they are utilized more automatically. These highly complex research topics make it crucial to ensure interdisciplinary cooperation between computer science, its subdisciplines, and library and information science.

CHAPTER REVIEW

1. Who are potential user groups for a large integrated information system?
2. What types of different searching interfaces are required to support these user groups?
3. What are the problems faced in mapping a KOS used by one culture to that of another?
4. Will there be two disciplines dealing with the topic of this book or will they merge into a single new discipline?

GLOSSARY
(*by Isto Huvila and Fredrik Åström*)

Computer science: The study of methods for organizing and processing data in computers. The fundamental questions of concern to computer scientists range from foundations of theory to strategies for practical implementation (Henderson 2009).

Empiricism: A theory of knowledge based on a premise that knowledge is acquired only or primarily from sensory experiences.

Epistemology: An area of philosophy which is concerned with the nature and scope of knowledge.

Historicism: A theory of knowledge based on cultural hermeneutical emphasis of the significance of historical context and traditions.

Information science: The science and practice dealing with the effective collection, storage, retrieval, and use of information (Saracevic 2011).

iSchool: Information School; an interdisciplinary university-level institution with "a fundamental interest in the relationships between information, people, and technology" (http://ischools.org/about/).

Library and information science (LIS): An interdisciplinary domain concerned with creation, management, and uses of information in all its forms (Estabrook 2010).

Ontology: The study of the basic categories and nature of being.

Pragmatism: A philosophical theory that focuses on the practical consequences of actions.

Rationalism: A theory of knowledge that regards reason as the primary source of knowledge.

REFERENCES

Åström, Fredrik. 2008. "Formalizing a Discipline: The Institutionalization of Library and Information Science Research in the Nordic Countries." *Journal of Documentation* 64 (5): 721–37.

Bowker, Geoffery C., and Susan Leigh Star. 2000. *Sorting Things Out: Classification and Its Consequences*. Cambridge, MA: MIT Press.

Douglas, Mary. 1966. *Purity and Danger: An Analysis of Concepts of Pollution and Taboo*. New York, NY: Praeger.

Estabrook, Leigh S. 2009. "Library and Information Science." In *Encyclopedia of Library and Information Sciences*, 3rd ed., edited by Marcia Bates, 3287–92. New York: Taylor and Francis.

Henderson, Harry. 2009. *Encyclopedia of Computer Science and Technology*. New York: Facts on File.

Hjørland, Birger. 2002. "Epistemology and the Socio-Cognitive Perspective in Information Science." *Journal of the American Society for Information Science and Technology* 53 (4): 257–70.

Olson, Hope A. 2001. "The Power to Name: Representation in Library Catalogs." *Signs* 26 (3): 639–68.

Saracevic, Tefko. 2009. "Information Science." In *Encyclopedia of Library and Information Sciences,* 3rd ed., edited by Marcia Bates, 2570–85. New York: Taylor and Francis.

Shannon, Claude E. 1948. "A Mathematical Theory of Communication." *Bell System Technical Journal* 27: 379–423, 623–56.

Smiraglia, Richard P. 2002. "The Progress of Theory in Knowledge Organization." *Library Trends* 50 (3): 330–49.

White, Howard D. 2011. "Bibliometric Overview of Information Science." In *Encyclopedia of Library and Information Sciences*, 3rd ed., edited by Marcia Bates, 534–45. New York: Taylor and Francis.

Zerubavel, Eviatar. 1991. *The Fine Line: Making Distinctions in Everyday Life*. Chicago, IL: University of Chicago Press.

Index

About the Author

KORALJKA GOLUB, PhD, is associate professor in the Department of Library and Information Science, School of Cultural Sciences, Linnaeus University, Sweden. Koraljka also teaches at the School of Information Studies, Charles Stuart University, Australia, as well as at several universities in Croatia. She has been involved in international research projects related to knowledge organization since 2003, including five years at UKOLN, University of Bath, United Kingdom.